Towards a Competitive, Sustainable Modern City

Towards a Competitive, Sustainable Modern City

Edited by

Peter Karl Kresl

Charles P. Vaughan Professor of Economics (Emeritus), Bucknell University, USA and Co-founder and Past President, Global Urban Competitiveness Project

 Edward Elgar
PUBLISHING

Cheltenham, UK • Northampton, MA, USA

Published by
Edward Elgar Publishing Limited
The Lypiatts
15 Lansdown Road
Cheltenham
Glos GL50 2JA
UK

Edward Elgar Publishing, Inc.
William Pratt House
9 Dewey Court
Northampton
Massachusetts 01060
USA

A catalogue record for this book
is available from the British Library

Library of Congress Control Number: 2020944680

This book is available electronically in the **Elgar**online
Economics subject collection
http://dx.doi.org/10.4337/9781839107481

ISBN 978 1 83910 747 4 (cased)
ISBN 978 1 83910 748 1 (eBook)

Typeset by Columns Design XML Ltd, Reading
Printed and bound by CPI Group (UK) Ltd, Croydon, CR0 4YY

Contents

v

Contributors

Leo van den Berg, Erasmus University of Rotterdam, the Netherlands.

Edward J. Blakely, University of Sydney, Australia.

Luis Carvalho, University of Porto, Portugal.

Cho Dong-Sung, Incheon National University, Republic of Korea.

Robert Huggins, Cardiff University, United Kingdom.

Gi-Chan Kim, Incheon National University, Republic of Korea.

Hyun-Woo Kim, Incheon National University, Republic of Korea.

Peter Karl Kresl, Bucknell University, United States of America.

Meenakshi Kumar, TERI School of Advanced Studies, India.

Isela Orihuela, Mora Interdisciplinary Center of Metropolitan Studies, Mexico.

Clemente Ruiz Durán, Autonomous University of Mexico, Mexico.

Shen Jianfa, Chinese University of Hong Kong, China.

Arnaud Scaillerez, University of Moncton, New Brunswick, Canada.

Shaleen Singhal, TERI School of Advanced Studies, India.

Jaime Sobrino, El Colegio of Mexico, Mexico.

Piers Thompson, Nottingham Trent University, United Kingdom.

Diane-Gabrielle Tremblay, University of Quebec, Canada.

Introduction

Cities and urban centers have, for the past 30 years, been increasingly focused on the competitiveness of their economies, firms and labor in the context of a global economy that has become extraordinarily integrated and mutually dependent. In the Fourth Industrial Revolution (I-4), of Klaus Schwab and the World Economic Forum, technological advance is giving way to interconnectivity and communication among all of the system's actors. This newly developing global economy imposes demands on each of the participating urban centers, if they wish to be active participating members. The key element in this economy is the labor force that it demands. These workers differ from their blue collar industrial predecessors in their education, specialized skills, mobility and demands relating to living amenities and lifestyles. They demand schools, public safety, good neighborhoods, recreation and cultural institutions, if only for their children. This has meant that cities must shape their urban spaces to accommodate these skilled workers, or they will move to a more congenial city, be it in another part of the country or to another country or continent – the world is literally at their feet.

It is also true that what the city has in terms of amenities, such as public health and recreation, must be sustainable in the longer term. Global warming is only the most obvious of the challenges they face: the vitality of neighborhoods, the quality of schools, recreation and cultural amenities must also be maintained into the future. Ongoing investments must be made in these institutions, as well as in infrastructure, including highways, rail and air travel facilities. Furthermore, cities feed off each other in terms of new approaches and new ideas that facilitate improvement in all of these areas.

Another more recent demand on competitive cities is the necessity of their being tolerant to workers from all countries, of all races, religions, sexual preferences, genders and ages. All of the truly competitive cities – in this new, I-4 – understanding of the term, must overcome long-lasting lack of tolerance, in one or more of the various ways of being intolerant and discriminatory.

For these elements of competitiveness to be worth pursuing, they must be sustainable in the long run. This is true for both the tangible aspects, such as facilities, institutions and structures, as well as "softer" ones, including social and governance relations, and tolerance. All economic entities have mobility, to varying degrees, and if the situation in a city becomes less congenial or productive they will simply move elsewhere. Local leaders must always look a decade or two into the future to ascertain, as best they can, whether it is likely that their economy will retain and increase its desirability to the mobile labor, capital and firms that give it its strength today.

The authors of the chapters in this book were convinced that these issues were of sufficient importance that we should choose the interaction of these two themes for this book. We have always found stimulation in the interaction of scholars and researchers from across the world coming together for an intense analysis and discussion of whatever theme was thought to be of importance at that time. We believe that a broader readership in the several parts of the world we represent, as well as those we do not, will find this to be a stimulating and useful volume to have and to study.

While we wrote with our professional colleagues in mind, we are all university teachers and have written our chapters in such a way that they will be accessible to students, such as ours. Issues such as smart technology, inclusive growth, tolerance, branding, innovation, entre-preneurship and sustainable competitiveness are subjects that are currently being studied and discussed both by scholars and by students, as well as being implemented in policy in cities throughout the world.

While knowledge occasionally advances in great leaps, it is almost always the case that it advances with smaller steps. We are convinced that our volume of studies contributes in this latter model. While there have been many books and much research on both competitiveness and sustainability, some of it recorded in earlier publications of the authors, our combination of the two subjects and the geographical variety in the presentations gives our book a character that distinguishes it from the many other books on these topics. We are convinced that it will make a contribution that will be recognized by readers throughout the world.

In Part I of the book, "The Sustainable City," Leo van den Berg and Luis Carvalho (Chapter 1) conclude from their research that for the modern city, its competitiveness is dependent upon its social cohesion and its environmental quality. So the environmental, the social and the economic are interlocked in the competitive city in a structure that embraces government, universities, not-for-profits, the private sector and citizen groups. Additionally, the interaction between the project level and the city level create a symbiotic relationship. This is revealed in their analysis of 24 cities in Europe, North and South America, Africa and Asia.

Sustainability and competitiveness now require new working spaces for creative workers; spaces that are examined by Diane-Gabrielle Tremblay and Arnaud Scaillerez (Chapter 2), using the city of Montreal for their analysis. This enhances collaboration, flexibility, improvisation and new possibilities for interaction. These workers now have the ability to rethink continually their specialization and their relationships with workers in related areas of creative activity. A co-working space facilitates the collaboration of independent workers, and frees them from traditional corporate structures, which are confining to many creative workers. It is just one more step to give these workers the opportunity to telecommute and to interact through increasing distances, and to create family and residential situations that are more congenial and productive.

In China, all of the problems of competitiveness and sustainability are exacerbated by demography. Shen Jianfa (Chapter 3) tells us that between 1982 and 2010, China's urban population tripled, with the largest increase being due to temporary migrants from rural areas. These migrants have no permanent status and lack access to basic services such as housing, sanitation, water, schools and health care. They lack skills and are used in the most menial types of work; they are one of the principal problems for urban areas. The situation is magnified by the application of advanced technology such as artificial intelligence (AI), robots and Internet communication. To resolve this problem, Shen argues for a regional approach to planning that will combine improvement of the economic life in smaller cities and towns along with planning for sustainable urbanization. The Hong Kong community of Ma On Shan offers a guide to this approach to the future of China's urban areas.

Australian Edward Blakely (Chapter 4) argues that the traditional elements of regional science focused on location and local assets, the comparative advantage of place of Christaller, and the competitive advantage approach have been supplanted, to a significant degree, by the concept of global innovative places. A truly innovative space is one that is inclusive of disadvantaged communities, and competitive spaces as suggested by Tremblay; creative entities need proximity, government must serve as a facilitator and utilize planning and financial levers in support, public–private partnerships are vital, and government also needs to facilitate data-driven solutions to pressing urban challenges.

In Korea, Hyun-Woo Kim and Gi-Chan Kim (Chapter 5) study the many natural disasters that have befallen Korea's major cities. They study the resiliency of local disaster planning of seven of the largest cities and find that the planning varies dramatically in the degree to which the city has an effective plan in place. They evaluate the seven cities according to a set of four consequences: health/well-being, society/economy, environment/ infrastructure and leadership/strategy, and 72 indicators, and find that, to varying degrees, the cities did not fully utilize residency principles in their planning. Unfortunately, leadership/strategy appears to be the least effect- ively implemented although Seoul does considerably better than the others. Seoul is the highest ranked in the second and fourth categories, Busan in the first, and Gwangju in the third. Resiliency enables the city to minimize damage from disasters and promotes sustainable planning and develop- ments, hence cities must plan their policy responses to all categories of disaster in advance and be prepared to implement these measures at very short notice.

Part II of the book, "The Competitive City," begins with a study by Cho Dong-Sung (Chapter 6) of one of Korea's largest cities, Incheon. This city has just passed 3 million in population, its airport is regarded as one of the best in the world, and Songdo is a district that is considered to be a "smart city." Incheon National University (INU) is one of the key elements in the strategy of the city for its future development. In addition to its current campus, INU plans to build a research campus, to support a curriculum that is based on biotechnology and its linkages to virtually all disciplines taught. The objective is to prepare students for the coming AI economy in which many traditional jobs will disappear. INU aims to be attractive to international students, with financial packages that make it a place they can consider; in part due to the expected decline in the number of Korean students. The city itself aspires to be the hub of north-east Asia, based on its transportation assets – the airport is ranked 8th in the world for passenger traffic and 2nd in international freight – the technology that is based on the Songdo smart city, and the biotechnology that is centered on INU.

Robert Huggins and Piers Thompson (Chapter 7) elaborate upon the importance of psychocultural behavior and economic competitiveness and development. Behavioral economics highlights the limitations of the rational-choice approach in explaining economic decision-making actions. In this approach they elaborate the role of individual and collective behavior and socio-spatial community culture in determining outcomes. This is far from being a static situation, since one set of personality patterns and behaviors that were eminently suitable for a blue collar manufacturing economy are quite inappropriate for the contempor- ary skill-based I-4 economy. In this transition from yesterday to tomor- row, a strong work ethic is still important; however, social cohesion is counterproductive as it leads to reduced openness to new ideas and people. Places with high cultural diversity and extraverted individuals have relatively high levels of competitiveness. Tolerance is highlighted in the next contribution (Chapter 8).

This necessity of inclusion is amplified by Peter Karl Kresl's (Chapter 8) observation that in the United States (US) the most competitive urban areas are linked to tolerance: tolerance of individuals of various religions, sexual preferences, ages, genders, races and national origins, as well as the homeless and the disabled. The increased competitiveness of cities in the US South and West is significantly linked to movements into historically intolerant places of skilled younger workers from centers of technology such as Boston, Pittsburgh, Seattle, Silicon Valley and San Diego, as well as from university centers such as Chicago, Minneapolis and Philadelphia. This has been exacerbated by development of the I-4 Economy of the World Economic Forum. Modern transportation and communication have opened these hitherto intolerant cities to these inflows of modernity and competitiveness in a sustainable way.

Cities can contribute to the mitigation of some of the world economy's principal problems relative to degradation of the environment, through imposition of policies to safeguard the ecosystem, in the analysis of Shaleen Singhal and Meenakshi Kumar (Chapter 9). The traditional method of resource use involved extraction, making a product and then disposing of the waste and often, ultimately, the product itself – referred to as "take, make, dispose." The result is inefficient resource utilization and production that leads to environmental degradation. Cities can participate in the creation of an economy that results in a more sustainable utilization of resources through energy management in all buildings, more effective waste management and recycling, more energy-efficient approaches to design and construction of buildings, facilities, and transportation equipment and systems. A nature-based economy is clearly needed as we enter the 21st century, in view of resource availability and the need to integrate all members of society in consumption of the products that are created with these resources. Solar and wind power and other renewable energy sources have been the first step in this effort. We now speak of "smart cities," robotics and artificial intelligence as components in the creation of the economy that the world needs, and cities have a central role to play in its development.

We close this book with three chapters on aspects of cities and regions in Mexico. Jaime Sobrino (Chapter 10) examines Mexico's evolution during the past half-century and links competitiveness with demographic change. One of the primary features of Mexican economic development during this period has been population deconcentration and economic decentralization. As is the case with many larger urban centers, Mexico

City has seen its periphery grow in relation to the city's historic center; however, in the recent period Mexico City's growth in relation to other categories of cities has been greater than during the earlier period. Furthermore, while national population growth between 1980 and 2015 was 70 percent, the country's 15 urban agglomerations tripled their populations. Within Mexico, the greatest growth was in the Center region, with the North growing the least. Regional growth was clearly linked to the dynamism of the regions' dominant industries: manufacturing exports in the North, automobiles and electronics in the West, and the slow-growing petroleum sector in the South. One of the striking features of this growth was the lack of effective local or regional planning activities on the part of the levels of government. Sobrino argues that this is a powerful requirement for Mexico and its regions and cities in the coming decades.

Clemente Ruiz Durán (Chapter 11) focuses on two major industries – automobile and pharmaceuticals, and two minor industries – pharmaceuticals and medical devices, and shows how the development of interaction in global production networks and global value chains (GVCs) has increased interaction between regions and cities and has led to positive complementarities with activity in nearby towns. Automotive production is concentrated along the US border and down the center of Mexico to Puebla. Electronics is located in Baja California and Chihuahua in the north and then in the center, principally in Jalisco, and the south of Mexico. Pharmaceuticals and medical devices are far less developed and are concentrated in the areas around Mexico City, to the east in Jalisco and along the US border. The challenge for smaller cities and regions is to insert themselves into GVCs in these industries and to develop growth in interactions among the larger cities.

Our final contributor, Isela Orihuela (Chapter 12) shows how urban competitiveness and sustainability are linked to urban planning and alliances. This is examined in a context in which a premium is placed on development of innovative industries during the two decades 1993–2013. Innovative industries are, of course, those that are dependent upon knowledge, learning and technology, with less reliance on traditional capital and labor. In Mexico, traditional manufacturing and innovative industry grew similarly during 1993–2008 but in the final period, 2008–2013, innovative industry stagnated. However, while innovative industry growth slowed in the largest cities, it experienced a substantial growth in smaller cities, especially those that are in proximity to larger cities that give access to an airport. Furthermore, the aeronautics industry develops city–university–enterprise networks, while other industries such as automotive goods tend to function more in isolation. Obviously the spread effects throughout a region are greater in the former than in the latter industry. The innovative industries, such as the aeronautical industry, are most closely linked to their regional social, legal and environmental structures.

OVERVIEW

This is a wide-ranging set of contributions, but they all treat the policy options and experiences of cities and urban areas in East Asia, North America and Western Europe with regard to what is necessary for the successful functioning of these entities in the years to come. On the one hand, there is a set of soft issues, such as social cohesion, environmental quality, cultural diversity, tolerance, regional planning and alliances. On the other hand, there are hard elements, such as suitable working spaces, demography (including rural to urban, age distribution and deconcentration of population), innovative work spaces, smart cities, innovative industries, robots and communications.

Both soft and hard elements have roles to play, and the interaction between them is of great interest and importance. The wide array of cities that are included in these chapters afford the reader the opportunity to see how these elements are operative in cities of different structures, systems of governance and administration, aspirations, population sizes, histories and geographic locations. This is not a book that attempts to conclude that one city or one approach is superior, but rather considers how city leaders and social groups can intervene in a way that works for the longer-term benefit of the residents of that city. There is clearly no one objective goal or end, nor is there a single "best way."

PART I

The sustainable city

1. Towards sustainable urban competitiveness? The role of organizing capacity and distributed leadership

Leo van den Berg and Luis Carvalho

INTRODUCTION: HEIGHTENED CHALLENGES FOR URBAN COMPETITIVENESS

Sustainability is a keyword of our time. Although the attention to urban sustainability issues goes back a few decades in academic and policy discourse (Campbell, 1996), the perception of the urgency to act is now very evident. If cities have been widely acknowledged as growth and competitiveness engines of their countries (e.g., Kresl and Ietri, 2014; McCann, 2013), modern and sustainable cities are also increasingly expected to be at the forefront of the fight against climate change and other intertwined societal challenges, such as fighting poverty and improving health conditions, among many others. Moreover, it is now also increasingly clear that in order to remain competitive in economic terms, a city's economic progress has to be holistically combined with environmental and societal dimensions. This raises gigantic challenges to urban policy-making and the way cities are managed by those in charge, at a time of rising populist concerns and the need to still unlock new growth paths in places that have been left behind for too long.

There are different normative viewpoints about what sustainability means or should be (Hopwood et al., 2005), when discussing its urban facets (Bulkeley et al., 2011). These different perspectives are very important in order to frame action and align different interests (Lombardi et al., 2011). In this chapter, we take a simplified approach, looking at sustainable urban competitiveness as "a city's ability to keep growing and developing over time while fostering social cohesion and environmental quality" (Carvalho et al., 2016, p. 1). Our main interest is to reflect on the challenges that emerge when urban competitiveness goals and strategies become infused with sustainability dimensions and, because of that, become increasingly multidimensional and multi-stakeholder.

In particular, we focus on the role of organizing capacity and urban leadership (van den Berg et al., 1997; van den Berg and Braun, 1999) in the ability of cities to engage multiple actors and constituencies in sustainable urban competitiveness ambitions and initiatives. We draw from recent reviews and work in the field (e.g., Beer and Clower, 2014; Sotarauta, 2006; van den Berg et al., 2014; Carvalho et al., 2016) to learn from past experiences and venture into what this implies in a context in which the stakes are higher; not only because social and environmental dimensions are increasingly important, but also because economic diversification is still a fundamental cornerstone of urban and regional development (Boschma, 2017). Overall, we argue that leadership will likely remain one of the most fundamental components of a city's organizing capacity, but it must be seen as a distributed, relational feature beyond the action of heroic individuals, chief visionaries and strong mayors.

To make this point, the chapter starts by briefly reviewing the changing context for urban leadership and the key role of organizing capacity, in times in which urban development has become – perhaps more than ever before – an open-ended process. It proceeds to discuss how organizing capacity has become largely a matter of distributed urban leadership, and its implications. Then, it looks at three types of actors and urban constituencies (lead firms, knowledge institutes and civic movements) whose influence in urban competitiveness affairs has been growing in many parts of the world, looking into how to frame their involvement in urban leadership. The chapter concludes with a number of observations about distributed urban leadership in times of new societal demands.

ORGANIZING CAPACITY AND THE EVOLVING CONTEXT OF URBAN COMPETITIVENESS

One of the reasons why organizing capacity and more demanding concepts of urban leadership are needed is because the playing field for urban development has changed substantially over the last decades. For example, in Europe during most of the 20th century – when the welfare state was being built – leadership in city councils and other agencies largely focused on the implementation of visions and policies emanating from the national level (Sotarauta, 2002; Pike et al., 2006). Change was slow, and many city departments grew substantially as a reaction to the demands of an industry-based economy, giving rise to municipal "silos" in land planning, utility provision, infrastructure and public works, and so on. Urban leadership tended to be formal and hierarchical, and organizing urban development was more about the ability to give and follow concrete instructions and intervene in case of deviations (Bass, 1991).

The context for urban leadership started to change over the last decades of the 20th century. From the mid-1980s onwards, globalization, the diffusion of information and telecommunication technologies, greater political integration of sovereign states and the consolidation of a knowledge-based economy with heightened factor mobility dramatically increased competition between cities to attract, among others, talent, capital and investments (van den Berg and Braun, 1999). This new context had many implications for cities and urban leadership. Urban development became an open-ended process, in which urban success increasingly depended on the strategic choices of those in charge. At this time, and building on previous studies of urban growth, decline and recovery, van den Berg et al. (1997) started to discuss the notion of urban organizing capacity as an increasing fundamental "ability to enlist all actors involved and, with their help, to generate new ideas and to develop and implement a policy designed to respond to fundamental developments and create conditions for sustainable development" (van den Berg et al., 2014, p. 1).

Therefore, more than controlling, repressing or simply throwing money at problems, the ability to organize and lead urban competitiveness became much more about managing, steering and organizing interests and networks (Sotarauta, 2006; Teisman and Klijn, 2002). This implied that, on the one hand, the resources needed – for example, knowledge, funding and legitimacy – became progressively not in the sole hands of the local administration but required partnerships with public and private actors. Moreover, on the other hand, and in order to combine these resources, urban management progressively called for trust-building, social capital, mutual understanding and even experimentation. Indeed, more than coordinating stable and formal relationships, urban leadership increasingly had to deal with uncertainty, ambiguity, bargaining and compromise (Lynn et al., 2000).

Although these shifts have been recognized for about two decades, the challenges they bring are still highly contemporary and quite far from being solved. It is clear that cities are fundamental arenas to tackle the complex societal challenges of our time, such as climate change, aging, migrations, diversity and exclusion, which go hand-in-hand with rising citizen expectations and the unfolding digital revolution. All the aforementioned pose challenges to sustainable urban competitiveness. At the same time, new modes of private engagement in urban provisions – for example, based on notions of shared value (Porter and Kramer, 2011) – promise to challenge the playing field of urban governance and power relations within cities, with firms increasingly willing to have a role in the development of local communities and to engage in urban affairs. All in all, urban dynamics became increasingly hard to predict, also as external changes can emerge fast and have very strong impacts, requiring local leaders to identify early signals, deal with ambiguity and adapt fast to new realities.

ORGANIZING CAPACITY AS A MATTER OF DISTRIBUTED LEADERSHIP

It seems self-evident that the challenging scope of contemporary urban challenges requires organizing capacity and committed leadership. However, a problem with many studies and previous accounts on urban competitiveness and change is that they tend to look at leadership as sort of a "black box," emphasizing single leaders, visionaries and influential persons (Carvalho et al., 2016; van den Berg et al., 1997; Wray, 2019) at the expense of the processes involved in leading and transforming.

Beer and Clower (2014) identified this limitation when reviewing some of the most influential perspectives of urban and regional leadership, pinpointing three key approaches. As explored by the authors, the first view on leadership – and one of the most influential – is the so-called "great person" approach. This approach links the success or failure of strategies and projects, whether in a company or in a city, to the virtues and traits of individuals, namely their charisma and capabilities. This view holds that organizations should find these people, and retain them in decision-making positions. Clearly, the political process associated with urban leadership renders this approach's applicability limited vis-à-vis firms (for example, appointing a chief executive officer); yet, translated to the context of cities, leaders would be the charismatic "visionaries" or "heroic" mayors who championed, for example, large urban transformation projects (such as Barcelona's Pasqual Maragall or Curitiba's Jaime Lerner, to name just two).

A second set of approaches relates individual leaders with the specific leadership context. These approaches suggest that different types of leaders are necessary according to the challenges they are faced with. In principle, no single person has the capacity to be a leader across the board, and leadership capacity is contingent on time, place and types of strategies. For example, in early studies of the organization of major urban development projects in European cities (e.g., van den Berg et al.,

1997) it was found that leadership was an essential enabler, but that the key individuals in charge often changed during the project, and good initiators were not necessarily as good at implementing visions and strategies. In other words, as elaborated by Beer and Clower (2014), effective urban leadership may be a temporary phenomenon and may rely on timely contributions.

A third group of perspectives on urban leadership focuses on behavior styles. Examples are the contrasts between authoritarian, democratic and laissez-faire approaches; ordinary versus heroic leaders; and socio-emotional versus task-oriented (Beer and Clower, 2014). In the same vein, in the context of urban economic development, Sotarauta (2006) distinguishes between "policy generalists" (leaders with a general view of the urban policy context and trends), "persons of substance" (with deep knowledge in a concrete field) and "persons of understanding" (able to mediate interests and bridge networks).

Valuable as they are, the above-mentioned approaches tend to associate leadership with the actions of individuals. Yet, recent studies in the field of urban and regional studies have started to discuss leadership as a distributed capacity: that is, an urban-level competence emerging out of a broader network of stakeholders whose actions, in one way or another, promote urban and regional development. For example, it has been argued that "in regional economic development leadership is by defin-ition shared … be they as powerful as possible, leaders can usually transform nothing major alone. Therefore, the question is not only how leaders lead their own followers, but also how they influence other leaders" (Sotarauta, 2006, p. 2). Such a way of understanding leadership has been gaining advocates in international urban policy spheres, and is arguably very important to tackle many of the intricate societal chal-lenges faced by cities, notably in Europe (Schlappa and Neill, 2013).

In fact, distributed leadership as relational capacity largely resonates with the leadership practices observed in recent surveys of urban projects combining economic, societal and environmental objectives (van den Berg et al., 2014; Carvalho et al., 2016). In such projects, a multitude of relevant actors, with different sorts of formal and informal resources, shape leadership constellations around projects, engaging in a multitude of tasks: brokering relations, shaping partnerships, thinking "outside the box," backing projects in complex political arenas, maintaining enthusiasm, avoiding capture by interest groups and bureaucratic units, keeping experimentation going on, assuring stability, speaking different "languages," among many other actions. In the literature on sustainability transitions, successful experimentation of new solutions to pressing urban challenges also rely on these types of agentic features, and the most impactful ones coalesce into dense, committed and distributed networks of individuals with a stake in the initiative (Schot and Geels, 2008). There are nowadays plentiful examples of such types of agency in energy and sustainability transitions in cities, in which some of the most relevant leadership positions are actually intermediation and not command-and-control positions (e.g., Kivimaa, 2014; van Winden and Carvalho, 2019).

Yet, a remaining question is: under which conditions can distributed leadership emerge in cities? It is clear that just "picking" and "getting" good leaders is, in practice, a very difficult (if possible) task. There is a time dimension involved, and thus "making" leaders may also not be a feasible option. For example, while networking skills can eventually be learned, a leader's network cannot be built overnight as it requires, among others, trust and social capital. And, even if theoretically possible, "picking," "getting" or "making" leaders would likely not suffice to make leadership a truly distributed and self-sustaining capability. This is the case because urban leadership sometimes emerges in communities – for example, through passionate individuals with an individual mission to change something – and not inside formal organizations. While in formal organizations there are appointments to be made (mayor, rector, chief executive officer, council member), this is less often the case with agents who exert informal leadership. Therefore, as put by Beer and Clower (2014), there are risks that leadership roles will not be taken up, and hence a key problem for cities is not only one of poor leadership, but also one of absence of leadership, which may endanger the feasibility of more challenging urban initiatives in many cities.

In this vein, an important notion is that it is important to create space to make leadership emerge. Building on the notion of organizational slack from management studies (Cyert and March, 1963; Geiger and Makri, 2006), Beer and Clower (2014) argue that a certain degree of slack in urban management increases the ability to take risks, experiment and innovate. Many cities and local administrations are increasingly engaging with this philosophy, for example by creating "design-thinking" units and other sorts of innovation and experimentation labs, in which new solutions are tested and new local constituencies are engaged. Moreover, it is fundamental that those in charge are willing to share power and resources. This may be particularly problematic within the public administration, in which there is a well-entrenched "instinct to control and constrain, in order to provide certainty" (Miles and Trott, 2011, p. 7).

Urban leadership may thus also rely on voluntary time contributions from experienced people from outside the local government, meaning that enough time to work on urban development issues has to be available in different organizations. In the aftermath of austerity and budget cuts in Europe, resources are still scarce in local governments, and this may hinder the ability to foster distributed urban leadership and engage in long-term envisioning (versus solving short-term problems). Yet, this space often has to be actively created by individuals, for example by doing things differently or doing different things in order to increase the time, capabilities and room for maneuver to act on urban leadership.

NEW ACTORS IN URBAN LEADERSHIP

It is increasingly accepted that urban leadership can (and in many cases should) go beyond the action of elected representatives and city council mandates, involving "unusual suspects." In many cities, and increasingly so, urban leadership has to be discussed in the light of the actions of other influential groups of stakeholders, notably lead firms, universities and civic movements. For example, large private companies tend to have an enduring, strong influence in urban policy-making and leadership, namely by signaling future developments and economic policy needs; the same goes for universities and knowledge institutes, in cities with high shares of student population. Many lead firms and universities are increasingly ready to collaborate, influence and take a strong role in urban leadership, and the same goes for organized groups of citizens and their associations. But is that an advantage or a threat for sustainable urban competitiveness? And what can local governments do to make the most of their involvement in urban leadership?

Lead Firms

The involvement of lead firms and private companies in urban manage-ment is framed in two rather contrasting ways in the literature (see van Winden, 2013, for a review). One influential research stream looks at private companies (namely, large corporations) as purely profit-maximizing agents, which put their own short-term, self-interest above the greater, long-term urban common good. They are seen as committed to urban progress to the extent that they can reap benefits from city assets (for example, labor, land) and influence policy agendas in a way that serves their own interests (Swyngedouw et al., 2002). Under this perspective, corporate involvement in urban development has been often linked to "urban boosterism" (for example, flagship urban redevelop-ment projects), so that corporations can reap most of the benefits under the argument that the developments will create jobs and other economic multipliers in the city, in a trickledown fashion. In a different yet related way, a classic example demonstrated that the industrial elites of the German Ruhr area were powerful enough to influence the regional economic agenda in the 1970s so that they could maintain privilege (support to the declining steel industries), at the expense of delaying a much-needed economic transition (Grabher, 1993). All in all, this perspective highlights the conflict between private interests and (long-term) urban benefits, advocating against private involvement in urban leadership.

In other literature strands, however, the role of lead firms and private corporations in urban leadership is viewed rather differently. An early study about the relation between city and enterprise framed cities as the "competitive context" in which companies operate, it thus being in their own interest to improve that context in the long run (van den Berg et al., 2004); the study analyzed how European and North American corporations (for example, Boeing, Diageo, BMW, Pfizer) contributed to social improvement in their local communities (physical regeneration, crime prevention, youth unemployment) under corporate social responsibility (CSR) schemes. More recently, it has been suggested that companies are increasingly moving beyond "tokenism" and piecemeal CSR initiatives to embrace notions of shared value and societal purpose; that is, placing the community's progress at the core of a company's strategy (Porter and Kramer, 2011). Under this perspective, improving urban development is no longer a peripheral concern of the company, but integral to competing and profit-making. Thus, lead firms would have considerable incentives to support urban leadership in a way that favors the long-term prospects of both city and enterprise.

These two views represent the extreme ends of scholarly thought on the link between private involvement in urban development; yet, they call our attention to important issues when involving lead firms in strategic urban leadership. On the one hand, the potential conflicts between private interest and sustainable urban development should not be underestimated, and this calls for enhanced accountability, and more skills in the city administration and governance systems to ensure a proper system of checks and balances. Yet, on the other hand, it is also clear that many contemporary sustainable urban competitiveness challenges require the knowledge, skills and resources of private companies, many of them with authentic ambitions to improve the "competitive urban environment" in order to strengthen the company's profile.

Two contemporary examples epitomize the challenging relation between lead firms and urban leadership. One concerns the involvement of large private companies in the design of "smart city" strategies. For example, leading technology companies (such as software providers, telecom companies) have significant technical knowledge that can support cities in the development of new urban solutions. Yet, it is also true that many such companies envision selling proprietary solutions, which may hamper a city's resilience in the long run by causing technological lock-ins (Townsend, 2013). Thus, a smart-city strategy strongly led by lead firms risks emphasizing techno-driven visions of sustainability at the expense of more inclusive and user-driven approaches (Carvalho, 2015).

Other examples concern the involvement of companies signaling the direction for regional innovation policies. Companies are the main innovators and are well positioned to identify promising market and innovation opportunities, hence the argument to involve them to the full. However, lead companies also have large incentives to influence policies to fit their own interests, which makes the involvement of companies in innovation policy a very challenging issue in cities and regions with weaker economic and industrial bases, in which the dominance of vested interests is a latent threat (Boschma, 2013).

Knowledge Institutes

The involvement of universities and knowledge institutes in urban leadership is much less contested in the literature: it is often seen as positive (Russo et al., 2007; van Winden, 2012), perhaps due to their typical not-for-profit nature. As urban economies become increasingly knowledge-intensive, the role of universities and their influence in urban development has grown. Just like firms, universities and research institutes are well positioned to spot innovative trends, and their researchers are often (yet, not always) connected to relevant business and knowledge networks, which are increasingly fundamental for urban development, economic renewal and many sorts of sustainability-oriented initiatives.

The involvement of universities in urban development issues can also be seen from a "shared value" perspective, in fields in which their interests may overlap (van Winden, 2012), for example:

● The promotion of the local and regional economy, entrepreneurship and innovation. The city has interests in new firm and job creation, exports and in enhancing the local tax base; while the university has growing interests in commercializing its research, for example through the support of incubators, science parks and knowledge transfer schemes.

- Marketing, attractiveness and internationalization. The brand of the city and of the university often become intertwined, and both have an interest in strengthening it: for example, to attract businesses and students.
- Finding solutions to societal problems, such as urban mobility, health, inclusion and greening the city. Universities may see cities as test-beds for new applied research in these domains; while cities may benefit from universities' knowledge bases to tackle some of those pressing issues.
- Urban planning and student life. Universities have an important stake in typical urban planning actions and public provisions (for example, public spaces, mobility, housing) as they directly affect the academic population; and at the same time, cities may benefit from the involvement of students in city life (leading to cultural and economic vibrancy, political activism, and so on).

For all these reasons and overlaps, universities may exert their power and take important roles in urban leadership. However, their involvement is also not always conflict-free. For example, residents, tourists and students increasingly compete for the use of space in cities, and universities may exert their power to assure that their specific interests are met in the first place. The increase in student and scientist mobility in many parts of world, being overall a rather positive development, creates new challenges in cities – for example, in Southern Europe – as housing prices rise and displace permanent residents, who are outcompeted by the higher purchasing power of floating urban populations.

Civic Movements and Public Engagement

There is a long history of civic movements exerting influence in urban development and local politics (Arnstein, 1969). Those have been widely documented in cases of controversial urban renewal projects, but also related to NIMBY (not in my back yard) reactions against transport and environmental infrastructure (for example, wind turbines, waste treatment stations). For these reasons, it has been argued that getting social support early on is a critical variable behind successful urban development strategies (van den Berg et al., 1997, 2014).

Yet, beyond protesting and engaging in radical politics, many civic movements and their representatives are becoming increasingly embedded in urban development initiatives. In Barcelona, for example, emerging movements against housing evictions in the aftermath of the financial crisis became institutionalized and are now represented in the city council on a very high level (for example, through the Mayor Ada Colau, a well-known social activist). Moreover, technology is empowering and facilitating the involvement of civic movements and new unusual suspects in urban leadership. There are many examples across contemporary urban development domains. Examples are the involvement of co-operatives of citizens in producing and aggregating renewable energy; movements of citizens claiming for and championing new environmental improvements in their districts; the development of new services and "smart" software solutions for cities based on open data, freedom of information and distributed communities of information technology (IT) developers; communitarian co-working spaces; charities; time bank organization; among many other formal and informal communitarian practices.

Notably, engaging with civic and grassroots movements is easier said than done. Contrary to lead firms and knowledge institutes, civic movements are often unstable, distributed, and their representatives are not always easy to find, calling for new ways to engage and involve them in urban leadership.

CONCLUSION

Cities are not short of challenges today, and the role of leadership and organizing capacity is only likely to increase in competitive, sustainable and modern cities. This chapter has reviewed a number of studies and conceptual viewpoints with an eye to providing a deeper perspective on what it takes to "lead" in order to deal with contemporary urban challenges. As argued, organizing capacity and urban leadership should increasingly be seen as distributed capacities, in which new constellations of actors are not only involved, but can also take pre-eminent leadership positions. So, how to make the most of such involvement in urban leadership?

Far from closing the debate, we would simply argue that the productive involvement of new stakeholders in urban leadership requires more – not less – skills and competences from city officials and local administrations. This is fundamental, so that cities may reap the benefits of their participation and avoid latent threats; for example, making sure that private involvement is not confused with replacement, "take-over" or privatization of a council's tasks and responsibilities. City officials need more reflexive, mediation and conflict management capacities and the ability to "speak different languages" (of business people, academics and activists). The involvement of new stakeholders in urban leadership may give rise to out-of-the-box initiatives, obliging city officials to step outside their comfort zones and embrace risk. In that vein, urban managers need to be able to balance risk with the need to maintain accountability for their initiatives. Yet, this also poses a challenge for other constituencies engaging in sustainable urban development affairs, as their knowledge on how the city council works is often very limited as well.

Moreover, city leaders and officials need more "urban intelligence" in order to discuss at the same level with lead firms and universities, as well as to identify and mobilize civic movements. This consists in knowing better what is going on in the city, and permanently assessing new trends, identifying new actors and the implications for a city. This may involve quantitative indicators and comparative rankings, but that is rarely enough to spot more subtle changes.

For example, some cities have put in place systematic economic trend-watching and foresight initiatives, and their staff attend conferences, meetings of informal groups, and so on, to pick up weak signals. This helps to spot new economic fields and entrepreneurs beyond "old boys' networks," and to open urban leadership to new players. Moreover, the involvement of lead firms and universities in urban leadership should go hand-in-hand with the development of systematic discussion platforms to identify and explore opportunities for "shared value" creation. For the specific case of civic and distributed grassroots movements, the role of digital tools is becoming absolutely central.

REFERENCES

Arnstein, Susan, "A ladder of citizen participation," *Journal of the American Institute of Planners*, Vol. 35, No. 4, 1969, pp. 216–224.
Bass, Bernard, "From transactional to transformational leadership: learning to share the vision," *Organizational Dynamics*, Vol. 18, No. 3, 1991, pp. 19–31.
Beer, Andrew and Terry Clower, "Mobilizing leadership in cities and regions," *Regional Studies, Regional Science*, Vol. 1, No. 1, 2014, pp. 5–20.
Berg, Leo van den and Erik Braun, "Urban competitiveness, marketing and the need for organising capacity," *Urban Studies*, Vol. 36, No. 5–6, 1999, pp. 987–999.
Berg, Leo van den, Erik Braun and Jan van der Meer, "The organising capacity of metropolitan region," *Environment and Planning C*, Vol. 15, No. 3, 1997, pp. 253–272.
Berg, Leo van den, Erik Braun and Alexander Otgaar, "Corporate community involvement in European and US cities," *Environment and Planning C*, Vol. 22, 2004, pp. 475–494.

Berg, Leo van den, Jan van den Meer and Luís Carvalho, *Cities as Engines of Sustainable Competitiveness: European Urban Policy in Practice*, Aldershot: Ashgate, 2014.

Boschma, Ron, "Constructing Regional Advantage and Smart Specialization: Comparison of Two European Policy Concepts," Papers in Evolutionary Economic Geography, No. 1322, Utrecht University, Section of Economic Geography, 2013.

Boschma, Ron, "Relatedness as driver of regional diversification: a research agenda," *Regional Studies*, Vol. 51, No. 3, 2017, pp. 351–364.

Bulkeley, Harriet, Vanessa Castán Broto, Mike Hodson and Simon Marvin (eds), *Cities and Low Carbon Transitions*, London: Routledge, 2011.

Campbell, Scott, "Green cities, growing cities, just cities? Urban planning and the contradictions of sustainable development," *Journal of the American Planning Association*, Vol. 62, No. 3, 1996, pp. 296–312.

Carvalho, Luis, "Smart cities from scratch? A socio-technical perspective," *Cambridge Journal of Regions, Economy and Society*, Vol. 8, No. 1, 2015, pp. 43–60.

Carvalho, Luís, Leo van den Berg, Hazem Galal and Peter Teunisse (eds), *Delivering Sustainable Competitiveness*, London: Routledge, 2016.

Cyert, Richard and James March, *A Behavioral Theory of the Firm*, Englewood Cliffs, NJ: Prentice Hall, 1963.

Geiger, Scott and Marianna Makri, "Exploration and exploitation innovation processes: the role of organizational slack in R&D intensive firms," *Journal of High Technology Management Research*, Vol. 17, No. 1, 2006, pp. 97–108.

Grabher, Gernot, "The weakness of strong ties; the lock-in of regional development in the Ruhr area," in Gernot Grabher (ed.), *The Embedded Firm: On the Socioeconomics of Industrial Networks*, London: Routledge, 1993, pp. 255–277.

Hopwood, Bill, Mary Mellor and Geoff O'Brien, "Sustainable development: mapping different approaches," *Sustainable Development*, Vol. 13, 2005, pp. 38–52.

Kivimaa, Paula, "Government-affiliated intermediary organisations as actors in system-level transitions," *Research Policy*, Vol. 43, No. 8, 2014, pp. 1370–1380.

Kresl, Peter and Daniele Ietri, *Urban Competitiveness: Theory and Practice*, New York: Routledge, 2014.

Lombardi, Rachel, Libby Porter, Austin Barber and Chris Rogers, "Conceptualising sustainability in UK urban regeneration: a discursive formation," *Urban Studies*, Vol. 48, No. 2, 2011, pp. 273–296.

Lynn, Laurence, Carolyn Heinrich and Carolyn Hill, "Studying governance and public management: challenges and prospects," *Journal of Public Administration Research and Theory*, Vol. 10, No. 2, 2000, pp. 233–262.

McCann, Philip, *Modern Urban and Regional Economics*, Oxford: Oxford University Press, 2013.

Miles, Emily and William Trott, *Collaborative Working Inside Out: A Series of Personal Perspectives on Government Effectiveness*, London: Institute for Government, 2011.

Pike, Andy, Andrés Rodriguez-Pose and John Tomaney, *Local and Regional Development*, Abingdon: Routledge, 2006.

Porter, Michael and Mark Kramer, "The big idea: creating shared value," *Harvard Business Review*, Vol. 89, No. 1–2, 2011, pp. 62–77.

Russo, Antonio Paolo, Leo van den Berg and Mariangela Lavanga, "Toward a sustainable relationship between city and university: a stakeholdership approach," *Journal of Planning Education and Research*, Vol. 27, No. 2, 2007, pp. 199–216.

Schlappa, Hans and William Neill, *Cities of Tomorrow – Action Today. URBACT II Capitalisation, From Crisis to Choice: Re-imagining the Future in Shrinking Cities*, Paris: URBACT, 2013.

Schot, Johan and Frank Geels, "Strategic niche management and sustainable innovation journeys: theory, findings, research agenda, and policy," *Technology Analysis and Strategic Management*, Vol. 20, No. 5, 2008, pp. 537–554.

Sotarauta, Markku, "Leadership, power and influence in regional development: a tentative typology of leaders and their ways of influencing," *Perspectives on Process-Based Regional Development Policy*, Stockholm: Nordregio, 2002, pp. 182–207.

Sotarauta, Markku, "Where have all the people gone? Leadership in the fields of regional development," *Sente Working Papers*, Vol. 9, 2006, pp. 1–16.

Swyngedouw, Erik, Frank Moulaert and Arantxa Rodriguez, "Neoliberal urbanization in Europe: large-scale urban development projects and the new urban policy," *Antipode*, Vol. 34, No. 3, 2002, pp. 542–577.

Teisman, Geert and Erik-Hans Klijn, "Partnership arrangements: governmental rhetoric or governance scheme?," *Public Administration Review*, Vol. 62, No. 2, 2002, pp. 197–205.

Townsend, Andy, *Smart Cities: Big Data, Civic Hackers, and the Quest for a New Utopia*, New York: W.W. Norton & Company, 2013.

Winden, Willem van, *EUnivercities: City–University Cooperation to the Next Level. A Baseline Study*, Paris: URBACT, 2012.

Winden, Willem van, "Delivering sustainable urban solutions: a new chapter of corporate involvement in urban management," in M.P. van Dijk, J. van der Meer and J. van den Borg (eds), *From Urban Systems to Sustainable Competitive Metropolitan Regions: Essays in Honour of Leo van den Berg*, Rotterdam: Erasmus University Rotterdam, 2013.

Winden, Willem van and Luís Carvalho, "Intermediation in public procurement of innovation: how Amsterdam's startup-in-residence programme connects startups to urban challenges," *Research Policy*, Vol. 48, No. 9, 2019, 103789 (pp. 1–11).

Wray, Ian, *No Little Plans: How Government Built America's Wealth and Infrastructure*, London: Routledge, 2019.

2. The modern city and third places: new sources of sustainable entrepreneurs and competitiveness

Diane-Gabrielle Tremblay and Arnaud Scaillerez

New technologies and competition are driving employers and cities to rethink how they work by looking for new ideas for city planning, new modes of work organization and space sharing for a more sustainable environment, as well as more sustainable entrepreneurs. At the same time, workers want to be given more autonomy in their work or to free themselves from hierarchical constraints. In short, the expectations of employers, as well as employees, are constantly changing and encourage us to rethink the organization of work and the spaces for work and reflection dedicated to this purpose.

The purpose of this chapter is to show the possibilities that third places (co-working spaces, fab labs and living labs) can offer for sharing and developing knowledge and tools, thus contributing to competitiveness and sustainability of entrepreneurs, firms and cities. In our work, we have used the theories on communities of practice and epistemic communities in relation with third places. We will present the definitions, the characteristics and the challenges observed in these places, since the benefits can be important for competitiveness and sustainability, but require some pre-conditions (Scaillerez and Tremblay, 2019a, 2019b, 2019c).

THIRD PLACES AND COMPETITIVENESS

Definitions

Co-working spaces, fab labs and living labs are third places, and it is necessary to start by defining these notions (Scaillerez and Tremblay, 2017a).

Third places: spaces that facilitate the exchange of knowledge

In the late 1980s, the sociologist Ray Oldenburg (1989) presented a new idea: that of working outside the walls of one's business and even outside one's home, especially in third places. It is not easy to define the concept of a third place (Brown, 2017). It is possible to say that the third places are a place in-between home and work, having characteristics that are common to the private sphere and to the professional sphere. These places were originally created to revive social interactions in cities in North America that were losing economic momentum. Since then, different authors have added some criteria to the definition, making it broader and more related to other circumstances (Smits, 2015) and other countries. Therefore, for this sharing model to be a third place:

- It must be neutral (therefore, neither at home nor at the employer's premises), hence the third place (Oldenburg, 1989), in-between the two, which contributes to reduction in car use and in greenhouse gas emissions, as well as sharing office space, thus contributing to sustainability of workers, entrepreneurs and cities.
- It must offer free access, and therefore be open to all without any restriction, especially as to the activity carried out (Oldenburg, 1999).
- Finally, it must facilitate meetings and exchanges: the configuration of the place must be conducive to conversation, with the presence of meeting rooms in particular, or simply places of conviviality such as those reserved for coffee breaks or lunch (Guenoud and Moeckli, 2010).

With these first elements, one could for example consider that cafes providing free wifi (such as Starbucks) could be considered as third places. However, this is not the case, because to be a third place, two other elements must also be introduced:

- Frequency of use by the same users; with this fourth element, Starbucks could represent a third place for customers accustomed to come to work and exchange ideas and knowledge (Gershenfeld, 2005).
- Above all, for a third place to be recognized as such, it is necessary that the knowledge (or product) that results and that emanates from exchanges between the regulars of the place subsists even after the end of the collaboration, even after a possible closure of the venue and the end of the meetings between the actors, and in this way it can contribute to competitiveness. Also, it is undoubtedly this

element that differentiates places open to the public (such as Starbucks, for example) from third places conducive to work and knowledge sharing (Liefooghe, 2016).

Co-working spaces, sharing space for more sustainability and competitiveness

Co-working is a phenomenon that appeared in the 1990s. The first co-working space was created ten years later, in 2005 in San Francisco (Lallement, 2015), to allow users of the place to develop their creativity and innovative spirit. Since then, co-working spaces have been multiplying every year across the world, and reached 13 800 spaces in 2017 (Deskmag, 2017). Recently, it has been indicated that these co-working spaces are developing everywhere, including in Asia, and even Africa. Regus and its mother house IWG have created 16 co-working spaces in Morocco, doubling its number in three years. In Africa and Asia it is often expatriates who work in these places, when their employer only has some 10–20 workers on site, and all the more so when they are often working out of their office. Business travelers can work in different co-working spaces when they are traveling, provided they have a membership card, which gives access to some 3300 sites all over the world (Gorwitz, 2019). This is one aspect of the picture, as the other refers to the local workers, who find here a place to work for a lower rental cost, and often without traffic congestion, with more proximity to home (Le Nadant et al., 2018). As they share equipment and space, they contribute to more sustainable work and entrepreneurs (Boutillier, 2017; Boutillier and Ryckelynck, 2017). Data indicate that co-working spaces could represent up to 30 percent of business office space in 2030 (Gorwitz, 2019, according to Jones, Lang Lasalle, Consultants).

A co-working space allows its users to share a physical space with all the elements that can be found in an office, and take advantage of the pooling of equipment and the sharing of expenses in exchange for a weekly or monthly rental fee (Capdevila, 2015; Scaillerez and Tremblay, 2016a). It is above all a place composed of chairs and offices (Scaillerez and Tremblay, 2016b; Fabbri, 2016), but also shared equipment (printers, photocopying machines, scanners, and so on), with this sharing contributing to less waste of equipment. The offices can be open (open space) to facilitate meetings, or closed for more confidentiality, depending on the firm's or individual's needs. Both forms of office contribute to reduce the isolation of co-workers (Oldenburg, 2000; Scaillerez and Tremblay, 2016a), and often increase knowledge sharing and the competitiveness of businesses, and also of cities, as international firms and expats appreciate finding co-working spaces in cities. Thus, for individuals, co-working space can become a new solution to the desire to work away from the office, but without necessarily being alone at home; while sharing space and equipment, which contributes to the sustainability of their business and of the city. For firms they present advantages for expats or other workers who they can place in these spaces; and finally, for many cities, co-working spaces are becoming a competitive and sustainable advantage to be put forward to attract businesses (the self-employed, entrepreneurs, as well as large firms who sometimes place some 10–20 workers in a given city).

Fab labs: places for sharing knowledge and tools
Fab lab is short for "fabrication laboratory." Fab labs have been created within the Massachusetts Institute of Technology's (MIT) Center for Bits and Atoms (CBA) to enable everyone to become main players in technology manufacturing, rather than just spectators (Gershenfeld, 2005). The first ever fab lab was established at MIT in the CBA, a research laboratory founded in 2001 by the National Science Foundation (NSF). Thus, in the same way that the Internet has enabled the collaborative web, and in fact the development of shared tools, the CBA wishes to make fab labs the logical consequence of the digital revolution by giving everyone the opportunity to manufacture digital tools, as Neil Gershenfeld, director of the CBA wished (Scaillerez and Tremblay, 2019a, 2017b). After participating in the digital revolution, MIT wanted to democratize digital manufacturing. The fab lab network, also initiated by MIT, has listed nearly 1000 so far (Deskmag, 2017). Fab labs are proliferating around the world, and are presented as new places of collaboration and exchange open to all and in which anything is possible. The main advantage of these places is that they contribute to sharing tools and equipment, thus leading to more sustainable entrepreneurs and businesses, but also the sharing of tools and equipment for non-work activities. These places allow the creation of many innovations and can facilitate meetings between creatives and designers, amongst other groups.

Living labs, places of appropriation and collective experimentation
A living lab is a technique that was developed for the first time in the late 1990s at MIT: in fact, at the MIT Media Lab. Its institutionalization has grown in Europe since 2006, with the creation of the European Network of Living Labs (EnoLL) in 2015. More than 370 living labs in some 40 countries around the world are currently members (Deskmag, 2017). The interest of a living laboratory is to develop a project on the basis of solutions from the users themselves. Living labs make it possible to

invent solutions collectively, usually responding to empirical issues, or answering territorial development issues through the implementation of innovative practices. These laboratories develop a methodology adapted to each situation in order to encourage individuals to collaborate, exchange ideas and then create innovations that meet the needs of users (Capdevila, 2015; Scaillerez and Tremblay, 2017b). These labs work on various types of projects, many being oriented towards the revitalization of cities or parts of cities, many also related to the sustainability of cities, much less to competitiveness per se, although the two are often linked. In this sense, when they work on sustainability projects, they also contribute to the sustainable city.

The sharing of space, equipment, tools and ideas is the basis for the competitive advantage and sustainability of businesses and cities. But this sharing of material and ideas is not always spontaneous, and our research sought to analyze the elements which can contribute to knowledge and the sharing of space and equipment. In this perspective, the concepts of epistemic communities and of communities of practice appear to be useful.

Conceptual Frameworks: Epistemic Communities and Communities of Practice

Epistemic communities and third places: drivers of discussion, production and knowledge transfer

As early as the 1960s and 1970s, the notion of an epistemic community developed (Holzner, 1968; Holzner and Salmon-Cox, 1977; Holzner and Marx, 1979). It refers to a group of people working together to develop some form of knowledge through the use of specific scientific methods, the value of which is recognized by all (Holzner and Marx, 1979). In the 1990s, the notion developed further in the literature on politics and international relations (Adler, 1992; Adler and Haas, 1992; Haas, 1989, 1992). An epistemic community is thus defined as a group of people with significant and recognized expertise and skills in a specific area.

Third places can thus be studied through the prism of an epistemic community, as this community bases its action on an exchange of knowledge and skills. We find this same type of exchange in co-working spaces, fab labs and living labs. In addition, this type of community only stays together until it reaches a goal; everyone can go their separate ways once the result has been attained, whether the result has to do with knowledge sharing for more productivity, competitiveness or sustainability. All these types of objectives are possible, and communities of practice can indeed be brought together for various objectives (Amin and

Cohendet, 2004; Bourhis and Tremblay, 2004). This same situation of knowledge production and sharing is found in third places, where even if the co-workers no longer work together, the project or the professional activity that results can continue. The same goes for manufactured products developed by exchanging knowledge and sharing tools in fab labs, or the final reflection or idea produced by the participants of a living lab approach, all of which can contribute to business competitiveness and sustainability, and to more sustainable individual entrepreneurs.

The difference between communities of practice and epistemic communities stems from the fact that epistemic communities refer primarily to interest in the exchange of ideas and may give rise to some form of political action (Amin and Cohendet, 2004; Akrich, 2010), which can often be related to sustainability. Communities of practice are based on practice, as the word suggests, and they are thus interesting for the study of third places and their activities, in the perspective of attaining better competitiveness or sustainability in workplaces, and thus in cities.

Communities of practice and third places: the development of knowledge exchange groups

The term "community of practice" refers to a group of people who share an area of expertise or professional practice, and who meet to exchange, share and learn from each other, face-to-face or virtually, such as originally defined by Lave and Wenger (1991). In the case of third places, there are face-to-face exchanges that we have been able to study, but we could also imagine that these exchanges take place between different places, at a distance.

Community members are usually bound by a common interest in a field of knowledge, and a desire or need to share problems, experiences, models, tools and best practices (Bourhis and Tremblay, 2004), which is similar to what is observed in co-working spaces and fab labs, that gather people working in the same field, often in the field of information technology (IT) or other related sectors, to share knowledge and tools.

Wenger et al. (2002) presented a model of the developmental stages of communities of practice, which could also be applied to third places such as co-working spaces, fab labs or living labs. Most of these places are in the early stages of developing knowledge exchanges, at least according to what we have seen in our research in Quebec. Nevertheless, they already share spaces, tools and equipment, which is an important element for sustainability, although knowledge exchanges could increase competitiveness also.

According to this model of Wenger et al. (2002), there would be five stages in the life of a community. This is of course a standard model, and the reality may differ from this theoretical model. In the first stage, from a more or less formal network of people, the community is at the stage of potential development. Then, the community is formed and it moves to the stage of unification, then maturity, with frequent knowledge and tool exchanges. It then reaches a momentum, a "cruising rhythm," in other words, despite ups and downs which are always possible during its course. Then, normally, an external event might trigger the need to transform itself. This model is only theoretical, and the duration of the various steps is different depending on the community. In any case, most research suggests that it takes several months – at least six – before a community reaches the stage of maturity and produces concrete results (Bourhis and Tremblay, 2004). It can then go on cooperating, sharing knowledge, tools and spaces for some time, and producing various innovative ideas, products or services, depending on its goal.

In terms of functioning, communities – unlike work teams – rarely have a defined work plan (McDermott, 1999), which may still be similar to third places. After reaching their goals, teams normally disintegrate; whereas in principle, communities of practice are created to last, continuing to develop knowledge and expertise. Here, on the other hand, they are different from co-working spaces because people who find themselves in these spaces do not necessarily form a long-term community; although this can sometimes be the case. Depending on the location of the space, its objectives and infrastructure, it can receive people on a short- or long-term basis, for a few or many days a week. This is also the case for fab labs, where users can use the same tool together or share their knowledge to make an object, and once the object is created, they can put an end to their relationship or continue on to another project. We also find this vision in living labs, since the people who participate in the sharing, do so during the time for reflection or the project, then this exchange ceases or people move on to another project. There is a certain diversity in objectives and duration of the collaboration.

Our research on communities of practice has shown that for know-ledge exchanges to develop, there must first be some trust between people, and they must have come to know each other somewhat. Then, once trust is established, a project or objective, sometimes simply a common interest in a theme or subject, must encourage them to exchange ideas and knowledge, and to network (Tremblay, 2004a, 2004b). These exchanges can be relatively simple in the beginning, but can then lead to exchanges of knowledge and expertise more relevant to both parties to the exchange, for example in relation to a project aimed at better competitiveness or sustainability. At the same time, the very existence of co-working spaces leads to more sustainable businesses and cities, as they contribute to equipment sharing, as well as reduction in car use and greenhouse gas emissions, thus being conducive to more sustainable cities through their simple multiplication. Communities of practice then proceed to the unification and maturity stages evoked by Wenger et al. (2002), and it is here that exchanges can lead to the development of new ideas, products or services, or simply new ways of doing things in an organization or a collective. Again, these ideas, products and services can lead to better competitiveness and sustainability for individuals, entrepreneurs, businesses and cities. In addition, the development of any community is obviously influenced by its environment, as well as by the background of each of its members; but it can also be influenced by the cultural, economic and political context in which it is embedded, an environment that can be more or less favorable to its development (Wenger et al., 2002). An environment with goals related to competitiveness or sustainability objectives will thus imprint itself on the objectives of the community, as we have seen in our research on communities of practice (Tremblay, 2004a, 2004b).

In the case of co-working spaces and fab labs, for example, they usually host self-employed people, entrepreneurs or small and medium-sized enterprises (SMEs), but present similarities to communities of practice, as we will show in the following sections. These self-employed people, entrepreneurs or SMEs will choose a co-working space which is closer to their home, thus reducing car use and greenhouse gas emissions, while sharing space and equipment. It appears that co-working can contribute to reduce greenhouse gases, reduce the number of cars on the streets and favor public transportation, or walking or cycling to work, inasmuch as the co-working space is sufficiently close to the home of the worker. The sharing of space and equipment also has a positive impact on the environment by limiting the volume of IT equipment, amongst other positive impacts. This will be developed somewhat further in the next section, before we go on to present our research on third spaces and their functioning.

Research Method

To carry out our investigation on these new forms of work and space organization, we conducted qualitative research and interviewed 20 co-working spaces in Quebec and ten living labs, in large cities and in smaller towns or medium-sized cities, some of which are located in less urbanized areas. We met 30 users of these co-working spaces and 20 community managers and facilitators who work in co-working spaces, living labs, but also fab labs. The average duration of each interview was 60 minutes. These semi-structured interviews were based on an interview grid that included open and closed questions. These interviews were then the subject of a thematic analysis to highlight results related to the origins of a community and the establishment of a collaborative spirit, which can lead to real sharing (of space, equipment, tools, ideas) and to concrete results. These themes were analyzed and are the basis for our results presented here.

RESULTS

Co-working Spaces, Strategies to Facilitate Networking and Collaboration

A co-working space can go beyond its basic purpose of sharing space, fees and equipment, or offering services to become a real place of knowledge sharing (Fabbri, 2016), market or non-market, or professional collaboration between its members (Scaillerez and Tremblay, 2017a). New cooperation between users can then be observed. Some co-working spaces bring together specific categories of workers, with professional links with one another (Tremblay, 2016a, 2016b). The principle of a co-working space is to rent several premises, the sharing of collective space and equipment contributing to reduce costs and waste, while encouraging networking and the exchange of knowledge (Scaillerez and Tremblay, 2016a). For cooperation to develop beyond sharing space and equipment towards knowledge sharing, people must find a common interest that will encourage these exchanges. To do this, some spaces have focused their activity on an ideological proximity (third sector of social economy, for example) which, without guarantee of success, can at least promote the interest and desire to collaborate. These places can encourage new cooperation and a different coordination between their users. Working together in a single space, users can find common solutions to facilitate their business and cope with an increasingly competitive environment, thus favoring competitive advantage for each.

In a co-working space, whether or not there are strategies to facilitate collaboration, exchanges can take many forms. They can be simple exchanges such as a friendship that is woven between two co-workers, but without professional links because the activities are very different; in this case, the space will have made it possible to improve the social networks of the people concerned. But it can also be the development of knowledge allowing the networking or the improvement of one's professional activity, making it more competitive or sustainable. It is also possible to find tacit or explicit exchanges of knowledge between people who are interested in the same project or the same subject, as in the case of epistemic communities (Cohendet et al., 2003), or who have common tasks in their work. In this case, the co-worker takes advantage of the advice or experience of other users to help with this task.

Our research highlights the importance of the financial, material and human resources available in the co-working space, especially with regard to animation resources. A space that is created without having these animation or intermediation resources is less likely to facilitate exchanges and collaboration, and it might even have some difficulty in sustaining its activity.

Fab Labs, Strategies for Sharing Tools for More Competitiveness and Sustainability

The existence of a collaborative environment is an important factor at the beginning of the innovation process, whether one is in a small business, or an entrepreneur, or self-employed, because success or failure depends on the ability to acquire external resources and knowledge complementary to those available internally (such as one's own knowledge or own material). To justify its existence, a fab lab therefore requires the help of intermediaries, individuals or organizations serving as an interface between two or more parties throughout each stage of the innovation process (Howells, 2006). Their role is then to try to develop a relationship of trust between the actors involved, by playing the role of "matchmakers" to encourage meetings and the sharing of tools and expertise.

This can be done by:

- the use of the fab lab's resources (Chesbrough, 2003), such as the pooling of a 3D printer or other specialized equipment; in itself, this contributes to the circular economy in reducing the amount of equipment bought individually, and contributes to a more collective use of resources;
- the development of an environment designed to facilitate exchanges between members of the group, such as creating within the fab lab open working spaces, places of conviviality to take lunch or coffee together, in order to facilitate knowledge exchanges, which can again contribute to more competitive or sustainable enterprises;

- or by facilitating the flow of knowledge and meetings (Fabbri and Charue-Duboc, 2016), by organizing workshops, discovery workshops or other types of meetings between users.

A fab lab is thus a place where this intermediation is possible through a variety of factors facilitating the culture of collaboration within it, thus allowing contacts to achieve the desired result, such as business opportunities, business sustainability, or product or service innovations. These manufacturing spaces make their machines and tools available to all people (free of charge or at a lower cost), with the aim of producing an object or digital innovations. They facilitate learning by doing, and sharing skills (Bosqué, 2015). In short, in a fab lab, anyone with an idea can benefit from a place to test (prototyping), and then create a physical or digital object freely and quickly, because the place provides the necessary means. In a fab lab, cooperation can, for example, allow various forms of creation with numerically controlled machines, such as a 3D printer or a laser cutting machine (Fastermann, 2014; Fleischmann et al., 2016).

Living Labs, Strategies for Sustainability and Revitalization Projects

The living laboratory is a different type of initiative. It must find the right actors (the heads of networks) who will be able to attract all the people (citizens' committee for example), public organizations (municipalities, boroughs, consultation table) and private (local) companies which should be part of the process. These network heads will then be able to put the managers in charge of the implementation of the living labs method in contact with the diversity of actors present in the territory (region, district or village) concerned.

The advantage of a living laboratory, in this context, is that these different participants would not always have opportunities to meet. The method allows them to discuss topics for which they did not yet have the opportunity to present their vision or analysis. The living lab approach then allows for the development of a reflection that uses the skills of its members, but which, above all, is based on the needs of those they serve; this is why the projects are carried out by the users themselves (Scaillerez and Tremblay, 2017a, 2017b).

To best serve the objectives, whether the revitalization of a building or city district, or other, the living lab will seek the most appropriate method to meet the right people and question them with the tools best suited to serve their purpose. The approach then leads to place the participants in a temporal and spatial situation favoring creativity and fruitful exchanges.

A living lab can achieve the goal by becoming a facilitator of meetings between individuals with varied knowledge in a space, whether physical or virtual. A living lab does not necessarily need a specific place to exist and carry out its action. This spatial flexibility also helps to adopt the most relevant modes of action to serve the objectives. According to the nature of the project, a living lab questioned during our research, told us that they used two spatial modes:

- either they use a specific place known to the greatest number, to meet the various users;
- or they organize meetings at the place of the object of reflection or the project, for example, a place or building to be revitalized.

For some projects, the two modes can be combined in order to maximize the results. Whatever the option chosen, the experiences created are intended to add concrete data to go beyond the simple exchange of visions and opinions, but above all to obtain an experience, a reality, and to add meaning to the reflection or project.

Among the stakeholders, whatever the approach adopted, the living lab solicits citizens' participation in reflection and thus mobilizes the territory's resources (Kalle et al., 2015). This increases the feeling of belonging to the territory, thereby stimulating concerted action (Fu and Lin, 2014). A living lab draws on both concrete data and intuitive data, both contributing to the building of the project, since each user contributes depending on the nature of their knowledge, whether practical knowledge or another form of expertise.

A living lab facilitates the stimulation of all forms of intelligence present in the territory (Bergvall-Kåreborn et al., 2009), whether the knowledge comes from experts or laypersons. The success of the method comes precisely from this mixture of different knowledge sources, without valuing one more than another (Giannetti and Simonov, 2009), but also from the diversity of external resources that are solicited, whether they are clients, users, regular or temporary users, businesses, associations or public institutions (Knudsen, 2007).

The advantage of soliciting users (experts or laypersons) is that these individuals are affected or concerned by the situation. They can provide more precise information, and are more motivated to participate in the process (von Hippel, 2005), so that appropriate solutions are found for their benefit and thus to improve their environment, or to contribute to a more sustainable building, place or environment (Leminen et al., 2015).

This diversity of knowledge and skills is the core of this approach which makes it possible to generate original recommendations that would never have emerged without this living labs approach.

THIRD PLACES: POSSIBLE CHALLENGES

Although third places can bring many benefits, they can also raise a number of questions or challenges. In particular, the question arises of whether one wants to ensure active knowledge exchanges that go beyond the dimensions of space and equipment sharing, which are already important in terms of the competitiveness and sustainability of the self-employed, entrepreneurs, businesses and cities, but can be improved with knowledge sharing.

Co-working Spaces, a Variety of Pictures

In many industrial and even emerging countries, co-working has become, over the last 20 years, a new way of organizing work based on a shared work space, set up with the aim of fostering exchanges and emulation between co-workers, in order to fuel innovation (Brown, 2017). The reality, however, is somewhat more complex, as co-working designates very diverse situations according to the territory or city in which it develops (Scaillerez and Tremblay, 2016a).

Co-working spaces as places of possible collaboration but no guarantees

The collaborative work culture that we presented in the previous section is not a constant in all co-working spaces, and although it has often been put forward as a co-working benefit, it has not necessarily been fully validated for all spaces (Scaillerez and Tremblay, 2019a, 2019b). Geographical or physical proximity does not automatically lead to collaborations between co-workers (Boschma, 2005). The logic of bringing together professionals in the same field does not always work, either (Scaillerez and Tremblay, 2019a). Of course, in any case, they are using resources (office space, equipment, tools) in a more responsible and sustainable way, but the objective is usually to go a little further. Among the co-workers interviewed, the professional relationship does not always bring people to cooperate and work together. For example, we have observed spaces that wanted to specialize in the cultural field, but which, in the end, received very little or no co-workers in this field of work. Even if the discourse is sometimes different, most of the managers want to welcome all categories of people, because without this inclusive vision there might not be enough customers to maintain the activity of the space, especially in small cities or outside of the metropolis. This is confirmed by other recent studies on the subject (Deskmag, 2018).

In addition, a co-working space can stimulate creativity, innovation, initiative and the feeling of belonging to the same community, but this is not always observed (Scaillerez and Tremblay, 2019b). Exchanges and collaboration seem to be easier between self-employed people than entrepreneurs, who sometimes see themselves as competitors, although this can also be the case for the self-employed. We have observed that some employees of the same company who work in co-working spaces may tend to work among themselves and usually occupy closed offices in this place without having much interaction with other co-workers. This is unfortunate, as it limits collaboration, although there is already a positive sustainability impact from sharing office space, equipment and tools, and possibly from working closer to home. However, a more open collaboration with others might lead to a more competitive business, and even possibly more sustainable business. This is why managers or animators of these spaces often seek to develop cooperation between the persons present in the co-working spaces.

Co-working spaces as individual workspaces at reduced cost
The relationship of trust is not always established between co-workers. Co-working spaces can also be used by people who prefer to work alone, or who already have their own clientele and who are looking for a way to have a business address, a more professional space, or the possibility of having a larger room for business meetings in order to appear more credible to their customers. In this case again, they are at least contributing to a more sustainable business and city by sharing office space and equipment, and possibly by reducing the distance between home and work, especially if they live in a large city, where there is an abundance of choice as concerns living and working spaces. Others can use a co-working space to enjoy the benefits they provide, such as reduced costs, sharing human resources (such as a common administrative office) or hardware (printer, photocopier, meeting rooms), or simply for the comfort of the place (such as common kitchen and coffee machine).

It can also sometimes be difficult to interact with co-workers who do the same job. Some may perceive themselves as competitors, and fear that others may take their customers or steal their ideas. Some co-working spaces refuse to welcome new people if their activity could compete with some of the users already present; others try to bring them to cooperate, for both to become more competitive and sustainable.

Risks Incurred by Fab Labs: Between Deskilling of Knowledge and New Occupational Risks

In fab labs, while the advantages of sharing resources (tools and space) are clearly important in terms of sustainability and collective access to specialized machines and tools, the risks are of two types: they can call into question certain expert skills, and possibly lead to new risks in health and safety at work.

Fab labs, sharing resources, but with a risk of skills disqualification

The fab labs place themselves in the do-it-yourself (DIY) movement (Kuznetsov and Paulos, 2010; Rognoli et al., 2015; Tanenbaum et al., 2013). This DIY movement is often celebrated for the potential it holds for the democratization of knowledge, for the development of citizen manufacturing, for the empowerment of ordinary people, and for its educational, economic and socio-cultural value.

In addition, fab labs also develop ways to communicate, domesticate and simplify; that is to say, to make more accessible and democratic the idea of "making by yourself." The DIY movement thus embodies the sharing of data and knowledge, as well as the opening of knowledge gates hitherto reserved exclusively to technological institutions. The DIY movement also advocates an entrepreneurial spirit, a community spirit, but also an underlying form of rebellion, individualism and mistrust of bureaucracy. Fab labs can thus sometimes imply some risks. Indeed, by facilitating DIY and the making of almost anything (Gershenfeld, 2005), these places could eventually contribute to the Uberization of knowledge and expertise (Scaillerez and Tremblay, 2017a). That this can be good at times is not to be questioned, but it can also lead to a negation of the skills acquired by some in favor of a pseudo-universal knowledge, which may imply some risks when people are creating scientific tools, or similar products. Previously, it was almost unthinkable that individuals could manufacture a multitude of products by themselves, because the purchase of technological equipment was expensive, difficult, rare, or simply impossible. However, the affordability and availability of scientific equipment has increased significantly in recent years. There are now various ways in which the cost of setting up a manufacturing community or workshop becomes more affordable, through the purchase of used equipment in particular. The possibility offered by these fab labs to build, or build by yourself, various goods (using 3D printers, DIY tools, mechanics, carpentry objects; Devendorf et al., 2016) is certainly interesting in terms of sharing resources in the perspective of a circular economy, but it could contribute to a loss of technical expertise (advanced technical and craft skills) and the real skills of professionals in favor of a generalization of amateur creations. Fab labs can cause some concern, since it can be dangerous to tinker with biology or technology outside scientific institutions, and this can lead to potential risks for people and the environment. One could fear a de-qualification effect of the actors who use these places and their devices, but also the risks of injury or health issues with non-standardized instruments. So while the sharing of resources is clearly interesting from a sustainability perspective, cities should be careful to ensure the right environment for such experimentation.

Fab labs: sharing resources, but with a risk of deterioration of work and health

The practices that are explored in fab labs carry a culture of "doing," of rapid experimentation and sharing, to a degree that depends on the forms considered (Lallement, 2015). Promoting autonomy and collaboration, these practices have also triggered a shift in working relationships. One of the goals is to undo the hierarchical relationships of previous systems, to install more horizontal, participatory and open modes of cooperation.

By bringing "make almost anything" into private garages, the boundaries between amateurs and experts, between scientists and citizens, between universities and homes are potentially transformed. Other limitations become particularly salient and problematic through these changes: between responsible and criminal uses, between safe handling and dangerous experiences, between the garage and the outside world. Again, we stress the fact that the sharing of resources is clearly interesting from a sustainability and circular economy perspective, but cities need to ensure that the various experimentations are contained to a certain extent, and that they ensure health and safety issues in these more open production environments, as well as security for the possible users of products created in these environments.

Living labs: a new approach with old methods

In the living lab approach, there is an open call for participation and collaboration, as well as sharing; in this case, mainly ideas. Here there are usually no physical risks, as in the case of fab labs, but there may be a risk that it will always be the same type of people involved in the process (retirees, students, certain social categories, socio-professionals). The risk could be that only those who feel capable and legitimate to express themselves will participate in the process. As a result, some more disadvantaged, marginalized or minority groups might hesitate to do so, by doubting their legitimacy to participate in the exchanges or doubting the value of their opinion, even while the revitalization project might concern them in the first place. Similarly, people who work full-time, have children and therefore are very busy in their daily lives may also not participate due to lack of time or compatible time slots. However, according to the themes, these people would have a vision that would be essential or even determinant in the understanding of a phenomenon or in the search for solutions, especially when the sustainability of their district or city is at stake.

One of the advantages of living labs also comes from the great diversity of stakeholders and the search for multiple stakeholders, so one must remain vigilant when organizing such an approach not to always use the same network or the same type of people. Using the same network can save time, but also reduces the relevance of results, and thus the acceptability or sustainability of a given project. Indeed, in a living lab, it is necessary to diversify the variety of the actors to be questioned according to the subjects, but also to change the practices and to modify methods according to the subjects or projects. To resort to the living laboratory is therefore to question oneself and be open, and to adapt the method and the actors according to the project. This complicates things, of course, but ultimately gives better results as concerns long-term sustainability. Even the place can or must be different, so everything is transformed, disrupted, and changes, evolves and moves. This is simultaneously the difficulty, or the challenge, but also the benefit of the method in terms of the long-term sustainability of projects, or cities.

CONCLUSION

While technologies and societal objectives such as sustainability now allow for new collaborative environments, these new spaces and approaches also refer to a series of issues and challenges. Also, while there are gains of using these various forms of initiatives for sharing of various resources (office space, tools, equipment, machines and knowledge), and thus long-term sustainability of entrepreneurs, businesses and cities, there are a few issues and challenges that arise from these new collaborative environments. This chapter has presented these new forms of resource sharing, and has also taken a critical look at the reality of these new forms of sharing or various types of resources (office space, tools, equipment, machines and knowledge).

In short, there is a great variety of third places, with realities that are more complex than they appear at first sight. It is necessary to nuance the statements of some promoters concerning the usefulness of these various forms of knowledge exchanges for creativity and innovation, but it is clear that these various initiatives do offer new and interesting forms of resource sharing, and these are particularly interesting in terms of competitiveness and sustainability of businesses and cities.

These new forms of resource sharing are perfectly in line with the objectives of the circular economy, which proposes to share, reuse and recycle resources. Also, these forms of sharing are informed from the bottom up, rather than the top down, as is often the case in more traditional contexts of work.

In our view, communities of practice, as well as co-working spaces, fab labs and living labs are all new formats which contribute to creating, sharing, using and managing (Girard and Girard, 2015) the knowledge, space, tools and equipment of an organization. The creation and sharing of resources can often go beyond the organization, as is the case for third spaces such as co-working spaces, fab labs or living labs, which make it possible to share resources such as office space, tools, equipment and knowledge beyond the boundaries of the firm, and to gain access to much more in this way. These forms of third spaces can thus all contribute extensively to simultaneously more competitive and more sustainable businesses and cities.

REFERENCES

Adler, E., "The Emergence of Cooperation: National Epistemic Communities and the International Evolution of the Idea of Nuclear Arms Control," *International Organization*, Vol. 46, No. 1, 1992, pp. 101–145.

Adler, E. and P.M. Haas, "Conclusion: Epistemic Communities, World Order, and the Creation of a Reflective Research Program," *International Organization*, Vol. 46, No. 1, 1992, pp. 367–390.

Akrich, M., "From Communities of Practice to Epistemic Communities: Health Mobilizations on the Internet," *Sociological Research Online*, Vol. 15, No. 2, 2010.

Amin, A. and P.P. Cohendet, *Architectures of Knowledge: Firms, Capabilities, and Communities*, Oxford: Oxford University Press, 2004.

Bergvall-Kåreborn, B., C. Eriksson, A. Ihlström, A. Ståhlbröst and J. Svensson, "A milieu for innovation – defining Living Lab," Communication présentée à la 2e ISPIM Innovation Symposium, New York, 2009.

Boschma, R.A., "Proximity and Innovation: A Critical Assessment," *Regional Studies*, Vol. 39, 2005, pp. 61–74.

Bosqué, C., "Enquête au cœur des FabLabs, hackerspaces, makerspaces. Le dessin comme outil d'observation," *Techniques and Culture*, no. 64, Essais de bricologie. Ethnologie de l'art et du design contemporains, 2015, pp. 168–185.

Botsman, R. and R. Rogers, *What's Mine is Yours: The Rise of Collaborative Consumption*, New York: Harper Business, 2010.

Bourhis, A. and D.-G. Tremblay, *Les facteurs organisationnels de succès des communautés de pratique virtuelles*, Québec: Cefrio, 2004.

Boutillier, Sophie, "Small Entrepreneurship, Knowledge and Social Resources in a Heavy Industrial Territory: The Case of Eco-innovation in Dunkirk," *Journal of Knowledge Economy*, 2017, https://doi.org/10.1007/s13132-017-0511-z.

Boutillier, Sophie and Phillip Ryckelynck, "Sustainable-Entrepreneurs: Quantifying Opportunities and Social Networks: Case Study on Sustainable Entrepreneurs in a Heavy Industrial Area," *International Journal of Entrepreneurship and Small Business*, Vol. 31, No. 1, 2017, pp. 85–102.

Brown, J., "Curating the 'Third Place'? Coworking and the Mediation of Creativity," *Geoforum*, Vol. 82, 2017, pp. 112–126.

Capdevila, I., "Les différentes approches entrepreneuriales dans les espaces ouverts d'innovation," *Innovations, revue d'économie et de management de l'innovation*, Vol. 48, 2015, pp. 87–105.

Chesbrough, H.W., *Open Innovation: The New Imperative for Creating and Profiting from Technology*, Boston, MA: Harvard Business Press, 2003.

Cohendet, P.F., O. Créplet and O. Dupouët, "Innovation organisationnelle, communautés de pratique et communautés épistémiques: le cas de Linux," *Revue française de gestion*, No. 147, Nov.–Déc., 2003, 99–121.

Deskmag, *Final Results of the Global Coworking Survey in Charts*, 2017.

Deskmag, *New Global Survey: Everything You Wanted to Know About Coworking*, 2018.

Devendorf, L., A. De Kosnik and K. Mattingly, "Probing the Potential of Post-Anthropocentric 3D Printing," *Proceedings of the 2016 ACM Conference on Designing Interactive Systems*, ACM, 2016, pp. 170–181.

Fabbri, J., "Les espaces de coworking: ni tiers-lieux, ni incubateurs, ni FabLabs," *Entreprendre & innover*, Vol. 31, 2016, pp. 8–16.

Fabbri, J. and F. Charue-Duboc, "Les espaces de coworking: nouveaux intermédiaires d'innovation ouverte?," *Revue française de gestion*, No. 254, 2016, pp. 163–180.

Fastermann, P., "FabLabs – wie sich in offenen Werkstätten weitere Möglichkeiten erschließen," *3D-Drucken*, Berlin and Heidelberg: Springer, 2014, pp. 57–59.

Felson, M. and J. Spaeth, "Community Structure and Collaborative Consumption: A Routine Activity Approach," *American Behavioral Scientist*, 1978, https://doi.org/10.1177/000276427802100411.

Fleischmann, K., S. Hielscher and T. Merritt, "Making Things in Fab Labs: A Case Study on Sustainability and Co-creation," *Digital Creativity*, Vol. 27, No. 2, 2016, pp. 113–131.

Fu, Z. and X. Lin, "Building the Co-design and Making Platform to Support Participatory Research and Development for Smart City," *International Conference on Cross-Cultural Design*, Springer, 2014, pp. 609–620, https://link.springer.com/chapter/10.1007/978-3-319-07308-8_58.

Gershenfeld, N., *FAB: The Coming Revolution on Your Desktop – From Personal Computers to Personal Fabrication*, New York: Basic Books, 2005.

Gershenfeld, N., "How to Make Almost Anything: The Digital Fabrication Revolution", *Foreign Affairs*, No. 91, 2012, pp. 43–57.

Giannetti, M. and A. Simonov, "Social Interactions and Entrepreneurial Activity," *Journal of Economics and Management Strategy*, Vol. 18, 2009, pp. 665–709.

Girard, J.P. and J.L. Girard, "Defining Knowledge Management: Toward an Applied Compendium," *Online Journal of Applied Knowledge Management*, Vol. 3, No. 1, 2015, pp. 1–20.

Gorwitz, N., "Coworking et réseautage font bon ménage. Les espaces de travail partagés pourraien représenter jusqu'à 30 % du portefeuille immobilier des entreprises d'ici à 2030," *Jeune Afrique*, No. 3039, 2019, https://www.jeune-afrique.com/mag/759436/economie/bureaux-coworking-et-reseautage-font-bon-menage/.

Guenoud, P. and A. Moeckli, Revue économique et sociale: RES; bulletin de la Société d'Etudes Economiques et Sociales. Lausanne: SEES, ISSN 0035-2772, ZDB-ID 208694-3. Vol. 68.2010, 2010, 2, pp. 25–33.

Haas, P.M., "Do Regimes Matter? Epistemic Communities and Mediterranean Pollution," *International Organization*, Vol. 43, No. 3, 1989, pp. 377–403.

Haas, P.M., "Epistemic Communities and International Policy Coordination," *International Organization*, Vol. 46, No. 1, 1992, pp. 1–35.

Hippel, E. von, *Democratizing Innovation*, Cambridge, MA: MIT Press, 2005.

Holzner, B., *Reality Construction and Society*, Cambridge: Schenkman, 1968.

Holzner, B. and J. Marx, *Knowledge Affiliation: The Knowledge System in Society*, Boston, MA: Allyn & Bacon, 1979.

Holzner, B. and L. Salmon-Cox, "Conceptions of Research and Development for Education in the United States," *Annals of the American Academy of Political and Social Science*, No. 484, 1977, pp. 88–100.

Howells, J., "Intermediation and the Role of Intermediaries in Innovation," *Research Policy*, Vol. 35, No. 5, 2006, pp. 715–728.

Kalle, K., S. Hirvonen-Kantola, P. Ahokangas, M. Iivari, M. Heikkilä and H.-L. Hentilä, "8th Nordic Conference on Construction Economics and Organization Urban Development Practices as Anticipatory Action Learning: Case Arctic Smart City Living Laboratory," *Procedia Economics and Finance*, Vol. 21, 2015, pp. 337–345.

Knudsen, M.P., "The Relative Importance of Interfirm Relationships and Knowledge Transfer for New Product Development Success," *Journal of Product Innovation Management*, Vol. 24, No. 2, 2007, https://doi.org/10.1111/j.1540-5885.2007.00238.x.

Kuznetsov, S. and E. Paulos, "Rise of the Expert Amateur: DIY Projects, Communities, and Cultures," *NordiCHI '10: Proceedings of the 6th Nordic Conference on Human–Computer Interaction: Extending Boundaries*, October 2010, pp. 295–304, https://doi.org/10.1145/1868914.1868950.

Lallement, M., *L'âge du Faire, Hacking, travail, anarchie*, Paris: éditions du Seuil, 2015.

Laursen, K. and A. Salter, "Open for Innovation: The Role of Openness in Explaining Innovation Performance among UK Manufacturing Firms," *Strategic Management Journal*, Vol. 27, 2005, pp. 131–150.

Lave, J. and E. Wenger, *Situated Learning: Legitimate Peripheral Participation*, Cambridge: Cambridge University Press, 1991.

Leminen, S., T. Turunen and M. Westerlund, "The Grey Areas Between Open and Closed in Innovation Networks," *Technology Innovation Management Review*, Vol. 5, No. 11, 2015, pp. 5–14.

Le Nadant, Anne-Laure, Clément Marinos and Gerhard Krauss, "Les espaces de coworking. Le rôle des proximités dans les dynamiques collaboratives," *Revue des sciences de gestion*, No. 272, 2018, pp. 121–137.

Liefooghe, C., "Tiers-lieux, coworking spaces et fab labs: nouveaux lieux, nouveaux liens et construction de communautés de connaissance créatives," in C. Liefooghe, *Lille, métropole créative? Nouveaux liens, nouveaux lieux, nouveaux territoires*, Lille: Presses universitaires du Septentrion, 2016, pp. 183–221.

McDermott, R., "Learning across Teams: How to Build Communities of Practice in Teams Organizations," *Knowledge Management Review*, Vol. 8 (May–June), 1999, pp. 32–36.

Oldenburg, R., *The Great Good Place: Cafes, Coffee Shops, Community Centers, Beauty Parlors, General Stores, Bars, Hangouts and How They Get You Through the Day*, New York: Paragon House, 1989.

Oldenburg, R., *The Great Good Place: Cafes, Coffee Shops, Bookstores, Bars, Hair Salons, and other Hangouts at the Heart of a Community*, New York: Marlowe, 1999.

Oldenburg, R., *Celebrating the Third Place: Inspiring Stories about the Great Good Places at the Heart of Our Communities*, New York: Marlowe, 2000.

Rognoli, V., M. Bianchini, S. Maffei and E. Karana, "DIY Materials," *Materials and Design*, Vol. 86, 2015, pp. 692–702.

Scaillerez, A. and D.-G. Tremblay, "Le télétravail, comme nouveau mode de régulation de la flexibilisation et de l'organisation du travail: analyse et impact du cadre légal européen et nord-américain," *ROR (Revue des Organisations Responsables)*, mai–juin, 2016a, pp. 21–31.

Scaillerez, A. and D.-G. Tremblay, "Les espaces de co-working, les avantages du partage," *Revue Gestion* (HEC), Vol. 41, No. 2, 2016b, pp. 90–92.

Scaillerez, A. and D.-G. Tremblay, "Coworking, fab labs et living labs, État des connaissances sur les tiers-lieux," *Territoire en mouvement; Revue de géographie et aménagement*, Vol. 34, 2017a, pp. 1–17.

Scaillerez, A. and D.-G. Tremblay, "Numérique, télétravail et développement des territoires ruraux. Analyse et résultats des politiques publiques québécoises relatives au déploiement," *Revue Économies et Solidarités* (RES), Vol. 44, No. 1–2, novembre, 2017b, pp. 103–121.

Scaillerez, A. and D.-G. Tremblay, "Travailler et collaborer autrement: les espaces de coworking, une approche apparentée aux communautés de pratique," in G. Krauss and D.-G. Tremblay (eds), *Tiers-lieux – travailler et entreprendre sur les territoires: Espaces de co-working, fab labs, hack labs*, Rennes, France and Québec, Canada: PUR and PUQ, 2019a.

Scaillerez, A. and D.-G. Tremblay, "Les livings labs, intermédiaires d'innovation ouverte: proposition d'une typologie des usagers," in J.L. Klein and B. Pecqueur (eds), *Living Labs; perspectives globales et applications*, Québec: Presses de l'université du Québec, 2019b.

Scaillerez, A. and D.-G. Tremblay, "Coworking spaces, new workplaces," in *Encyclopedia of Organizational Knowledge, Administration, and Technologies*, IGI Global Editors, 2019c.

Smits, M., *Les tiers-lieux sont-ils reproductibles à grande échelle? Étude de la viabilité de l'intégration de ces espaces dans un processus d'aménagement formalisé*, Projet de fin d'étude, ENPC, 2015.

Tanenbaum, J., A. Williams, A. Desjardins and K. Tanenbaum, *Democratizing Technology: Pleasure, Utility and Expressiveness in DIY and Maker Practice*, ACM Press, 2013.

Tremblay, Diane-Gabrielle, "Communities of Practice: Towards a New Mode of Learning and Knowledge Creation?," in R. Ruzicka, J.H. Ballantine and J.A. Ruiz San Roman (eds), *Key Contexts for Education and Democracy in Globalizing Societies*, Actes du colloque Education, Participation and Globalization, Agentura Action, 2004a, pp. C117–124.

Tremblay, D.-G., "Les communautés virtuelles de praticiens: vers de nouveaux modes d'apprentissage et de création de connaissances?," *Possibles*, numéro spécial sur la formation, Automne 2004b, pp. 66–79.

Tremblay, Diane-Gabrielle, "Trade Unions and Work–Life Rights: The Challenge of Work–Life Interface in a Union Environment," *Employee Responsibilities and Rights Journal*, Vol. 28, No. 3, 2016a, pp. 171–187.

Tremblay, Diane-Gabrielle, "Temps de travail, charge de travail et articulation travail-famille; enjeux pour les milieux syndicaux," *Revue de l'IRES*, No. 85–86, 2016b, pp. 145–169.

Trott, P. and D. Hartmann, "Why 'Open Innovation' Is Old Wine In New Bottles," *International Journal of Innovation Management*, Vol. 13, December, 2009, pp. 715–736, http://www.hamafarini.com/images/EditorUpload/1.pdf [archive].

Wenger, E.C., R. McDermott and W.M. Snyder, *Cultivating Communities of Practice: A Guide to Managing Knowledge*, Boston, MA: Harvard Business School Press, 2002.

3. Urbanization and sustainable urban development in China

Shen Jianfa

INTRODUCTION

Urbanization, along with marketization, decentralization and globalization, has contributed significantly to the profound urban and regional development and transformation in China since 1978. Shen (2018) provides an overview of urbanization and development, urbanization and hukou reform, urban and regional restructuring, and regional development and governance in China. After nearly three decades of under-urbanization in China (Ran and Berry, 1989), the urbanization process in China has accelerated since the early 1980s with a massive inflow of migrants from rural areas (Shen, 2002, 2005a, 2015). According to recent population censuses (NBS, 2011a, p. 96), the urban population in China more than tripled in the period 1982–2010, increasing from 210.82 million in 1982 to 458.44 million in 2000 and 665.57 million in 2010. The level of urbanization reached 56.1 percent in 2015 (NBS, 2016).

Differently from other countries, the population of a Chinese city does not just consist of local residents, due to a unique hukou (household registration) system. It actually consists of three parts: the local population (with local hukou), permanent migrants (with local hukou) and temporary migrants (without local hukou) (Shen, 2005b). The temporary migrants are defined as a floating population (temporary population) who have left their place of hukou for over six months. They contribute to the bulk of the increased urban population. This is one outstanding feature of the recent rapid urbanization in China.

Under the hukou system, China formed a dual society, separating urban and rural areas rigidly, with limited migration from rural to urban areas in the pre-reform period (Wu and Treiman, 2004). There was an unequal urban–rural relation, as industrialization and urban development was largely built on the "scissors" difference in the planned prices of industrial and agricultural products. While the rural migrants have been allowed to move in to urban areas as a temporary population in the reform period, the unequal urban–rural relation has been shifted into urban areas in the form of unequal intra-urban relation between residents with local hukou and the floating population without local hukou. Thus current urbanization of China is incomplete and not inclusive. The realities, theories and strategies of migration, floating population and urbanization in China have been discussed in a previous paper in Chinese, focusing on the theories of urbanization, and integration and assimilation of migrants (Shen, 2019). This chapter will focus on sustainable urbanization in China.

The chapter will first discuss the problems of migration and urbanization in China. A regional people–nature symbiotic systems approach to sustainable urbanization is then proposed. Finally, a new town example from Hong Kong is used to illustrate how and what sustainable cities and communities can be built under scientific planning. Some conclusions are reached in the final section.

PROBLEMS OF MIGRATION AND URBANIZATION IN CHINA

The floating population from rural China has a number of disadvantages in Chinese cities, including an institutional barrier (no local hukou), social discrimination and a low education level (usually with primary and lower secondary education), similar to international migrants in foreign countries (Shen, 2011). The floating population faces a series of problems, including low income; high personal risks; poor social protection; poor access to public services such as education, social housing and basic public health; and poor legal protection (PTRISC, 2006). These problems are so serious that they have become a major source of social unrest and protest in China. There has been keen debate on promoting the rights of internal migrants and "urban citizenship" with full rights in the destination cities (Solinger, 1999). Wang et al. (2002, p. 542) argued that though the institutional barriers may decline over time, a subtler social barrier in the form of cultural discrimination would persist.

One major focus of previous studies is on the labor market performance and social status of temporary rural migrants in cities (Wang and Fan, 2012; Fan, 2002; Wang et al., 2002). Case studies based on different groups of the floating population project an image of either rich migrant groups or a poor class of migrants struggling for survival (Yang and Guo, 1996; Ma and Xiang, 1998). Temporary migrants are often compared with permanent migrants or local population in terms of their social and economic status (Wang et al., 2002; Liu and Xu, 2017). Sun and Fan (2011) showed that the gap between interprovincial permanent migrants and temporary migrants widened from 1990 to 2000. The temporary hukou status was considered to be the main cause of discrimination against migrant workers (Fan, 2002; Wang et al., 2002). Due to the impact of the 2008 global economic crisis, some migrants became unemployed and returned to rural areas (Wang, 2010).

Housing market performance is an important aspect of integration. Wu (2004) examined the institutional and socio-economic factors affecting housing conditions of migrants in China. She found that market-related factors such as income and education had a significant positive impact, but the institutional restrictions associated with the hukou system out-weighed the combined effects of socio-economic factors. Wu (2010) found that the majority of migrants were renters even after a long period in the cities, and they tended to invest little income to improve housing conditions. Many rural migrants were found to live in urban villages and urban periphery areas, resulting in a pattern of social and spatial segregation (Gu and Shen, 2003; Wu, 2010; Fan, 2011).

Some studies have compared the old and new migrants and their social and economic status. Zhu and Lin (2014) examined the new generation migrants and their differences from and similarities to the first generation migrants. They confirmed some common understanding of the differences between the first and the second generations of migrants in the literature, but there were still some similarities between the two generations in their socio-economic status and their readiness for integration into the destination cities. They argued that the existence of rural–urban disparity and the dominance of labor-intensive industries constrained more fundamental changes in the generational transition of migrants in China.

Wang et al. (2002) found that there was a clear division between rural migrants and local residents in terms of industrial and occupational compositions, living conditions and income; and that rural migrant laborers were far from being integrated into Chinese cities. This is inconsistent with the assumption that migrants pay a higher price at the beginning, but that they will gradually assimilate into the Chinese urban society.

The rapid urbanization in China has been contributed to by the growth of a temporary population in an informal urbanization process. For simplicity, the increase in non-agricultural population may be termed a formal urbanization process while the increase in agricultural population may be termed an informal urbanization process (Zhu, 1998; Shen et al., 2002; Shen, 2015; Lin and Shen, 2019).

According to an estimation based on census data, the urban non-agricultural population increased by 147.3 percent in the period 1982–2010. The formal urbanization process is strong, following the pace of the total urban population growth in China. As a result, the total urban non-agricultural population increased from 144.95 million in 1982 to 309.41 million in 2000, and 358.2 million in 2010 (Shen, 2015; PCO and DPES, 2012). The formal and informal urbanization can also be indicated by the growth of the urban hukou population and the temporary population. The temporary population increased from 6.57 million in 1982 to 39.63 million in 1990, 144.39 million (including 35.38 million from the same urban district) in 2000, and 260.94 million (including 39.96 million from the same urban district) in 2010 (PCO and DPES, 2012; NBS, 2011b).

Figure 3.1 presents detailed information of the distribution of temporary population by administrative area type (Township, town and sub-district), hukou population and total population in city, town and rural areas of China in 2010 as defined by the 2010 census. Urban population equals to populations in city proper and town proper. According to Figure 3.1, 85.60 percent of the temporary population (225.96 million) was

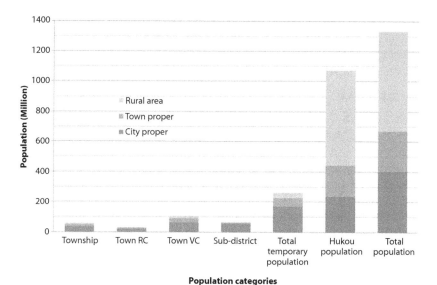

Figure 3.1   Temporary population by administrative area type, hukou population and total population in city, town and rural areas of China in 2010

found in urban areas (city proper and town proper) in 2010. In 2010, among the urban population of 670.01 million, 444.04 million had local hukou in urban areas (close to the size of urban non-agricultural population of 358.42 million). Overall, 66.27 percent of the urban population had local hukou in China in 2010.

The informal urbanization process – that is, the increase of the temporary population – is very significant in post-reform China. In 2010, the temporary population in urban areas totaled 225.96 million persons. A temporary population of 79.04 million came from the same county, city or urban district; 75.33 million from another county, city or urban district of the same province; and 71.59 million from other provinces.

The 2010 census also revealed the extent of the housing shortage, and the housing quality, in urban China (PCO and DPES, 2012). The floor space per person in 6.82 percent of households was less than 8 square meters; 9.97 percent of households lived in housing units without a kitchen, 15.63 percent in households without a toilet, and 13.35 percent households were without piped water. These figures indicate that a high proportion of urban residents in China do not have access to basic housing utilities such as a kitchen, toilet and piped water. The standards of urban housing and utility provision have to be raised, particularly for disadvantaged and poor urban residents. Much has to be done to reduce inequality and improve the social and economic status of the temporary migrants and low-income residents, to achieve sustainable urbanization.

A REGIONAL PEOPLE–NATURE SYMBIOTIC SYSTEMS APPROACH TO SUSTAINABLE URBANIZATION

Urbanization and urban development are profound processes which will shape global, national, regional and local systems dramatically. The studies on urbanization and urban development have been conducted by various disciplines with different focuses. Even in geography, different sub-disciplines and scholars with different backgrounds use different approaches and focus on different issues, such as the floating population, land use, urban villages, new towns, transport, housing, urban planning and urban governance (Chen, 2007; Florida et al., 2008; Li and Wu, 2013; Wei et al., 2016; Shen, 2014; Shen and Kee, 2017; Scott, 2019; Friedmann and Sorensen, 2019). These studies are valuable to address various issues, but a systematic and integrated solution is lacking in the current studies.

This author argues that the system approach should be used to study the urbanization and urban development issues. A logical understanding of various systems and sub-systems is essential. Indeed, the systems approach has been proposed to study world systems, ecological systems and epigeo-sphere systems by various scholars. Wallerstein (1974) introduced the concept of the "world-system," which is defined as a unit with a single division of labor and multiple cultural systems. It divides the world into core countries, semi-periphery countries and the periphery countries, and studies the relations among various countries. The Chinese ecologist Shijun Ma proposed "ecological system engineering" and the theory of "social–economic–natural integrated ecological system" in the 1980s (Ma, 1983). The "epigeosphere system" concept was proposed by Xuesen Qian in the 1980s, which promotes integrated research on nature and human society as one single epigeosphere system using a systems approach (Qian et al., 1986). The concept has further stimulated discussions on the development of epigeosphere science, quantitative geography, constructive geography, earth system science and geographical science in China (Qian et al., 1986; Chen, 1988; Zhang and Shen, 1993; Huang, 1996).

This author suggests using a regional people–nature symbiotic systems approach to sustainable urbanization, by considering physical and human sub-systems in greater detail. It is not possible to discuss this approach in detail in this section. But a general framework of various systems is proposed. First, spatial systems can be defined according to different scales. Thus there are the earth system, super-national system (such as the East Asian system), national system, regional system, city system, town system and village system. The systems at different scales are interrelated. Thus a system approach will link these systems together and help to solve system problems at a particular scale. For most issues of urbanization and urban development, the national system, regional system, city (town) system and village system are of main concern. The following discussion will use the city system as a reference.

Second, a city system at city scale may consist of hard systems and soft systems. Hard systems include the following: the environmental system, biological system, infrastructure system, living system, population system and production system. The environmental system (such as land, air and water) and the biological system (such as plants and animals) are natural systems which may be affected by the urbanization process. Nature conservation measures are needed to protect them for sustainable ecological development. The infrastructure system (such as gas and electricity supply, ports, airports, highways, railways and metro lines) and the living system (such as food supply, housing, health service and public space) are largely man-made systems to support the flows, life and operation of population and production systems. The people in the population system are consumers, residents and laborers. They are responsible for production and the reproduction of the population. They are the ultimate target for meeting the needs and achieving a high quality of life. The production system refers to factories, service outlets and office buildings which are spatially organized and used for economic activities. More studies are needed to build an optimal and efficient production system, infrastructure system and living system using fewer resources and also having a minimal impact on the environmental system and biological system.

To human society, the soft systems are also very important. They include economic, financial, social/cultural, and political/governance systems. The economic system operates on top of the physical production system and determines the income, employment and wealth distribution for residents in the city system. It links with the external economy via trade and capital flows. The financial system is becoming increasingly important in supporting the operation of the economic system via stock markets, capital investment, capital flow, fund-raising, wealth management, insurance, interest rates and exchange rates. The economic and financial systems work together to determine the income, wealth and distribution among residents in the city. It also affects the exchange of value of the city with the rest of the country and the rest of the world. It has been well argued that leading world cities are the base for global capital and capital accumulation, with a dominant role in the world economy and global value chains (Friedmann, 1986, 1995; Huang et al., 2007; Taylor and Derudder, 2016; Gereffi, 2018).

The social/cultural system is important to social and cultural activities and life of residents in cities. It determines the quality of life in the social and cultural dimensions, and is supported by the economic system. The political/governance system is critical to ensure fair and just distribution of political power, and the rules of the social/cultural and economic/financial systems. The healthy operation of the political/governance system affects the efficient operation of the economic system and the quality of life of residents. An open, fair and transparent political/governance system is important to the sustainability of a city system.

Clearly, these hard and soft systems are interrelated and will affect each other. Many academic studies on urbanization and urban development focus on specific issues. There is a great need to promote integrated and transdisciplinary research to address the system problems of sustainable urbanization and urban development. The research group led by this author has been promoting a sustainable approach for urban competitiveness studies by evaluating a city's performance in social, economic and environmental dimensions for many years (Jiang and Shen, 2013; Shen and Yang, 2014; Shen and Wang, 2016). Systematic study of the efficient, effective and sustainable organization, building and operation of these systems is needed, taking into account the systems at upper and lower scales. The approach can be applied to the planning, development, construction and expansion of people–nature symbiotic systems at various scales.

SUSTAINABLE COMMUNITIES: MA ON SHAN NEW TOWN IN HONG KONG

Hong Kong has been a model city to many cities in mainland China. The land market, commercial housing and urban planning in mainland China have been influenced by Hong Kong significantly since the opening of China to the outside world in 1978. Hong Kong has an effective system of urban planning. It has implemented a large-scale public housing programme and a new town programme. These two programmes go hand in hand, as land development of the new town programme provides essential land for public housing development.

Assessment of the new town programme is mixed. On the one hand, new towns provide comprehensive community facilities, transport infrastructure and green space to create a livable community for many residents. On the other hand, new towns have failed to attract industrial and commercial development to create jobs for their residents to achieve the original goal of self-contained development. Job opportunities in Hong Kong still concentrate in major urban centers in Kowloon and Central, so that millions of residents have to travel 30–90 minutes or more in commuting to their work places. The pressure on commuting costs in terms of time and money are so high that some residents prefer to live in poor and small subdivided housing units in old urban areas to stay close to their work places. In recent years, Hong Kong SAR government has provided subsidies to public transport to relieve the acute problem. This chapter will use Ma On Shan new town in Hong Kong as an example to demonstrate what kind of sustainable communities may be planned and developed to meet the rising aspirations of urban residents for a high quality of life in modern cities.

There are 18 districts in Hong Kong. Ma On Shan is a new town in Shatin district (Figure 3.2). The new town has been developed since the early 1990s. It has a total area of 819 hectares. According to census data, its population increased from 138 000 in 1986 to 184 540 in 2001, and 202 431 in 2011, when it had almost completed all development. Mixed development takes place in the new town. It has a good mix of the population in public and private housing with different income levels. As shown in Table 3.1, 75 439 people lived in private permanent housing, 93 292 people in subsidized home ownership housing, and 28 935 people in public rental housing.

Source: Photo by the author, 2015.

Figure 3.2   Ma On Shan new town

Table 3.1   Population and households by type of housing in Ma On Shan new town in 2011

Type of housing	Households	Population
Population in domestic households		
Public rental housing	9 171	28 935
Subsidized home ownership housing	29 416	93 292
Private permanent housing	24 492	75 439
Non-domestic housing	647	1 454
Temporary housing	38	94
Population in non-domestic households		3 217
Total	63 764	202 431

Source: Compiled from CSD (2012).

The labor force participation rate was 63.7 percent. Most of the working population was employed in the services sectors, including 25 491 in import/export, wholesale and retail trades; 19 749 in public administration, education, human health and social work activities; 12 943 in real estate, professional and business services; 11 523 in miscellaneous social and personal services; and 9204 in transportation, storage, postal and courier services (Table 3.2). As Hong Kong is an advanced service center, only 5114 people from Ma On Shan were employed in the manufacturing sector. As Ma On Shan is designed as a new town, there are not many economic activities. Only 7583 people worked in Ma On Shan and the nearby area of the same Shatin district. Over 88.3 percent of the working population worked in other districts. Some 5193 people worked outside Hong Kong (Table 3.3).

Table 3.2   Working population by industry in Ma On Shan new town in 2011

Industry	Male	Female	Total
Manufacturing	3 497	1 617	5 114
Construction	7 495	1 067	8 562
Import/export, wholesale and retail trades	12 820	12 671	25 491
Transportation, storage, postal and courier services	7 010	2 194	9 204
Accommodation and food services	3 363	2 933	6 296
Information and communications	2 370	1 381	3 751
Financing and insurance	2 727	3 016	5 743
Real estate, professional and business services	6 733	6 210	12 943
Public administration, education, human health and social work activities	7 913	11 836	19 749
Miscellaneous social and personal services	1 805	9 718	11 523
Others	656	167	823
Total	56 389	52 810	109 199

Source: Compiled from CSD (2012).

The Ma On Shan Railway, 11.4 km long with an investment of HK$14 billion (HK$8 billion from government), started construction in 2001 and operation on December 21, 2004. It serves a population of about 0.48 million. The trip time from Ma On Shan reduced to 15 minutes to Tai

Table 3.3   Working population by district in Ma On Shan new town in 2011

Place of Work	Male	Female	Total
In same district	2 948	4 635	7 583
In another district:			
Hong Kong Island	9 713	8 839	18 552
Kowloon	16 729	15 047	31 776
New towns	14 775	12 728	27 503
Other areas in the New Territories	2 315	1 144	3 459
No fixed places/marine	5 422	1 423	6 845
Work at home	348	7 940	8 288
Places outside Hong Kong	4 139	1 054	5 193
Total	56 389	52 810	109 199

Source: Compiled from CSD (2012).

Wai and 30 minutes to East Tsim Sha Tsui which is the urban core of Kowloon and opposite the Central across the Victoria Harbour.

Ma On Shan is a well-designed new town with various shopping and service facilities. In the town center, there are a central park, library, swimming pool and three main shopping centers: Ma On Shan Plaza, Ma On Shan Center and Sunshine City Plaza (Figure 3.3). These shopping centers are connected to each other and to Ma On Shan MTR station by sky bridges, facilitating safe and convenient movement of residents and shoppers. There are two bus terminuses on the ground floor of Ma On Shan Plaza and Sunshine City Plaza. The convenient shopping and public services make Ma On Shan a pleasant place to live. It is supported by good public transport (Figure 3.4).

Ma On Shan also has a lovely living environment. In addition to Ma On Shan park, most residential buildings face the Tolo harbor. The waterfront along the Tolo harbor has been developed for recreational use with pedestrian and cyclist paths (Figure 3.5). In short, the new town has been well planned and designed to provide a high-quality living environment which serves as a good example for building sustainable communities.

Source: Photo by the author, 2019.

Figure 3.3 Shopping center in Sunshine City Plaza

Source: Photo by the author, 2017.

Figure 3.4 Public transport in Ma On Shan town center

Source: Photo by the author, 2015.

Figure 3.5   Residential buildings and waterfront area in Ma On Shan

CONCLUSIONS

China has undergone rapid urbanization and urban growth in the past four decades. Urbanization, along with marketization, decentralization and globalization, has contributed significantly to the profound urban and regional development and transformation in China. But the current urbanization in China is incomplete and not inclusive, with many problems. The unequal urban–rural relation existed in the pre-reform transformation in China. The unequal urban–rural relation in the pre-reform period has shifted into urban areas in the form of unequal intra-urban relations between residents with local hukou and the floating population without local hukou.

China has a large temporary population (floating population); 85.60 percent of the temporary population (225.96 million) was found in urban areas in 2010, and 66.27 percent of the urban population had local hukou in China in 2010. Some urban residents do not have access to basic needs and facilities. In China in 2010, 9.97 percent of households lived in housing units without a kitchen, 15.63 percent of households were without a toilet and 13.35 percent of households were without piped water. Much has to be done to reduce inequality and improve the social and economic status of the temporary migrants and low-income residents, to achieve sustainable urbanization.

This author argues that the system approach should be used to study the urbanization and urban development issues. The spatial systems can be defined according to different scales. A city system may consist of hard systems and soft systems. The hard and soft systems are interrelated and will affect each other. Systematic study of the efficient, effective and sustainable organization, building and operation of these systems is needed, taking into account the systems at upper and lower scales. The approach can be applied to the planning, development, construction and expansion of people–nature symbiotic systems at various scales. This chapter has used a new town example from Hong Kong to demonstrate what kind of sustainable communities may be planned and developed to meet the rising aspirations of urban residents in modern cities.

REFERENCES

Chen, C., "Physical geography, epigeosphere science and integrated geography," *ACTA Geographica Sinica*, Vol. 43, No. 3, pp. 258–264, 1988 (in Chinese).

Chen, X., "A tale of two regions in China: rapid economic development and slow industrial upgrading in the Pearl River and the Yangtze River Deltas," *International Journal of Comparative Sociology*, Vol. 48, No. 2–3, pp. 167–201, 2007.

CSD (Census and Statistics Department), *2011 Population Census – Fact Sheet for Tertiary Planning Unit 757*, Hong Kong: Census and Statistics Department, 2012.

Fan, C.C., "The Elite, the natives, and the outsiders: migration and labor market segmentation in urban China," *Annals of the Association of American Geographers*, Vol. 92, No. 1, pp. 103–124, 2002.

Fan, C.C., "Settlement intention and split households: findings from a survey of migrants in Beijing's urban villages," *China Review*, Vol. 11, No. 2, pp. 11–42, 2011.

Florida, R., C. Mellander and K. Stolarick, "Inside the black box of regional development – human capital, the creative class and tolerance," *Journal of Economic Geography*, Vol. 8, pp. 615–649, 2008.

Friedmann, J., "The world city hypothesis," *Development and Change*, Vol. 17, pp. 69–83, 1986.

Friedmann, J., "Where we stand: a decade of world city research," in P.N. Knox and P.J. Taylor (eds), *World Cities in a World-System*, Cambridge: Cambridge University Press, pp. 21–47, 1995.

Friedmann, J. and A. Sorensen, "City unbound: emerging mega-conurbations in Asia," *International Planning Studies*, Vol. 12, No. 1, pp. 1–12, 2019.

Gereffi, G., *Global Value Chains and Development*, Cambridge, UK and New York, USA: Cambridge University Press, 2018.

Gu, C. and J. Shen, "Transformation of urban socio-spatial structure in socialist market economies: the case of Beijing," *Habitat International*, Vol. 27, No. 1, pp. 107–122, 2003.

Huang, B., "On earth system science and sustainable development strategy (I)," *ACTA Geographica Sinica*, Vol. 51, No. 4, pp. 351–354, 1996 (in Chinese).

Huang, Y., Y. Leung and J. Shen, "Cities and globalization: an international cities perspective," *Urban Geography*, Vol. 28, No. 3, pp. 209–231, 2007.

Jiang, Y. and J. Shen, "Weighting for what? A comparison of two weighting methods for measuring urban competitiveness," *Habitat International*, Vol. 38, pp. 167–174, 2013.

Li, Y. and F. Wu, "The emergence of centrally initiated regional plan in China: a case study of Yangtze River Delta Regional Plan," *Habitat International*, Vol. 39, pp. 137–147, 2013.

Lin, L. and J. Shen, "Spatial patterns and driving forces of uneven dual-track urbanization in Fujian province: an approach based on employment sectors," *Urban Studies*, Vol. 56, No. 12, pp. 2568–2584, 2019.

Liu, Y. and W. Xu, "Destination choices of permanent and temporary migrants in China, 1985–2005," *Population Space Place*, Vol. 23, e.1963, 2017.

Ma, L.J.C. and B. Xiang, "Native place, migration and the emergence of peasant enclaves in Beijing," *China Quarterly*, No. 155, pp. 546–581, 1998.

Ma, S., "Ecological engineering – application of principles of ecological systems," *Issues of Agricultural Economy*, Vol. 9, pp. 20–22, 1983.

NBS (National Bureau of Statistics), *China Statistics Yearbook 2011*, Beijing: China Statistics Press, 2011a.

NBS, *Statistical Communiqués on Major Data of Sixth National Population Census*, 28 April 2011, Beijing: National Bureau of Statistics, 2011b.

NBS, *China Statistics Yearbook 2016*, Beijing: China Statistics Press, 2016.

PCO (Population Census Office) and DPES (Department of Population and Employment Statistics, National Bureau of Statistics), *Tabulations on the 2010 Population Census of the People's Republic of China*, 1–3, Beijing: China Statistics Press, 2012.

PTRISC (Project Team of the Research Institute of the State Council), *Survey Report on Peasant Workers in China*, Beijing: Yanshi Press, 2006.

Qian X. et al., *On Geographical Science*, Hangzhou: Zhejiang Education Publishing House, 1986.

Ran, M. and B.J.L. Berry, "Underurbanization policies assessed: China, 1949–1986," *Urban Geography*, Vol. 10, pp. 111–120, 1989.

Scott, A.J., "City-regions reconsidered," *EPA: Economy and Space*, Vol. 51, pp. 554–580, 2019.

Shen, J., "A study of the temporary population in Chinese cities," *Habitat International*, Vol. 26, pp. 363–377, 2002.

Shen, J., "Analysis of the trends of urbanization levels in Chinese provinces since 1982," *ACTA Geographica Sinica*, Vol. 60, No. 4, pp. 607–614, 2005a.

Shen, J., "Counting urban population in Chinese censuses 1953–2000: changing definitions, problems and solutions," *Population, Space and Place*, Vol. 11, No. 5, pp. 381–400, 2005b.

Shen, J., "Migrant labour under the shadow of the hukou system: the case of Guangdong," in T.C. Wong and R. Jonathan (eds), *Asian Cities, Migrant Labor and Contested Spaces*, London: Routledge, pp. 223–245, 2011.

Shen, J., "Not quite a twin city: cross-boundary integration in Hong Kong and Shenzhen," *Habitat International*, Vol. 42, pp. 138–146, 2014.

Shen, J., "Urbanization process and policies for sustainable urbanization in China," in P.K. Kresl (ed.), *Cities and Partnerships for Sustainable Urban Development*, Cheltenham, UK and Northampton, MA, USA: Edward Elgar Publishing, pp. 61–73, 2015.

Shen, J., *Urbanization, Regional Development and Governance in China*, London, UK and New York, USA: Routledge, 2018.

Shen, J., "Migration, floating population and urbanization in China: Realities, theories, and strategies," *Geographical Research*, Vol. 38, No. 1, pp. 33–44, 2019.

Shen, J. and G. Kee, *Development and Planning in Seven Major Coastal Cities in Southern and Eastern China*, Berlin: Springer, 2017.

Shen, J. and L. Wang, "Urban competitiveness and migration in the YRD and PRD regions of China in 2010," *China Review*, Vol. 16, No. 3, pp. 149–174, 2016.

Shen, J., K.Y. Wong and Z. Feng, "State sponsored and spontaneous urbanization in the Pearl River Delta of south China, 1980–1998," *Urban Geography*, Vol. 23, No. 7, pp. 674–694, 2002.

Shen, J. and X. Yang, "Analyzing urban competitiveness changes in major Chinese cities 1995–2008," *Applied Spatial Analysis and Policy*, Vol. 7, No. 4, pp. 361–379, 2014.

Solinger, D., *Contesting Citizenship in Urban China: Peasant Migrants, the State and the Logic of the Market*, Berkeley, CA: University of California Press, 1999.

Sun, M. and C.C. Fan, "China's permanent and temporary migrants: differentials and changes, 1990–2000," *Professional Geographer*, Vol. 63, No. 1, pp. 92–112, 2011.

Taylor, P.J. and B. Derudder, *World City Network: A Global Urban Analysis* (2nd edn), Abingdon: Routledge, 2016.

Wallerstein, I.M., "The rise and future demise of the world-capitalist system: concepts for comparative analysis," *Comparative Studies in Society and History*, Vol. 16, No. 4, pp. 387–415, 1974.

Wang, F., X. Zuo and D. Ruan, "Rural migrants in Shanghai: living under the shadow of socialism," *International Migration Review*, Vol. 36, No. 2, pp. 520–545, 2002.

Wang, M., "Impact of the global economic crisis on China's migrant workers: a survey of 2700 in 2009," *Eurasian Geography and Economics*, Vol. 51, No. 2, pp. 218–235, 2010.

Wang, W. and C.C. Fan, "Migrant workers' integration in urban China: experiences in employment, social adaptation and self-identity," *Eurasian Geography and Economics*, Vol. 5, No. 3, pp. 731–749, 2012.

Wei, Y., X. Bi, M. Wang and Y. Ning, "Globalization, economic restructuring, and locational trajectories of software firms in Shanghai," *Professional Geographer*, Vol. 68, pp. 211–226, 2016.

Wu, W., "Sources of migrant housing disadvantage in urban China," *Environment and Planning A*, Vol. 36, pp. 1285–1304, 2004.

Wu, W., "Drifting and getting stuck: migrants in Chinese cities," *City*, Vol. 14, No. 1, pp. 13–24, 2010.

Wu, X. and D.J. Treiman, "The Household Registration System and social stratification in China: 1955–1996," *Demography*, Vol. 41, No. 2, pp. 363–384, 2004.

Yang, Q.H. and F. Guo, "Occupational attainments of rural to urban temporary economic migrants in China, 1985–1990," *International Migration Review*, Vol. 30, No. 3, pp. 771–787, 1996.

Zhang, C. and J. Shen, *Geographical System Engineering*, Beijing: Science Press, 1993.

Zhu, Y., "'Formal' and 'informal' urbanisation in China – trends in Fujian Province," *Third World Planning Review*, Vol. 20, No. 3, pp. 267–284, 1998.

Zhu, Y. and L. Lin, "Continuity and change in the transition from the first to the second generation of migrants in China: insights from a survey in Fujian," *Habitat International*, Vol. 42, pp. 147–154, 2014.

4. In search of an innovation economic geography

Edward J. Blakely

GOOSE CHASING TECHNO-NOVATION SPACES

In many respects, there is nothing noticeably clear or intelligent about the location of new technology innovation locations. But what is phenomenal is that modern regional science is progressing to provide a geo-economics base for innovation. Regional science was founded on clear fundamental principles regarding the juxtaposition of natural systems as they interact with one another over limited geography. The most straight-forward and most evident example is the location of steel mills at the juncture of river transport. So, cities like Pittsburgh in the United States or Liverpool in the UK are easily understood and explained using this essential understanding of resources connected by transportation forces. Geoscience from this formula helped explain a prescriptive science for the location of places producing exportable goods. Human settlement algorithms are now deeply rooted in geographic distances and travel speeds. Settlements are formed in a linear predictable fashion. Walter Christaller (1933), a Bavarian scholar, generated the base roots of modern regional science with his notion of economic laws determining the location and arrangement of towns across geography correlating the size and location. Central cities locate at measurable optimal or primary transport and natural resource extraction. Christaller's work "Central Place Theory" is the bedrock of modern regional economic science. An important element of central place theory is that cities and towns are arranged at distances convenient for the movement or consumption of certain goods or services. Barry et al. (1958) provide mathematic algorithms of the maximum radius of sales related to resource production and consumption. Today the notion that any good or service has physical limits seems incredible given the rapid changes in information science. But the concept of central places or a hierarchy of cities and small towns forming a region remains a core concept of regional science and economic geography.

CENTRAL PLACE THEORY REVISED

Anna Lee Saxenian offered a new regional economics paradigm to explain the rise of Silicon Valley (Saxenian, 1996). Saxenian's central place offers a different configuration of place economics moving away from the centralized natural resources manufacturing approach offering to a more decentralized model of economic activity taking place over a larger territory, for example, Silicon Valley as a geo-node with multi-centers. Saxenian's model allowed for a milieu of small places forming an interdependent hub without a center. Each place in the hub contributing a fundamental resource (Figure 4.1) re-enforcing but not dominating the economic geography.

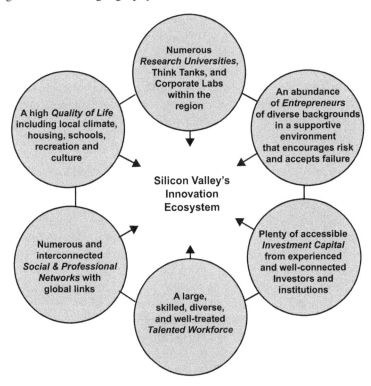

Figure 4.1   Saxenian economic geography

This approach created a system approach rather than the linear model of a dominating central city that smaller cities provided resources to and from which they received services and finished goods. Saxenian network methodology provided for a more footloose geography suggesting human mental resources act as strong attractors as natural ores and minerals. Michael Porter (Porter, 1980), a Harvard management scientist, added flexible specialization in Figure 4.1 as the basis for regional competitive construct for economic geography versus the comparative or least cost distance perspectives of Central Place theory.

> Because of its specialization in components and the relative weakness of electronic system industries, Silicon Valley depended almost exclusively on faraway markets. Firms in Silicon Valley shipped most of their output to the Department of Defense, to military electronics system firms, and later to consumer-oriented industrial sectors in the East, Midwest, and Southern California. As it grew, Silicon Valley became remarkably rich and heterogeneous. It gained many types of firms, bodies of knowledge, skills, and manufacturing formats (such as flexible specialization and mass production). The district, which at first specialized in vacuum tubes, acquired new capabilities in manufacturing silicon transistors and integrated circuits. (Lécuyer, 2006, p. 86)

GEO-ECONOMIC SCIENCE TO ECONOMIC POLICY

Regional science was shaken by these new concepts that seem to defy the role of fixed natural resources as anchors for firms and towns. Christaller posited:

1. Humans will always purchase goods from the closest place that offers them.
2. Whenever the demand for a certain good is high, it will be offered near the population. When demand drops, so too does the availability of the good. (Christaller, 1933)

Economic development based on the above Christaller thesis is the science of attracting firms and producing jobs by rearrangement of transportation to induce economic activity by creating comparative advantages for nearby natural resources. Economic development professional practice grew from Christaller based on the assumption that places with deep and thick natural resources links to the national and international transport networks became the comparative advantage (*transport + resource = jobs*) economic winners (Rostow, 1960). This concept is deeply ingrained as the basic platform for the economic development profession globally. In the United States the National Rural Development Administration built dams, created new rail and other infrastructure to induce factories to move from the northern part of the United States to the South. This was enormously successful. Entire university programs created the first quantitative simulation models for regional economics-based quantitative rationale for crafting of economic locations to replace declining agricultural enterprises and related activities. In Bradshaw and Blakely (1999), a counter argument was offered re-focusing agriculture and natural resources into small places loosening their bounds to central core cities by using the Internet to refine their natural and human resources into more globally competitive goods and services forming *local economic development programs.* Bradshaw and Blakely (1999) argue economic capacity can be built from the place (*endogenous wealth*) and not merely have the location as a responder to external transport and natural resource forces. Smaller places as local economic fulcrums using existing locational characteristics can remain competitive even after transport or natural resources declined or transformed. This notion is best reflected in our assertion,

> The ... task of economic development planning is to target the geographic scope. Areas or zones of concern can be as small as a city block that needs support or as large as a county, multicounty region, state, or even multistate region. Most important is that the economic area be a unit with internal consistency and cohesion. The area's economic configuration should be determined carefully because, despite political boundaries—especially in areas with large counties—these seldom correspond to economic regions. The key to effective planning is to realize that no economy begins and ends with neighborhood or city boundaries.
>
> The reality of economic development is that all small areas are ultimately nested in a larger regional enterprise that, of necessity, involves all communities sharing a common market, transportation system, and flow of goods and materials. The area to be focused upon is usually determined by the regional labor force (labor shed) or an equivalent interconnected zone physically and economically integrated. However, smaller, and larger areas may also be the focus of effective economic development if desired. At its most efficient, the economic development process plans for an entire economic zone, maximizing the area's total resource base. (Bradshaw and Blakely, 1999)

Thus, regional economics was and is being reshaped to fit the evolution of economic structures that required fewer physical resources and more institutional capacity is related to the assembly of institutions, natural resources and new technologies that forge relationships among these components as the basis for forming non-linear economic systems at a micro level in our competitive milieu within a region, across regions and even globally. Other important voices contribute to this new form as Ted K. Bradshaw labels this economic development movement as the third wave of economic/regional geography based on the human attributes of locations as a prime resource with little attachment to natural resources as a turning point in economic geography (Bradshaw and Blakely, 1999). This approach generated a new thrust economic development-based global connective capacity based on human interactions via the Internet not restrained by natural resources or ground transports. Michael Porter of Harvard (1980) coined the concept of competitive advantage versus resources constrained comparative advantage. Porter's concept of hundreds of cluster initiatives has flourished throughout the world. In an era of intensifying global competition, the pathbreaking book *The Competitive Advantage of Nations* (Porter, 1990) Porter suggests sustainable economies can be formed at a micro city and even neighborhood level with new Internet connectivity.

A VALLEY OF CHANGE

Saxenian's work (1996) on Silicon Valley inspired an introspection of regional economics as the science of linkage of resource-based rationality that accommodated various domains of regionalism into the Valley technology firm concept. Agglomeration became the new pet idea of regional development. That is if you add to the package of resources human activity and preferences you are still framing a set of economic densities using trails of linkage based on the earlier conceptualizations of regional science. Agglomeration became the new buzzword in both regional science and regional economic development. This led to a rush to create agglomerative packages called technology parks or tech nodes or science precincts. In the 1980s and 1990s and the beginning of the 2000s, any region worth its salt was investing heavily in trying to forge new techno-parks or similar copycat efforts of Silicon Valley to spawn industrial activity with some science components. Much of this activity had little value which is pointed out in numerous research papers since it was the cart in front of the horse literally. These parks proceeded from the notion that the park itself was an agglomerate because many firms could be in the same dense spatial areas and thus new mini Silicon Valleys would arise much like steel mills came up along the rivers leading to Pittsburgh and Cincinnati. These were add-ons to regional science since they were all embedded in a set of structures within a locale and simply appendages to the old resources with adding a new-found starter engine – *regional agglomeration theory* is the natural cousin to earlier regional science. Richardson (1969) models employment share in the region across manufacturing as the primary marker. Some regions simply possess better natural environments for certain industries. Nobel Laureate Paul Krugman weighed into this space asserting that places can alter theory of economic destinies by linking a new assembly of selected economic activities. For example, despite few transport and natural resources, tech firms in Massachusetts can induce new tech anchors that rely less on the old manufacturing roots of the Eastern Massachusetts Bay.

Economists are also discovering geography. Over the past decade, a "new trade theory" and "new economics of competitive advantage" emerged assigning importance to the role of human institutions like universities and science clusters to alter the internal geographic economic performance. Paul Krugman's (2019) work is a pivotal force promoting the generation of a new economic geography based on institutional agglomeration. According to Krugman, in a world of imperfect competition, international trade is driven as much by increasing returns and external economies as by comparative advantage. These external economies are more likely to be realized at the local and regional scale than at the national or international level. To understand trade, therefore, Krugman argues (in Ellison et al., 2010, pp. 1195–1213) that it is necessary to understand the processes leading to the local and regional concentration of production.

An agglomeration of institutions like the Harvard–MIT cluster naturally leads to the notion that one can stimulate agglomeration creating new or attracting universities to new locations. This idea led to the movement to university anchored science and technology parks around the world. Regional economics was misused as the scientific base for these products. However, closer inspection proves Silicon Valley could not be explained simply by science parks or university resources.

> Critics have also questioned the job-creation effect of such parks … Even in Japan, where the science park concept has been raised to the level of a national movement, truly … There is little evidence that parks have contributed to local economic growth or to the viability of localities. (Lécuyer, 2006, p. 19)

Until this point, regional economics/science matched economic transformations with only slight modifications in the theoretical underpinnings. Location within the spatial context remained central to the understanding of economic location and economic activity. Even the computer did not alter this paradigm. Admitting explanations fit nicely thus the notion that nature combined with interventions that alter the special economy still held forte in regional economic conceptualizations. But all this was about to change as people and human resources took the main stage and spatial relationships no longer dominated the economic paradigms governing commerce. We turn now to the central theme of this chapter designing a new understanding of human place as the core for regional economics.

PEOPLE SPACE

From the beginning of the intersection of space in economics natural factors and natural resources form the basic algorithm calculations of regional science. But at the turn-of-the-century in 2000, a new regime was firmly taking hold. Endogenous resources of the place that had earlier been central to the economic strength of the city or region, such as rivers, roads, extractive resources or physical geographic assets, are no longer able to define and sustain competitiveness in the rapidly developing economy based on innovation and techology based spatial systems. We already trace the paradigms shift back to the Silicon Valley search for a Holy Grail of new augmenting approaches to validate regional economic formation. But this was no longer holding when Richard Florida's *Rise of the Creative Class* (2002) disrupted the entire field with his work.

Richard Florida (2002) theorizes creativity (not locality) is the driving force of enterprise. Regional endowments are not physically creative. But creativity has no finite spatial attributes.

> At the beginning of civilization, the innovation of agriculture was a massively creative advance. People extracted more value per unit of land than they ever did as hunters. The Industrial Revolution was the next big step that brought further specialization and labor division.
>
> Society is in another significant influx of creative development. The pressure between creativity and organization is among today's most important issues since creative individuals do not adjust well to charge-and-control direction.
>
> Creativity comes in various shapes and forms; mechanical, economic, cultural, and artistic creativity all interact among themselves. For instance,
>
> A shared commitment to imagination and creativity fuels our economy and society. No format yet exists for the social and monetary framework that will recognize the coming Creative Age. (Greene, 2017)

However, two things are clear.

> First, innovation will not set us free since it does nothing to enhance human instinct. To be valuable, technology should be bolstered by social, organizational, and financial components. Second, large organizations will not vanish. An innovative economy needs big, little, and medium size associations. Independence is not limitless. Free market activity will always dictate the balance of power between companies and individuals. A few people may succeed being free agents, yet others will search for stable careers with set up businesses. Last, the economy is going Hollywood. In the past times, individuals moved to places where organizations were, trying to work for them. These days, however, companies move to places where creative individuals live to create jobs. (Ellison et al., 2010)

It is difficult to imagine an economy where people determined location and not resources. Richard Florida presents *creativity from place as a product*. Florida's work is now the bedrock of regional thinking and economics. Institutional economics is manifested in the largest world organizations that impart economic development notions and ideas are now captive of the Florida paradigm. Florida has produced several reinforcing works which we will not discuss here but the older common features regarding *the stickiness of place*. So, Silicon Valley cannot be replicated because *the people who occupy the valley want to be in the valley and nowhere else*. So, we find an economic landscape being transformed by people's desire to co-locate in certain specific places. Bradshaw and Blakely's (1999) economic development work reinforces the people aspects of economic formation by suggesting footloose of innovation technology making old rules of transport less relevant,

> Local economic development has been based on the notion that a locality can provide all of the resources to build and sustain an economic base. It is unclear in a cyberspace age whether any resources that a city controls are germane for economic development. Nonetheless, cities and states continue to invest enormous amounts of resources in the old models of attracting and retaining industry, despite clear evidence that this approach is no longer working. It is increasingly evident that the 21st-century economy is being shaped more by global than by local forces. This essay argues that the local economic development paradigm must be rethought, and that only communities taking a new path have a chance of success in a new global economy. (Blakely, 2007)

Florida's work combined with several other scholars builds on global versus local economies being formed with knowledge/creativity as centrality. Saskia Sassen in *Cities in the World Economy* (2019) moved from national regions within nation state systems as the competitive fulcrum for economic competitiveness to a thrust towards information systems unleashing geo-spatial relationships. Florida's *People* place can be translated into Sassen's *Globalness* meaning *Urbanity* as the new formula for geo-economic competitiveness. "As global hub cities emerge, the communities that build infrastructure to connect to this network will thrive" (Sassen, 2019, p. 42). Places with requisite urbanity, which must not be confused with community size, do not forecast or predict competitiveness. Thus, the roots of regional science have not disappeared but are overlaid. Creative places offer unique identities that attract the right human resources just like rivers and exploitable natural resources did. Place as location still matters, but how and why?

FROM FACTORY TO PLACE LABORATORY

The emergence of innovation place literature is still difficult to trace. A recent book *Crafting Innovative Places for Australia's Knowledge Economy* (Blakely and Hu, 2019) presents a new form of space-economics. Blakely and Hu (2019) replace the old models of industrial design as tools for making places attractivity nodes for creative people. Policymakers understand the Blakely–Hu approach to revitalize and energize old spaces into attractive milieus for Florida's creative class. The battle lines are drawn between those that believe that the old industrial forms can be recaptured and rekindled to form environmentally sustainable attractive places against some economic development professionals who cling to the old transport plus resources paradigms. Political lines and alliances using climate change and environmental regulatory frameworks are battle grounds across the globe. This revolution is deep and profound because it touches all forms of enterprise. The old anchor of business arising from the natural resource locations and the transportation hubs remains strong in political rhetoric. Thus, the rush among economic development practitioners is to find ways economic development can meld together new settlement systems that thrive without factories. The nature and dynamics of this new people place system, without large-scale manufacturing firms, is mystifying to local government in previously dynamic, but now dying, industrial towns. The literature is increasingly clear that the playing field is very uneven for the masses of people and the places that can be incorporated into this new knowledge base, and one that is muscle based, are limited. Unfixed geo-propensity is too hard for most politicians to fathom. Firms like Google can exist by transforming information with no spatial identity without centralizing hubs. Knowledge companies point out that their locations are not random but the intersection of well documented human economic geography. Amazon or similar platforms allow new sciences to come together generating or disseminating new products globally with no attachments to fixed transit or roads. Current research shows merely naming a place and sprinkling it with buildings re-branded tech park does not cultivate creativity. Tech parks, as described earlier are universal failures because they only concentrated on real estate as the essential feature. Others have assumed that the university is the inspiring source from which the emerging technology golden goose will spring. But it is difficult to build universities everywhere with the expectation they will spawn new globally competitive products. Clearly some aspects of this new formula seem accidental, while others are more fixed and provide guidance as to what forces and factors are essential.

WHAT ARE THE REGIONAL INNOVATION FACTORS?

Blakely and Hu (2019, pp. 121–153) suggest the emphasis should be on *elaboration* networks linking vast interconnections of science across the world into clear geo-nodes. We aggregate four factors to form with the core new economic geography. These factors or dimensions capture the essence of a new regional network science setting itself apart from the old approach of causal linearity not relevant with the evolution of knowledge space articulated here.

BOUNDED INTEGRITY

One of the most salient features of techno spaces is that they are named and the geographic extent of each space is well known and well-marked. In a regional sense, Silicon Valley, which covers many political jurisdictions and natural boundaries and barriers is still a well-defined geography; those who are within it know it. San Jose, California forms the central location from which this technology space is easily identified. Silicon Valley incorporates San Francisco and Oakland in a relatively large well-recognized geography around the southern portion of the San Francisco Bay. But it does not go north of San Francisco to relatively good city complexes such as Santa Rosa or Sacramento. Nor does it go south or east into the great California Valley. There seem no rational reasons for this, but the human resources agglomerate in this bounded geographical space. Attempts to extend the area have been unsuccessful (Figure 4.2).

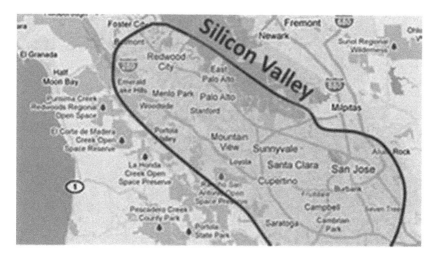

Source: https://dabrownstein.com/2015/02/06/the-swarming-of-silicon-valley/.

Figure 4.2   Silicon Valley bounded geography

Similarly, other technology geographies are easily in clearly marked creating innovation agglomeration dense clusters. These clusters of people and places and institutions are not random. But unlike extraction resource location are attractive settings for living and learning not merely for resource extraction. These places see the beauty of the environmental setting as a backdrop to attract people rather than to extract minerals and ores which spoil the environment. Emeryville, California is a prime example of setting old factory spaces reconditioned into biotechnology labs that require the old fortified factory walls as biohazard shields. This approach uses the old to build the new. Old mine shafts are now used as digital storage – the cloud. Re-using old space to generate new science is a creative future for Emeryville (Figure 4.3).

Emeryville is not just a place; it is an identity; it is a feeling; it is an expectation and an agglomeration place.

COLLABRATORIUMS

Moving to a multi-collaborative cluster is the second dimension. Earlier notions of science were based on the model that scientists were locked up in labs pursuing singular goals and objectives not even collaborating with one another but the single investigators working alone to create patentable products. This notion is dead. Large firms are now breaking down

Figure 4.3   Author artistic rendering: Emeryville Recast factory

into smaller units urged to collaborate across space and disciplines with one another. The best-known innovation incubation spaces are conglomerates of scientists and artists, along with venture capitalists, housed together in a single facility or group of facilities pursuing vaguely related scientific pursuits that yield new ways of presenting, performing, organizing or building some new approach to solving relevant problems. These aggregations can be as complex as the Tesla enterprise that combines groups of scientists working on energy, manufacturing and space travel with alternate forms of energy storage for initiatives including automobiles, and medical technology, in addition to space travel. Similarly, Amazon is a collection of activities with a single mission of transforming goods over all forms of information technology. The Bayer *Co-Lab* at the University of California, San Francisco represents a new research science institution that combines scientists interested in joint research with no fixed agenda. Co-labs usually come together as attractive open science ventures, not forced together by external government or private firms (Figure 4.4).

The shared science spaces are defined indefinable locations that attract collections of scientists in a similar locational environment such as what is known is Townhall in Boston and the MIT Innovation Centre in nearby Cambridge, Massachusetts. These places are known for the science and sciences across disciplines that find the spaces and the places attractive because they offer a form of urbanity that melds the arts and sciences

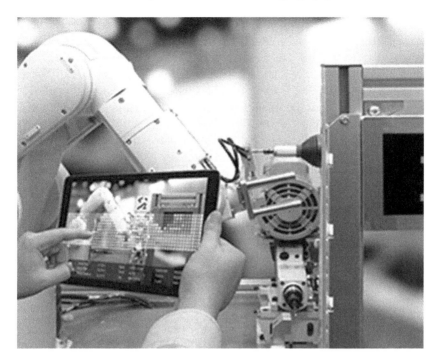

Figure 4.4   Co-Lab BioInformation Science, Adelaide, Australia

spatially enriching the environment for sharing and learning but making it *a cool place to be.*

Another feature of these environments is the attraction and retention of financial risk-takers who invest not just in the firms but are housed in the same buildings. Venture money is essential and must be both spatially and product flexible. These financers are seldom established bankers. The United States financial laws are ideal for such people because bankruptcy on a single product does not mean the loss of money from other endeavors. So, the adventurous capitalist with nimble financial structures. Agglomerative global capital is a pillar in this co-laboration system (Yigitcanlar and Inkinen, 2019, pp. 239–259).

GLOBAL-COSMOPOLITAN CONNECTIVITY

The third dimension is the most difficult special demographic issue associated with innovation technology – *cosmopolitan connectivity*. Many places in the world are international. Interestingly, there are a few places *designated cosmopolitan*. The new tech hubs are an unusual place because they go beyond a good airport and a few exciting locations for foreigners. Tech hubs are genuinely globalized in form, features, and international malleus. We know many cities that are international. Tokyo is international. Beijing is international. Los Angeles is international. But the cities are not cosmopolitan. Even cities such as Paris and London that have residents of many nationalities may or may not feel cosmopolitan simply by blending these global human resources into a new culturally distinctive space. So, San Francisco is globally connected cosmopolitanism inclusive of race, ethnicity across genders. While many urban centers are well-positioned to achieve global cosmopolitanism, few do. Berlin meets this standard for Europe as a Euro-cosmopolitan global milieu. Silicon Valley and Boston are the epitomai of this global cosmopolitan connectivity where people can share Paris cultures and be involved in a Boston–New York globalism (Figure 4.5).

Richard Florida (2002) shows places like Pittsburgh, Pennsylvania have become crucibles of human mixtures that liberate this form of global cosmopolitanism. But size is no restrictor; there are small places in the United States like Rochester, Minnesota, the home of the Mayo Clinic, which offer a high level of cosmopolitanism. An international airport nearby in a globally ranked university is vital but again, these cannot be manufactured easily. Berlin, Germany still struggles to have the right airport, yet it has the right milieu. So, there are aspects of these new spaces with the same characteristics as the old natural resource-based places where rivers and roads with bridges form the backdrop for the emergence of a place's centrality. There are steps that cities can take to create connected global urbanism. Austin, Texas for example, is an attractive community that innovates community-building social solidarity for people from across the globe.

> Once you have an innovation culture, even those who are not scientists or engineers – poets, actors, journalists – they, as communities, embrace the meaning of what it is to be scientifically literate. They embrace the concept of an innovation culture. They vote in ways that promote it. They do not fight science, and they do not fight technology. (Neil deGrasse Tyson, www.brainy quote.com)

The fourth dimension is the *magnet infrastructure* which is a grouping of institutional scientific resources densely located to form a web of innovation. The MIT–Harvard–Boston tech belt is an epitome of a magnet that continually pulls and reforms itself to meet the needs of innovators. The Lower West side of New York housing the Highline and

Figure 4.5   Future Lab Boston

Google, along with a plethora of incubators and startups, is another illustration. But such webs are not limited to the United States, Israel has a similar attracting network in bioengineering along with new attractors like Zhanjiang Science City emerging in China. These places all act as forceful attractors with a combination of dedicated science expertise and open avenues for collaboration across sciences.

FINAL WORD

As a final thought, this is an area of social template that all places can tackle if they have the requisite technological connectivity with a supportive government. Most sites can build private-firm-university and community tolerance for human capital across a region to become an incubator for globally competitive firms. Creative places must be re-created and re-stimulated, unlike factory environments that rely on identical routine outcomes. Innovation is driven from the inside by the constant mixing and re-mixing of the forces that spawn it.

REFERENCES

Barry, Brian J., L. Barry and William L. Garrison, "A Note on Central Place Theory and the Range of a Good", *Economic Geography*, Vol. 34, No. 4, 1958, pp. 304–311.

Blakely, Edward J., with Ted Bradshaw and Nancey Leigh Green, *Planning Local Economic Development*, Thousand Oaks, CA: SAGE Publications, 6th edition, 2000–2018.

Blakely, Edward J., "Competitive Advantage for the 21st-Century City: Can Help a Place-Based Approach to Economic Development Survive in a Cyberspace Age?", *Journal of the American Planning Association*, pp. 133–141, published online 26 November 2007.

Blakely, Edward J. and Richard Hu, *Crafting Innovative Places for Australia's Knowledge Economy*, Singapore: Palgrave, 2019.

Bradshaw, Ted K. and Edward J. Blakely, "What Are 'Third-Wave' State Economic Development Efforts? From Incentives to Industrial Policy", *Economic Development Quarterly*, Vol. 13, No. 3, 1999, pp. 229–244.

Christaller, Walter, *Central Places in Southern Germany* [*Die zentralen Orte in Süddeutschland*], Jena, Germany: Gustav Fischer, 1933.

Ellison, G., E.L. Glaeser and W.R. Kerr, "What Causes Industry Agglomeration? Evidence from Conglomeration Patterns", *American Economic Review*, Vol. 100, No. 3, 2010, pp. 1195–1213.

Engel, J.S., *Global Clusters of Innovation: Entrepreneurial Engines of Economic Growth around the World*, Cheltenham, UK and Northampton, MA, USA: Edward Elgar Publishing, 2014.

Florida, Richard, *The Rise of the Creative Class*, New York: Basic Books, 2002.

Greene, Robert, "The 48 Laws of Power", https://blog.12min.com/the-48-laws-of-power-pdf-summary. Published online 3 September 2017.

Krugman, Paul, *Regional Economics: Understanding the Third Great Transition*, CUNY, https://www.gc.cuny.edu/CUNY_GC/media/LISCenter/pkrugman/REGIONAL-ECONOMICS-3rd-transition.pdf, September 2019.

Lécuyer, Christopher, *Making Silicon Valley: Innovation and the Growth of High Tech, 1930–1970*, Cambridge: MIT Press, 2006.

Porter, Michael, *Competitive Advantage: Creating and Sustaining Superior Performance*, Cambridge: Harvard University Press, 1980.

Porter, Michael, *The Competitive Advantage of Nations*, New York: Free Press, 1990.

Raymond, Susan, "Listening to the Critics: Enlarging the Discussion of Policy for Science-based Development", *Annals of the New York Academy of Science*, December 1996.

Richardson, H.W., *Regional Economics. Location Theory, Urban Structure and Regional Change*. Westport, CT: Praeger, 1969.

Rostow, W.W., *The Stages of Economic Growth*, Cambridge: Cambridge University Press, 1960.

Sassen, Saskia, *Cities in the World Economy*, Thousand Oaks: SAGE Publications, 2019.

Saxenian, Anna Lee, *The Regional Advantage*, Cambridge: Harvard University Press, 1996.

Schumpeter, J., *Capitalism, Socialism and Democracy*, New York: Harper, 1942.

Yigitcanlar, T. and T. Inkinen, "Global Knowledge Precinct Best Practice", *Geographies of Disruption*, Baset: Springer Nature Switzerland, 2019, pp. 239–259.

5. Evaluating the quality of comprehensive plans for urban resilience: the case of seven metropolitan cities in South Korea

Hyun-Woo Kim and Gi-Chan Kim

INTRODUCTION

The occurrence of large-scale natural disasters (for example, flood, drought, snowstorm) has continuously increased and the extent of hazard damage has enlarged over the past two decades (Berke, 1996; Sim et al., 2008). In the past, hazard management was mostly conducted by physical improvement, since the size and scale of disasters were quite consistent and the urban structure was comparatively simple. However, abnormal climate changes, advancement of urban functions, and increased complexity of land uses within a city made it difficult to rely only on physical recovery after disasters. For instance, the amount of runoff caused by recent flooding often exceeded the existing designed stormwater capacity, which exacerbated the flood damage in urban areas (Kim and Tran, 2018). Thus, the establishment of sustainable urban systems that could minimize the damage from large-scale disasters is becoming more important.

The term "urban resilience" has emerged in recent years in various academic fields and policy discourses (Brown, 2013; Meerow et al., 2016). As populations and developments within urban areas continuously grow, cities are more exposed to diverse uncertainties and challenges (Carmin et al., 2012; Leichenko, 2011). One of the greatest threats that cities experience today is the problems caused by climate change, which has worsened multiple hazard issues. This has made the resilience concept more important in the field of hazard management and recovery. The definition in this field is widely understood as the capacity of urban systems to adapt, prepare and transform in the face of expected and unexpected hazards (100RC, 2019; Meerow et al., 2016). Because the urban system is complex and adaptive, municipalities should not only pay attention in a specific place that has been impacted by a certain hazard, but also need comprehensive resilient approaches to revitalize the overall urban systems after a disaster (Godschalk, 2003). While a number of studies focused on assessing physically and socially vulnerable areas in the past, recent research is examining multiple factors that may make cities more resilient to various disasters (Berke and Campanella, 2006; Godschalk, 2003). However, there still remains a gap in the previous literature, in that urban resilience has not been substantially addressed at the planning level. As each city has different thresholds to hazards (for example, different degrees of disaster impact as well as adaptability), their plans should primarily reflect local conditions while incorporating the concepts of resiliency. A comprehensive plan is a long-term document that envisions community growth for the next 20–30 years, generally covering current conditions, goals, policies and action strategies in various areas (for example, population, land use, environment, hazards, transportation) (Kim and Li, 2017). Considering that resilience is a broad concept that needs to be encompassed in a variety of planning disciplines, a comprehensive plan, which represents the highest planning hierarchy among urban management plans, should adopt the key principles of resiliency to properly guide other sub-plans.

This chapter attempts to explore the degree to which local comprehensive plans in South Korea have substantially incorporated the key concepts of urban resilience. Seven metropolitan cities in South Korea were selected for the study sample, and their plans were evaluated by employing the plan quality assessment method. The following section defines the concept of urban resilience that has been discussed in previous literature, and establishes the key principles of urban resiliency by reviewing earlier resilience studies and guidelines. Plan evaluation indexes (or indicators) are then derived for three plan components (factual basis; goals and objectives; and policies and strategies). Based on the evaluation protocol, plans are assessed with a total score of 120 points. Finally, a discussion aids in understanding urban resilience and providing policy implications for local planners of Incheon to better fill the current gaps of existing plans.

LITERATURE REVIEW

Urban Resilience

The origin of "resilience" came from the Latin word *resilo*, which means the ability to go back to the previous state. Holling (1973) first employed the topic of resilience in academia by applying it in the field of ecology. The ecological resilience concept was defined as the ability to absorb modification and disturbance while maintaining the previous relationship between multiple variables (Hassler and Kohler, 2014). From the early 1970s to the 1990s, it was understood as an ecosystem capability to endure external threats; but after the late 1990s, the framework was extended to a more general theory, which has been applied in a variety of fields (Hassler and Kohler, 2014; Seo et al., 2014). Urban resilience has been used dynamically in the urban planning field after Vale and Campanella (2005) adopted the concept in disaster recovery. ARUP (2014) stated that urban resilience is an ability to maintain the central function of a city, and emphasized the interactions of various assets, systems and stakeholders. They suggested that seven characteristics are necessary to secure these functions: reflectivity, resource mobilization, durability, substitution, flexibility, inclusion and integration. The seven characteristics were presented in conjunction with four categories, which are health/well-being, economy/society, infrastructure/environment, and leadership/strategy (Korea Land and Housing Research Institute, 2015). Thus, the concept of resilience goes beyond the previous concept of preventive management, which has relied on the disaster risk from past experience. It can also be interpreted as a regional capability to create a pleasant urban environment by maintaining the function of a city while resisting and adapting to unpredictable external shocks and stresses.

Previous Plan Evaluation Indexes and Case Studies

Previous studies with regard to urban resilience show two forms of research: index assessment, and case study through application. By reviewing the previous research, we have established our indicators for plan assessment. Jung et al. (2016) evaluated the comprehensive plans covering populations of more than 1 million and established the evaluation indexes based on the seven attributes that the Rockefeller Foundation and the Organisation for Economic Co-operation and Development (OECD) have suggested for urban resilience. Those indexes are classified and presented as: (1) reflectivity (population density, development plan, and so on); (2) resource mobilization (zoning, building criteria, and so on); (3) durability (system, urban infrastructure, and so on); (4) substitution (urbanization rate, preservation ratio, and so on); (5) flexibility (continuity of operation plan, and so on); (6) tolerance (intercommunication, and so on); and (7) integration (efficiency of internal institutions, and so on). Kim et al. (2018) established the assessment indicators in terms of four aspects (economy, society, infrastructure and ecology) through literature reviews and experts' surveys for the purpose of assessing the level of urban resilience in Suwon, South Korea. Specifically, their indicators were developed in terms of social (for example, vulnerable social group, handicapped person), economic (for example, participation rate of women's labor), infrastructural (for example, building construction year, cooling facility), and ecological (for example, urban park, impervious surface ratio) aspects. Han and Lee (2017) drew the urban resilience-related indexes among the 17 goals of the United Nations (UN) Sustainable Development Goals (SDGs) and conducted an expert survey and group interview to pull out the detailed evaluation indexes. These indexes are classified into nine sectors: (1) population structure (for example, elderly population ratio); (2) labor market (for example, economic activity participation); (3) stability and sustainability (for example, number of the national pension subscribers); (4) housing (for example, elderly housing ratio); (5) land use (for example, urbanized area percentage); (6) public space; (7) transportation (for example, public transport share); (8) environment and energy (for example, greenhouse gas emissions); and (9) infrastructure (for example, sewer/water line supply). Jeon and Byun (2017) yielded several assessment indexes for comprehensive resilience systems through a thorough literature review and applied it in 66 municipalities within the Seoul metropolitan area. Their indexes were grouped into six categories, which are: society, economy, institution, infrastructure, community capacity and environment.

With regard to case studies, Jeon and Lee (2018) proposed specific application alternatives for urban resilience in terms of four aspects (physical/environmental, economic, social and institutional aspects). They maintained that the application of resilience is necessary to achieve sustainable development. By analyzing the current conditions of Ulsan, South Korea, Yoon (2018) reviewed policies and projects to strengthen the city's resiliency. As a way to strengthen the city's resiliency, he emphasized six policy tasks, including the establishment of an urban safety research center, revitalization of residents' participation, redevelopment through applying the resilience concept, and adoption of an urban safety strategy plan. In addition, Pyo and Kwack (2017) analyzed the resilience enhancement project that was conducted by the United Nations Office for Disaster Risk Reduction (UNDRR), the OECD, and ARUP and the Rockefeller Foundation. Based on the results, she suggested urban design alternatives to enhance the concept of resiliency. While Jung et al. (2016) examined comprehensive plans regarding the level of urban resilience in South Korea, only limited research has investigated the quality of plans in terms of resiliency. Through content analysis, this chapter examines whether seven metropolitan cities in

South Korea have sufficiently incorporated the key concepts of resiliency. Policy suggestions are discussed in the conclusion, to enhance Incheon's resiliency in the long term.

RESEARCH METHODS

Study Areas, Principles and Plan Evaluation Indexes Setting

The seven largest metropolitan cities (Seoul, Busan, Incheon, Daegu, Daejeon, Ulsan and Gwangju) in South Korea were selected for the study areas. Since one of the main purposes of this study is to provide policy suggestions in enhancing overall urban resiliency for Incheon's comprehensive plan, cities that have similar urban structural and socio-economic characteristics were selected for the study sample (see Figure 5.1).

Following the four categories (health/well-being, economy/society, infrastructure/environment, and leadership/strategy) that ARUP (2014) established for resiliency, we developed our principles and evaluation indexes for assessing the comprehensive plans in terms of urban resilience. In addition, indicators that have been used in prior studies, projects and guidelines were considered while creating our own indexes. While reviewing the previous studies, the assessment index on the health/well-being sector was mainly mentioned with regard to socially disadvantaged groups, such as basic livelihood recipients and the elderly population. In addition, health and medical services, as well as guarantees for basic rights, were often mentioned in this field. In the economy/society sector, terms related to job creation were mentioned most, followed by citizen participation and safety-related words (for example, crime rate and crime prevention measure). Disaster-related indicators were generally presented in the infrastructure/environment sector, indicating that they play an important role in enhancing urban resilience. Other indicators, such as forest, green land, infrastructure provision, and land use, have also been widely revealed. Although the number of indicators in the leadership/ strategy sector was relatively small compared to other sectors, cooperation and communication between the government, citizens and stakeholders was emphasized in the majority of previous studies.

Based on these findings, the principle of the health/well-being sector focused on enhancing the quality of residents' life through satisfying their basic needs; while the economy/society sector concentrated on securing local self-sustaining power through the creation of jobs and enhancing safety from diverse crimes. The principles of the infrastructure /environment field focused on creating green areas and providing

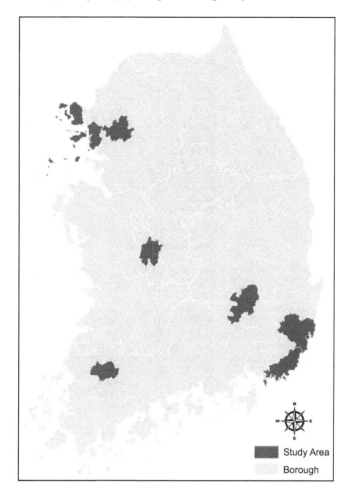

Figure 5.1   Study area

adequate public infrastructure to minimize disaster damage and to create a safe living environment for residents. Finally, the leadership/strategy sector aimed at promoting cooperation between multiple stakeholders, enhancing different stakeholder capabilities and continuously monitoring the execution of various policy strategies. A total of 72 indicators were developed by referring the four principles, and they were allocated to three plan components (factual basis: n = 33, goals and objectives: n = 15, policies and strategies: n = 24). Table 5.1 illustrates the detailed indicators for each sector and component.

Table 5.1   Plan quality evaluation indexes

Sector	Principles (n = 9)	Factual basis indicators (n = 33)	Goal indicators (n = 15)	Action plan indicators (n = 24)
Health and well-being	Improving the quality of life by meeting basic needs	Number of basic living security recipients, Water supply rate, Number of social welfare facilities, Number of deteriorated housing, Owner-occupation rate, Number of medical personnel, Number of medical facilities	Providing minimal services	Support for the renovation of deteriorated housing, Provision of welfare services, Provision of medical services
Economy and society	Continuous participation by residents	Civic group, Election turnout, Number of community facilities	Promotion of social network continuity, Enabling resident participation	Enabling civic group, Securing community facilities
	Securing regional self-sustaining power through job creation	Number of economically active participants, Number of people in the knowledge-based service industry, Business scale, Number of employees of small and medium-sized enterprises compared to large enterprises, Women's labor participation rate	Expanding employment support, Development and innovation of regional business	Enabling women's economic activities, Promotion of social enterprises, Promotion of specialization industry, Establishment of a link with the universities

Sector	Principles (n = 9)	Factual basis indicators (n = 33)	Goal indicators (n = 15)	Action plan indicators (n = 24)
	Improving social safety	Crime rate, Crime prevention measures	Creation of a city safe from crime	Preparing measures to prevent crime
Infrastructure and environment	Improving the sustainability of the environment through creation of green spaces	Green space rate, Urban park, Forest area	Expanding urban green space	Applying LID techniques, Creation of biotope, Creation of a park
	Securing a safe living environment by preparing measures to cope with disasters	Status of damage to storm/flood, Status of capacity of evacuation facilities, Disaster prevention facility	Preparing measures against disasters	Establishment of disaster prevention map, Installation of a temporary shelter, Establishment of a comprehensive disaster prevention system, Establishment of a disaster alert notification system
	Improving the quality of life through efficient land use and infrastructure provision	Mixed use development, Status of public transportation operations, Status of fire, police, emergency relief services, Status of roads	Establishment of transportation environment focused on public transportation, Efficient land use, Expanding and improving infrastructure	Enabling mixed use developments, Supply of basic living infrastructure, Activating the use of public transportation
Leadership and strategy	Successful establishment and execution of strategies through monitoring	Monitoring indicator, Regular updates of the plan	Establishment of a comprehensive monitoring system, Need for long-term, integrated strategy	Establishment monitoring indicators, Establishment of long-term, integrated strategy

Table 5.1 (continued)

Sector	Principles (n = 9)	Factual basis indicators (n = 33)	Goal indicators (n = 15)	Action plan indicators (n = 24)
	Empowerment stakeholders through information provision, training, and cooperation	Status of good case sharing, Status of stakeholder cooperation, Response training and education, Creation of a public awareness of risks	Continuous training and information provision, Preparing a plan for empowerment	Implementation of civic education, Establishment of a government–citizen communication system

Plan Quality Evaluation

Plan quality scores were measured by developing a plan coding protocol, which was employed by several prior plan evaluation studies (Brody, 2008; Kim and Tran, 2018). Particularly, plan scores were obtained for four sectors by considering three plan components (factual basis; goals and objectives; and policies and strategies), with each plan component receiving from 0 to 10. Each index within a plan component scored ranging from 0 to 2 (0 = index was not mentioned within a plan; 1 = index was mentioned, but not in detail; 2 = index was mentioned with detailed information). Indexes within the goals and objectives component, however, obtained scores only from 0 to 1, since the goals typically contain comprehensive visions that are difficult to measure in terms of the concrete contents.

Indexes within the factual basis component were evaluated by scoring two types of contexts: narration and visuality. Each context received scores on a 0–2 scale and then they were divided by 2 in order to convert the scale into 0 to 2. While indexes within the goals and objectives were scored on a 0–1 scale, indicators for the policies and strategies had the same scale as the factual basis. After each index was scored, all the scores within a plan component were added and then divided by the total possible scores that each plan component can receive (that is, if there are 33 indexes within the factual basis component, the added index scores were divided by 66 (33 × 2)). That score was multiplied by 10 to standardize into a scale of 0–10. Finally, three plan components' scores were added for a specific sector. Since each sector can receive up to 30 points, the total score for the three plan components ranges from 0 to 120. The evaluation process can be described as the equations shown below (Brody, 2008):

$$PCS_j = \frac{10}{2m_j} \sum_{i=1}^{m_j} IS_i \qquad (5.1)$$

$$SS_i = \sum_{j=1}^{3} PCS_j \qquad (5.2)$$

where PCS_j refers to the jth plan component score; m_j indicates the total number of indexes within the jth component; I_i indicates the ith index's scores; SS_i refers to the i sector's total plan quality score.

To minimize the threat of reliability and personal bias in judgment, seven plans were assessed twice by the same coder. A second evaluation was made approximately a month later, using the same evaluation protocol. The percentage agreement score of two assessments was about 88 percent, indicating that the agreement score can be considered as an acceptable level. According to Miles and Huberman (1994), a percentage agreement score above 80 percent generally has an acceptable reliability level.

RESULTS

The total average score for seven comprehensive plans was 67.7 out of 120. A large variation existed between sampled cities (Figure 5.2). Plans that rated higher than the average score were for Seoul (81.2), Busan (74.1) and Gwangju (70.8). Daegu (67.3), Incheon (66.6), Daejeon (59.0) and Ulsan (54.6) scored lower than the average score. While Seoul had the highest plan quality score and received the highest ratings in three categories except for the infrastructure/environment sector, Ulsan obtained the lowest scores in two categories (economy/society and leadership/strategy). Incheon had a score gap of 14.7 points with Seoul, and the leadership/strategy sector accounted for more than half of the total gap (8.3 points).

The images for the following sectors are given in Figure 5.3. Regarding the health/well-being sector, seven cities' average standardized score was 21.5. Busan received the highest score of 26.9 out of 30, while Daejeon scored the lowest score of 17.7. Only Busan (26.9), Seoul (25.0) and Incheon (23.0) scored higher than the average. In the factual basis component, water supply and medical facilities/services-related indicators were mentioned in all plans. The number of social welfare facilities,

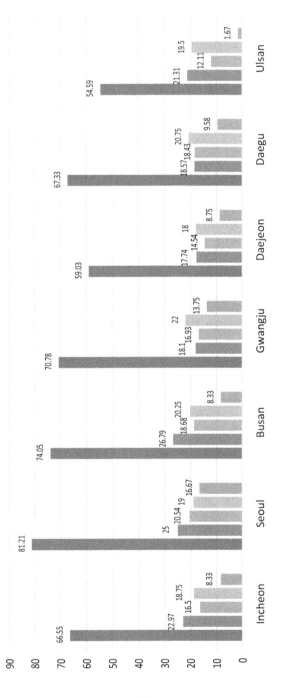

Figure 5.2   Total plan quality evaluation scores

basic livelihood recipients and doctors per 1000 people were often mentioned in all sampled cities. While there was only one goal for this sector (providing minimum required service), all cities mentioned this goal within their plans. Three indexes within the policies/strategies component were stated relatively well in all plans, except supporting for the renovation of old housings.

Seoul scored the highest within the economy/society sector (20.5 points), while Ulsan received the lowest score of 12.1. In terms of identifying the current conditions of economic and social status, the rate of participation in economic activities was revealed in the entire plan, while the number of civic groups, the election turnout, the percentage of employees in the knowledge-based services, the number of workers in small and medium-sized enterprises, and the crime prevention alternatives were not substantially mentioned in sampled plans. Daegu was the only city to have presented the status of female labor. Cities sufficiently mentioned the five goals that have been developed from this study. Ulsan was the only city that did not include the goal related to enhancing the social network sustainably. Within seven policies and strategies, every city mentioned installing CPTED or CCTV for preventing crime. Seoul was the only city to have mentioned vitalizing civic organizations, whereas Incheon solely failed to mention the index on promoting specialized industries.

The average standardized score of the infrastructure/environment sector was 19.75, with a relatively small variation between the highest (Gwangju: 22.0) and lowest (Daejeon: 18.0) scored cities. When it comes to the factual basis, every sampled city failed to include conditions regarding the capacity of evacuation facilities and the status of disaster prevention facilities, as well as mixed land-use developments. Busan and Gwangju only indicated the present conditions of police/fire stations in their plans. Six general goals were mentioned in all plans. Action strategies with regard to establishing urban parks, supplying basic infrastructure and promoting public transportation were readily seen in the plans. However, the disaster risk map was only partially mentioned in Ulsan, and the disaster alert notification system was insufficiently recognized in most plans. Cities also were not successful in establishing biotopes and temporary shelters. Overall, there was no large variation in the factual basis and goals within this sector, but Gwangju's plan only stated detailed strategies in terms of management of various hazards.

Finally, a large variation existed in the leadership/strategy sector, with a gap between Seoul and Ulsan of 15 points. Most indicators in this sector were poorly mentioned compared to the other sectors, indicating that existing plans still have huge limitations in cooperating with multiple

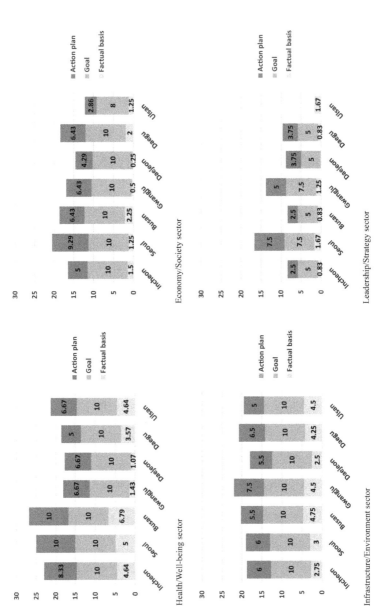

Figure 5.3 Plan quality score for each sector

stakeholders and monitoring and updating their past resilient-related policies. A number of plans did not show the present conditions of six indicators. Daejeon and Ulsan, particularly, received no scores on every index. Goals on providing continuous education and information to residents, and enhancing various stakeholders' capacity, were properly mentioned in the samples; while long-term strategies and comprehensive policy monitoring were missing in the majority of plans. Regarding action strategies, Seoul identified the needs of communication between the government and citizens, monitoring policies, and providing various residents' education programs. However, the plans focused on developing short-term policies rather than creating long-range comprehensive action strategies.

DISCUSSION AND CONCLUSION

While the scale of damage from various disasters is continuously increasing due to unpredictable climate change, the complexity and unexpected disturbance in urban areas make it difficult to completely prevent hazard damage in localities. Thus, it is necessary to create a resilient urban environment that can minimize disaster damage and promote sustainable development. One of the primary approaches to enhance urban resilience is to establish a long-range comprehensive plan that could embrace the key concepts of resiliency. Considering this aspect, our study has evaluated the degree to which metropolitan cities have sufficiently incorporated the key resiliency principles within their comprehensive plans. The findings show that the majority of sampled cities in South Korea did not fully integrate the key resiliency principles, with a mean score of 67.6 out of 120. A large variation existed between seven cities on the resilience score. While Seoul received the highest plan quality score (81.2), Ulsan obtained the lowest score, which was not initially expected. Since Ulsan has repeatedly experienced several earthquakes in recent years, it was assumed to have a relatively high plan quality score on resiliency. Among four resiliency sectors, plans have well-specified indicators related to the health/well-being sector (average score: 21.5 out of 30). However, the leadership/strategy sector (average score: 9.4) needed significant improvement for all sampled plans. Particularly, plans should regularly update their current status, goals and policies, and a concrete policy monitoring system that could check the policy implementation is highly required. Regarding the three plan components, goals and objectives were generally well mentioned in the sampled plans, with various specific resilient goals and visions. Present conditions regarding the urban resilience were stated relatively well, except in the leadership/strategy sector. Action strategies and policies should be further improved by incorporating more detailed technological and sophisticated land-use tools that could increase the overall urban resiliency.

The City of Incheon ranked #5 out of seven metropolitan cities, indicating that the level of urban resilience was relatively low within the comprehensive plan. The evaluation result for the health/well-being sector was generally mentioned well, but some indicators need to be further addressed in the near future. Specifically, indexes for the recipient of basic living and health professionals should be supplemented in the factual basis, and action strategies related to providing medical services need to be provided. For the economy/society sector, the number of civic groups and the election turnout have not been sufficiently reflected in the factual basis. In addition, the existing status and action strategy for community facilities and female labor participation activation should be addressed in the future amendment. Policies regarding the promotion of specialized industries should also be mentioned during the plan revision process. With regard to the infrastructure/environment sector, additional information on the capacity of evacuation facilities, disaster prevention facilities and mixed land-use developments are needed. Planning tools should be developed for creating the biotope/disaster maps and building strategic temporary shelters. Since the City of Gwangju has clear information and policies in terms of these indexes, Incheon should refer to its plan to establish a decent disaster management system. As mentioned earlier, indexes within the leadership/strategy sector were poorly mentioned in all sampled plans. For both factual bases and action strategies, a greater number of disaster preparedness education programs should be provided to different stakeholders. Moreover, a communication system between the government and citizens needs to be added and improved to better prepare for multiple disasters. Since Incheon has recently released a comprehensive hazard mitigation plan, goals and policies within the comprehensive plan should embrace the visions that have been established in the hazard mitigation plan, in order to create a consistent planning framework for urban resilience.

Although the findings in this study may provide some insightful suggestions to local planners and policy-makers, some limitations still exist which should be addressed in further research. First, surveys of urban resilience experts and professionals were omitted while developing the plan evaluation indexes due to the lack of financial and human resources. Since guidelines and previous studies on urban resilience were only referred to for creating the evaluation indexes, further study should increase the objectivity of indicators by conducting surveys or focus group interviews. Second, the evaluation in this study only focused on the quality of plans. Although the strength of a plan on urban resilience can be somewhat explained through the assessment of quality, we may not fully recognize whether the goals or policies have been implemented in practice. Examining both the quality and the implementation effect of plans in the future will allow municipalities to better understand their current level and status in terms of urban resilience. Finally, the study area of this research only covers seven metropolitan cities in South Korea. Further study may better assess, identify and compare the characteristics of plan quality associated with urban resilience by adding more samples.

REFERENCES

100RC (100 Resilient Cities), "What is Urban Resilience?," retrieved from: https://www.100resilientcities.org/resources (accessed on August 11, 2019), 2019.

ARUP, "City Resilience Index," retrieved from: http://www.arup.com (accessed on August 19, 2019), 2014.

Berke, Philip, "Enhancing Plan Quality: Evaluating the Role of State Planning Mandates for Natural Hazard Mitigation," *Journal of Environmental Planning and Management*, Vol. 39, No. 1, pp. 79–96, 1996.

Berke, Philip and Thomas Campanella, "Planning for Postdisaster Resiliency," *Annals of the American Academy of Political and Social Science*, Vol. 604, No. 1, pp. 192–207, 2006.

Brody, Samuel, *Ecosystem Planning in Florida: Solving Regional Problems Through Local Decision-Making*, Burlington, VT: Ashgate Publishing Company, 2008.

Brown, Katrina, "Global Environmental Change I: A Social Turn for Resilience?," *Progress in Human Geography*, Vol. 38, No. 1, pp. 107–117, 2013.

Carmin, JoAnn, Nikhil Nadkarni and Christopher Rhie, *Progress and Challenges in Urban Climate Adaptation Planning: Results of a Global Survey*, Cambridge, MA: MIT, 2012.

Godschalk, David, "Urban Hazard Mitigation: Creating Resilient Cities," *Natural Hazards Review*, Vol. 4, No. 3, pp. 136–143, 2003.

Han, Sanmi and Myunghoon Lee, "Analysis of Evaluation Indicator for the Development and Management of Sustainable and Resilient City: Focusing on the Goal 11 of UN Sustainable Developments Goals (SDGs)," *Journal of the Korean Regional Development Association*, Vol. 29, No. 3, pp. 1–24, 2017.

Hassler, Uta and Niklaus Kohler, "Resilience in the Built Environment," *Building Research and Information*, Vol. 42, No. 2, pp. 119–129, 2014.

Holling, Crawford, "Resilience and Stability of Ecological Systems," *Annual Review of Ecology and Systematics*, Vol. 4, pp. 1–23, 1973.

Jeon, Eunyoung and Byungsul Byun, "A Study on the Development and Application of Community Resilience Evaluation Indicators for Responding to Climate Change," *Journal of the National Geographic Society*, Vol. 51, No. 1, pp. 47–58, 2017.

Jeon, Yumi and Jaeseon Lee, "A Comparative Analysis of the Level of Urban Resilience in the Comprehensive Plan – Focused on Metropolitan Cities in Korea," *Journal of the Urban Design Institute of Korea Urban Design*, Vol. 19, No. 3, pp. 21–32, 2018.

Jung, Eunjoo, Bongyung Jeong and Jumong Na, "A Study on the Sustainability and Resilience of City," *Journal of the Korean Regional Development Association*, Vol. 28, No. 4, pp. 87–108, 2016.

Kim, Eunyoung, Kyungmin Jung and Wonkyung Song, "Evaluating and Improving Urban Resilience to Climate Change in Local Government: Focused on Suwon," *Journal of Environmental Impact Assessment*, Vol. 27, No. 4, pp. 335–344, 2018.

Kim, Hyun Woo and Ming-Han Li, "Managing Stormwater for Urban Sustainability: An Evaluation of Local Comprehensive Plans in the Chesapeake Bay Watershed Region," *Journal of Environmental Planning and Management*, Vol. 60, No. 10, pp. 1702–1725, 2017.

Kim, Hyun Woo and Tho Tran, "An Evaluation of Local Comprehensive Plans Toward Sustainable Green Infrastructure in US," *Sustainability*, Vol. 10, No. 11, p. 4143, 2018.

Korea Land and Housing Research Institute, "A Research on Urban Resilience for Urban Regeneration," retrieved from: http://lhi.lh.or.kr (accessed on September 16, 2019), 2015.

Leichenko, Robin, "Climate Change and Urban Resilience," *Current Opinion in Environmental Sustainability*, Vol. 3, No. 3, pp. 164–168, 2011.

Meerow, Sara, Joshua Newell and Melissa Stults, "Defining Urban Resilience: A Review," *Landscape and Urban Planning*, Vol. 147, pp. 38–49, 2016.

Miles, Matthew and Michael Huberman, *Qualitative Data Analysis*, 2nd edition, Thousand Oaks, CA: SAGE Publications, 1994.

Pyo, Heejin and Dognwha Kwack, "Types and Resilience Characteristics of Urban Disaster Prevention Design," *Journal of the Korean Society of Disaster Information*, Vol. 13, No. 1, pp. 59–72, 2017.

Seo, Jeeyoung, Byungwon Park, Sungho Lee, Kyujin Jo and Jeonghyun Yoon, "Future Risk and Resilience," Korea Institute of Science and Technology, Survey Research, June 2, 2014.

Sim, Woobae, Kwangik Wang, Bumhyun Lee and Moonwon Lee, "A Study on the Disaster-Prevention Urban Planning for the Creation of Safe City," Korea Research Institute for Human Settlement (in Korean), 2008.

Vale, Lawrence and Thomas Campanella, *The Resilient City: How Modern Cities Recover from Disaster*, Oxford: Oxford University Press, 2005.

Yoon, Youngbae, "A Study on the Strengthening of Urban Resilience in Ulsan," retrieved from: https://www.udi.re.kr/bbs/board.php?bo_table=research_report&wr_id=1169 (accessed on August 22, 2019), 2018.

PART II

The competitive city

6. "Focused Research University" and "Matrix College": Incheon National University's strategies based on combination and permutation

Cho Dong-Sung

INCHEON METROPOLITAN CITY, SONGDO AND THE BIO INDUSTRY

Located 30 km west of Seoul, Incheon Metropolitan City (hereafter: Incheon) connects the world and Korea through Incheon International Airport. Incheon's population is increasing while the other major cities' populations have declined. Incheon's population surpassed 3 million in 2018; the population of Seoul, the largest city in Korea, was reduced to less than 10 million; the population of Busan, the second-largest city in Korea, was also reduced to less than 3.5 million. Incheon has out-performed Busan in gross regional domestic product (GRDP), with 84.1 trillion won ($74.8 billion) in 2017.

At the center of Incheon's population and economic growth is Songdo International Business District (IBD), which is on the southwestern corner of Incheon and facing the Yellow Sea. Songdo IBD has been developed from 2003 with a plan for completion in 2022 on reclaimed land of 51.36 km² with a population target of 265 611 and a budget of $19.59 billion. It was designated as one of three districts of Incheon Free Economic Zone (EFEZ), in which income taxes are exempted for international investment in the first ten years of operation.

Songdo IBD has been widely recognized as a model "smart city" or "ubiquitous city." Being ubiquitous means that technology is used everywhere in the way the inhabitants live:

> computers are built into the buildings and streets. For example, Songdo IBD residents can video-conference with their neighbors, or even attend classes remotely. They can control lighting, heating, air conditioning and more, all with

the push of a button on a control panel. Sensors gather information on things like traffic flow and energy use. This kind of information can be converted into alerts that tell citizens when a bus will arrive, or notify the authorities when a crime is taking place. The water pipes are designed to prevent drinkable water from being wasted in showers and toilets. (Wikipedia, n.d.)

Incheon, with Songdo IBD as one of its districts, was chosen by an international organization as the world's most crimeless city in 2016.

Being a bridge away from Incheon International Airport, Songdo IBD has a distinct advantage in the transportation of biomedicine products at the deep freezing temperature of −70 degrees Celsius. Biomedicine companies have chosen Songdo IBD to locate their production facilities. Following Samsung Biologics and Celltrion, two leaders in the global biomedicine industry, approximately 350 bio companies have flocked together in Songdo IBD and its vicinity, creating a robust bio industry cluster. Songdo cluster's capacity of biomedicine products reached 560 000 liters equivalent in 2020, taking more than 10 percent of the industry's global market of 5.5 million liters equivalent. With the expansion plans of 1 million liters equivalent underway, the Songdo IBD is expected to surpass San Francisco and become the leader in the biomedicine industry in 2030.

Incheon National University (INU)

INU is a young university, yet it has been through a series of major changes. Established in 1979 as a private engineering university, it was taken over in 1994 by Incheon City Government and became a city university. In 2009, it moved to Songdo IBD as one of the District's first inhabitants. In 2013, the Korean government took it over, and made it the second incorporated national university in Korea. Seoul National University (SNU) became the first incorporated national university in 2011. The government's objective to make INU the second incorporated national university was intended to put competitive pressure on SNU so that there would be a healthy rivalry between the two. The reasoning behind the choice of INU was the population size of 16.5 million in Incheon and nearby Kyunggi Province, which far exceeded that of Seoul with less than 10 million. Although there are older and bigger national universities in Busan, Daegu and other regional cities, the government thought that the smaller sizes of these cities' populations and corresponding regional economies would not be sufficient to support the cities' universities as potent forces to compete with SNU. Having been chosen as one of two representative universities in Korea, INU has chosen to be not the best one, but the only one of its kind, among universities in the world. To this end, INU has strategically chosen two programs: "Focused Research University" as a research-centered strategy, and "Matrix College" as an education-centered strategy.

Focused Research University as a Research-Centered Program

There are three types of research-centered universities. The Comprehensive Research University (CRU) is the first type of research-centered university, in which professors conduct research into their choice of research topics without any interventions by the university presidents, college deans or department chairpersons. The school administrators can control professors by the quality of research outputs such as the number of journal papers and their impact upon society, but not by the research topics themselves. Harvard University, the University of Oxford, Peking University, and SNU may fall into the category of CRUs.

The Intensive Research University (IRU) is the second type of research-centered university in which professors and the school administrators behave in the same way as in a CRU. The only difference from a CRU is that professors' major fields are narrowly defined to such fields as social sciences, engineering or business. The École Normale Supérieure, MIT and London Business School may fall into the IRU category.

INU created a new type of research-centered university, and named it the Focused Research University (FRU). In the FRU, professors in various majors, in addition to pursuing their own choices of research, are encouraged to conduct research into the topics which are predetermined by the university. INU was a Comprehensive Research University, but became an FRU by choosing "bio" as its first focus in 2017, and a few more focuses in the following years. Since then, INU has been encouraging all INU professors to choose one of these as their research topic in addition to their original respective topics. INU is most likely the only FRU in the world.

Figure 6.1 graphically shows the characteristics of the CRU, IRU and FRU. The CRU is a university which has no restrictions on both of the two axes. The CRU provides no guidelines to professors (on the X axis) in their choice of research topics. The CRU also has no limits on the portfolio of colleges and departments (on the Y axis). The IRU is a university which has no restrictions on the X axis, but has a guideline on the Y axis. The IRU, like the CRU, provides no guidelines to professors (on the X axis) in their choice of research topics. The IRU has, at least in its founding philosophy, certain limits on the portfolio of colleges and departments (on the Y axis). The FRU is a university which has no

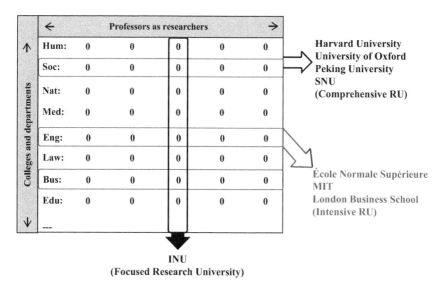

Figure 6.1   Three types of research universities: CRU, IRU and FRU

restrictions on the Y axis, but has a guideline on the X axis. The FRU, like the CRU, has no limits on the portfolio of colleges and departments (on the Y axis). The IRU has certain guidelines to professors (on the X axis) in their choice of research topics (on the X axis).

Let me explain INU's FRU approach in detail. Taking into account the emergence of the bio industry cluster in Songdo IBD, INU chose bio as the first focus. INU professors in 54 departments of 11 colleges have been encouraged to conduct research into bio in addition to their original major fields. At INU's annual Global Bio-Convergence Forums, which started in 2018, more than 50 professors in various fields presented their bio-related papers to the audience composed of bio professors and scholars.

The papers presented in the Global Bio-Convergence Forums can be categorized into two types. The first type of papers are the approaches by professors without a bio background on the bio-related subjects. For example, three professors of English language and literature and a professor of business administration presented their research result on bio. Titled "Biotechnology Manifested in Literature: Past, Present, and Future" (Cho et al., 2018; Cho et al., 2019), their paper compared the periods when key bio-related words such as "cell," "gene," "RNA," "DNA" and "cancer" first appeared in novels and in scientific journals. Using big data approaches, they tested the hypotheses, "Literature precedes science in the use of bio words," and "Time gaps between literature and science reduce in the use of newer words." They are moving to the next research project on predicting when the word being used in literature but not in science will appear for the first time in science journals.

Three other professors of English language and literature presented papers on "The Imagined Post-human in Eighteenth-Century Britain" (Ha, 2018), "The Anthropocene and the Ecological Imagination" (Jeon, 2018), and "Created to 'Donate'? Homo Deus and (Re)Definition of Humanity in Kazuo Ishiguro's *Never Let Me Go*" (Lee, 2019), respectively. A professor of history education presented a paper on "The Role and Status of Official Doctors in Chosun Dynasty" (Shin, 2018).

A professor of early childhood education presented a paper on "A Developmental Analysis on Children's Death Concepts" (S.L. Kim, 2018). A professor of management presented a paper on "New and Renewable Energy of Korea's Shift from FIT to RPS" (C.H. Kim, 2018). A professor of economics presented a paper on "An Analysis of Socio-Economic Impact from Change of Emotional and Health Status Caused by PM" (Kang, 2019).

A professor of sign art and design presented a paper on "Interplays between Art and Biomedical Science" (Youn, 2018). A professor of fashion industry presented a paper on "Smart Clothing Design for Health Monitoring" (S.H. Kim, 2019). A professor of architecture and urban design presented a paper on "Basic Study on Architectural Characteristics of Bio-engineering Research Facility" (J.H. Kim, 2019).

A professor of sport science presented a paper on "A Study on the Improvement of the Effective Physical Stability Control Mechanism of Adolescent Idiopathic Scoliosis by Three-Dimensional Approach" (Jeon, 2019). A professor of electronics engineering presented a paper on "Low-Dimensional Semiconductors Enabled Wearable Electronics for Eco-friendly Bio-Sensors Platforms" (Jin, 2019). The list continues.

The second type of papers are the approaches by professors of bio science and engineering or related fields on seemingly non-bio-related subjects in their appearances. For example, a professor of chemical and biological engineering presented a fascinating paper on "Biotechnology in Movies" (Park, 2018), in which he identified various applications of biotechnologies imbedded in the movies such as *Jurassic Park*, *Spider Man* and *XMan*. In 2018, a professor of molecular and medical science presented a paper on "History of Change in Viruses Presented in Culture and Arts" (Yeh, 2018), in which he visually showed the dangers of viral agents from the acts of bioterrorism, laboratory accidents and space in such movies as *Outbreak* (1995), *Resident Evil* (2002), *The Bourne Legacy* (2012) and *Train to Busan* (2016). In 2019, he narrowed down the research focus to gene therapy in his sequel paper, "Understanding of Viruses: Gene Therapy in Films" (Yeh, 2019). He showed that with the advancement of science on viruses, movie makers changed their description of zombies, vampires and superheroes from being the subjects of myth to the results of gene therapy.

Time versus space, the basic issue in the philosophy of science, was discussed from the point of view of bio science by a professor of nano-bioengineering in his series of papers on "Time-to-Space Conversion" (S.G. Yang, 2019) and "Time-to-Space Conversion in Brain" (S.G. Yang, 2019). His series of papers became the theoretical basis of his twin brother's paper on "Macroscale Brain Map Remodeling at the Cortical Surface" (S.C. Yang, 2019).

Although I separated the papers presented at the Global Bio-Convergence Forums into two categories of research, there was not much difference in the implications of the papers at the end of the day. The professors in bio and its related majors found friends among the professors without a bio background, and they talked about bio issues which they would never be able to with their colleagues in the same department. The professors without a bio background were pleasantly surprised to find themselves talking about bio issues with the professors on the other side of the table. They ate, drank, talked, argued and eventually laughed in the nearby restaurants after the forums were over. Convergence took place in real lives.

However important it may be, "bio" cannot attract all of the INU professors' attention to convergence. INU, therefore, has chosen five more topics as its focuses. They are "Post-unification integration (of two Koreas)," "Belt-and-road policies (of Chinese government from the point of view of China's partner nations)," "Smart city and smart energy," "Climate change," and "Big data and AI."

Matrix College as an Education-Centered Program

The following excerpt of a case titled "Matrix College Program by Incheon National University" (Cho et al., 2020) shows why this program was started, and how it has been implemented at INU:

> Dr. Cho Dong-sung, who was about to take office as President of Incheon National University (INU) after 36 years as a full-time Professor of business administration at Seoul National University (SNU) and two years as a full-time professor of strategy at China's Cheung Kong Graduate School of Business (CKGSB), met his longtime friend, President Kim Tae-Han of Samsung Biologics. It was the early summer of 2016.

Kim opened a dialogue. "I've been afraid to meet with university professors and presidents since I took office."

"Are you afraid?" asked Cho.

Kim: "Most of them come to ask for employment of their graduates."

Cho: "I think it would be helpful to your company if a good person is recommended …"

Kim: "That's true, but hiring recommended graduates often results in less than expected."

Cho: "Oh, really?"

Kim: "The new recruit we want is not a person who has taken two more biology courses. We teach biology well, too."

Cho: "Then, what kind of talent do you want out of university graduates?"

Kim: "A person with integrity based on humanity. A person who is committed to the organization, who goes well with colleagues, and who is dedicated to his or her role in a sincere manner. Humanity is hard to teach in a company. Please nurture students with humanities and send them to our company."

Cho: "—."

The conversation with President Kim ended, but the word "humanity" and "humanities" he mentioned three times left a deep impression in President Cho's mind. The "Matrix College," an innovative program representing Incheon National University's innovative endeavors, was seeded on the day.

Since taking INU's presidency in July 2016, President Cho has analyzed its structure and curriculum. "Reflecting needs of the industry, new departments have been created in such names as the Department of Creative Human Resources Development and the Department of Embedded System Engineering. However, they coexisted with traditional departments such as the Department of Korean Language and Literature and the Department of Mechanical Engineering, confusing prospective students' choice of major."

President Cho asked himself, "Why don't we delegate the authority to develop curricula and courses to companies which employ our graduates?" "Let's create a new axis, say Y-axis, and put the company-developed curricula in that axis. Certainly, existing curricula will be placed in the original X-axis. This way, company-developed curricula will be complementary to, rather than competitive with, the existing curricula developed by university faculty." Cho soon began to draw a table on a piece of paper. The existing 54 Majors within 11 Colleges were drawn on the X-axis, while new majors and colleges entered the Y-axis. Those in the Y-axis were called the "Matrix College."

By using the new education system called Matrix College, the total of 130 credits, which was the minimum required of INU students for graduation, would be split to 3 parts: 42 credits which were the minimum required to complete a major; 42 credits which were the standard credits for each curriculum that a company developed; and the remaining credits for liberal arts education and electives. The Matrix College was born on a piece of paper as shown in [Figure 6.2].

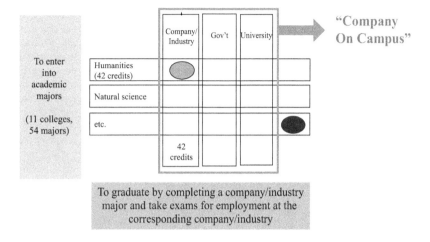

: The students who want to work for a company, government or as professionals.
: The students who do not want to work.

Figure 6.2 "Matrix College" of Incheon National University

Concerned that College of Humanities which offers many liberal arts courses as students' elective courses would protest, President Cho asked Dean Hwang Mi-Ok of College of Humanities her opinion after explaining the Matrix at the Deans' meeting. "It's a very good idea. It's a necessary program for our students who want to work in the industrial field." Dean Hwang was the first to express positive opinions, which surprised other Deans and made them question her: "Don't you worry that the courses taught by humanities professors will shrink?" She answered "Didn't you tell us that humanities education is what companies want the most? Let's trust the company."

Dean Hwang's belief that companies would want humanities education soon turned out to be a reality. For example, Agrich Global, a global operator of providing feedstock to cattle farmers, included 10 courses in humanities such as "Presentation and Discussion," "The World of Logic," "Critical Thinking Exercise," "Human Relations and Leadership," and "Creative Thinking and Problem Solving" as part of the 20 courses which they designed and brought to INU.

Lee Chang-yeon, Director of the Educational Innovation Institute, described the features of Matrix College: "Many universities run industry-academic cooperation education programs. However, Incheon National University will build a roadmap for the curriculum and create new subjects without disturbing the existing academic structure. There are no universities in the world in which formal education programs are initiated and designed

100% by companies with no involvement of professors. Incheon National University's "Matrix College" is the only program in the world that differentiates itself from other universities."

The Times Higher Education [THE], a UK-based global university evaluation organization, invited President Cho as a keynote speaker at the Emerging Economies Summit held on May 8–10, 2018, in Casablanca, Morocco. In front of some 500 university presidents and delegates from around the world, Cho introduced INU's Matrix College as a device to induce participation of private sectors to higher education. During the question and answer session that followed, a university president commented: "Many universities have programs similar to INU's Matrix College. At my university for example, there is an academia–industry cooperative educational program in which corporate executives are teaching directly to students." Cho asked him, "Are you sure that your faculty members do not participate at all in the process from designing of the curriculum to implementing it as an educational program?" His question silenced the audience.

"Matrix College has three functions to three groups. First, it provides the students with opportunities to develop the skills desired by the companies which they want to work for. Second, it allows the participating companies to directly groom the students who they want to recruit in the way the company wants them to become. Third, it helps the university and professors to educate the students into the talents whom the society want, without artificially reorganizing their academic systems and restructuring," said Team Manager Choi Jae-Woong.

For the 2019 school year, 47 companies and institutions including CJ Korea Express, POSCO Engineering & Construction, Dongwon Systems, Blackyak, Incheon Chamber of Commerce and Industry, and the Institute for Industrial Policy Studies, signed memorandums of understanding. Twenty-seven of them completed the curriculum development and started the courses.

In the 2019 school year, 474 courses, or 18.9 percent of the total 2,504 courses were opened as part of the Matrix College. In the job-linked Matrix, three TF teams signed MOUs with five companies and 10 subjects were provided to students. The number of professors, staff, and teaching assistants participating in the Matrix College program reached 170.

Choi Yong-soo, CEO of BSP Partners, which is participating in the Matrix College, commented with a positive assessment of Matrix College: "By educating students in advance with the curriculum that companies need for their incoming employees, we can reduce the amount of education which we provide to them after they join the companies. Also, by meeting students continually for a long period of time, we can effectively nurture them into the outstanding human resources whom our companies want. As a result, we can save time and money in the process and develop desirable talents as a result."

The Ministry of Education welcomed the "Matrix College" as the Ministry's model of the university innovation as stipulated in its "University Improvement Plan for Bachelor's Program." The Ministry cited INU's Matrix College as a representative case of university innovation in the course of soliciting the innovative cases from 41 national universities in March 2018. The Ministry's positive assessment of INU's Matrix College soon led to budget allocations. The Ministry approved of the annual budget of 2.5 billion won (approximately $2.1 million) for Matrix College in the 1919 budget, and again in the 2020 budget.

COMBINATION AND PERMUTATION AS A NEW PARADIGM IN STRATEGY

In this section I will explain how the strategic paradigm that underlies the Focused Research University in research and the Matrix College in education, the two main pillars of INU's innovative approaches towards the future, has been developed. Comparing Figure 6.1 and Figure 6.2, one can immediately notice a common feature in the frameworks of the two programs: a "cross" which is made of the X axis and the Y axis. Using the case of INU, the diagram of the Focused Research University in Figure 6.1 has INU professors as researchers on the X axis, and INU's 11 colleges and 54 departments on the Y axis. Again, using the case of INU, the diagram of the Matrix College in Figure 6.2 has some 50 programs which companies, governments and other universities bring to the campus of INU on the X axis, and INU's 11 colleges and 54 departments on the Y axis.

Strategic Paradigm of Focused Research University

The framework of a cross is the strategic paradigm which I used to design Focused Research University and Matrix College. Let me use the mathematical jargon of "combination and permutation" instead of the physics jargon of "convergence" as the logic of the strategic paradigm. It is because combination and permutation allow us to understand the content and the process of what INU has been doing, while convergence only shows the outcome or the result of INU's research and education. In other words, one can see a ceaseless activity of combination and permutation taking place within a black box called convergence. One may say that convergence can be done through a series of combinational and permutational activities.

INU's bio-focused research allowed and motivated INU professors of humanities and social science, so-called soft sciences, to tackle bio science and engineering, which is by any means a hard science. I call the resulting convergence which takes place within each professor's brain an outcome of combination (of heterogeneous objects) and permutation (of them by reverse order). This pattern of combination and permutation goes against our common sense that ordinary convergence takes place between different but related fields, and that people in hard sciences can more easily move to soft sciences than the other way around.

The heterogeneous combination of hard science and soft science enabled participating professors to identify the research topics which are not easily dealt with in conventional settings. This phenomenon may be regarded as a social science application of the natural science theory. In chemistry, the bigger the difference of between two liquid materials, the faster the speed of diffusion between the two.

More important than the heterogeneous combination was the permutation by reverse order. This approach by participating INU professors in soft science, tackling the hard science of bio, allowed them to generate a number of pioneering research agendas such as the papers presented in the Global Bio-Convergence Forums described above. Professors in soft sciences can provide professors in hard sciences with inspiration about what we should be doing today, and where we should be moving to in the future. Using this approach of unusual, and somewhat odd, combination and permutation, INU has been generating differentiated results of convergence, and may become the only university in the world in the not so distant future.

Strategic Paradigm of Matrix College

INU's Matrix College is another example of the strategic use of unconventional combination and permutation. The combination of academia and industry in traditional universities, as commented by a university president in THE's 2018 Casablanca Summit, is common. The combination of academic professors as spectators and industrial experts as designers of educational programs at INU is rare, if it happens at all. The permutation, or sequential process, of professors moving to industry often takes place in the real world, albeit not necessarily successfully. The permutation of industry experts coming to INU's campus to teach in their self-designed courses is less imaginable.

Table 6.1 shows a list of universities which I call "neo-boutique universities." These universities are small in size compared to regular universities, and they were established only in the past 20 years or so. Many of them do not have the legal status of university or college given by their respective governments. Among them is San Francisco-based Minerva Schools, which has become an icon in university innovation with its multi-campus approaches and revolution in memory-based pedagogy. Singularity University, founded by the American genius Peter Diamandis, is popular among young people wishing to become entrepreneurs. SADI, founded by Samsung Electronics has become a mecca

Table 6.1   A partial list of "neo-boutique universities"*

No.	Name	Founder	Nation	Starting year	Degree	On-line only	Number of students(1)	Period (year)	Tuition(2)	Legal status	Profit motive
1	Toyota Technological Institute	Toyota Motor Corporation	Japan	1981	O	X	389	4	¥3 119 610		
2	ICD Business School	Vincent Barry	Ireland	1990	X	O	1 000	3	€7 500		
3	University of the POTOMAC	Victor Berlin	USA	1991	O	X	72	5	$33 300		
4	SADI	Samsung Electronics	Korea	1995	X	X	40	3	₩4 240 000	Limited co.	Profit
5	Olin College of Engineering	Franklin W. Olin	USA	1997	O	X	350	4	$51 080		Non-profit
6	Chicken University	BBQ	Korea	2000	X	X	580	2 weeks	₩2 090 000	Limited co.	Profit
7	Cheung Kong Graduate School of Business (CKGSB)	Li Ka-Shing	China	2002	O	X	1 200	1.5	780 000(Yuan)		Non-Profit
8	London School of Business & Finance	Aaron Etingen	UK	2003	X	o	40 000+	3	£11 250		Profit
9	Seoul University of Science (aSSIST)	IPS	Korea	2004	O	X	400	1.5	$36 000		Non-Profit
10	Digital Hollywood University	Tomoyuki Sugiyama	Japan	2005	O	X	1 121	4	¥5 610 000	Limited co.	
11	UBIS (Univ. of Business & International Studies)	A group of professors	Switzerland	2006	O	X	500	3	58 800–85 000 (CHF)		profit
12	Cyber University	Masayoshi Son	Japan	2007	O	X	2 669	4	¥2 938 000		
13	MTA	Jose Mari Luzarraga	Spain	2007	X	X	180	4	Private		
14	Samsung Heavy Industries Engineering College	Samsung Group	Korea	2007	O	X	40	2	0	Limited co.	Non-Profit
15	Foundry College	Stephen Kosslyn	USA	2009	O	O	70	2	$12 000		Non-Profit
16	Singularity University	Peter Diamandis	USA	2009	X	O	80	12 weeks	$1 485		Non-profit
17	University of the People	Shai Reshef	USA	2009	O	O	20 000+	4	$4 060		Non-profit

No.	Name	Founder	Nation	Starting year	Degree	On-line only	Number of students(1)	Period (year)	Tuition(2)	Legal status	Profit motive
18	Business Breakthrough University	Ohmae Kenichi	Japan	2010	O	O	1.1	4	¥5 422 500		Non-profit
19	Minerva Schools at KGI	Ben Nelson	USA	2011	O	X	575	4	$50 000	Limited co.	Non-Profit
20	SPC Food Science College	SPC Group	Korea	2011	O	X	26	2	0	Limited co.	Non-Profit
21	Daewoo Shipbuilding & Marine Engineering College	Daewoo Shipbuilding Co.	Korea	2013	O	X	100	2	0	Limited co.	Non-Profit
22	Ecole42	Xavier Niel	France	2013	O	O	2 550	3+	0		Non-Profit
23	HYUNDAI Heavy Industries Technical College	Hyundai Heavy Industries Co.	Korea	2013	O	X	60	2	0	Limited co.	Non-Profit
24	KDB financial university	Korea Development Bank	Korea	2013	O	X	40	4	0	Limited co.	Non-Profit
25	LH Land & Housing University	LH	Korea	2013	O	X	40	4	0	Limited co.	Non-Profit
26	POSCO Technology University	Pohang Steel Corporation	Korea	2013	O	X	50	2	0	Limited co.	Non-Profit
27	Hupan University	Jack Ma	China	2015	X	X	30–40	3	360 000(yuan)		
28	Innovation Academy	Korean Government	Korea	2019	X	X	500	2	0		Non-Profit
29	SK University	SK Group	Korea	2019	?	?	?	?	?	?	?

Notes:

* The list is partial and exemplary, and the data have not been fully checked for accuracy.

(1) Numbers of full-time/part-time students.

(2) Total tuition for a 4-year bachelor's degree or 2-year Master degree.

for aspiring designers. Ecole 42, founded by French billionaire Xavier Niel, grooms creative software designers without interventions by professors. Cyber University was founded by Masayoshi Sohn, the richest entrepreneur in Japan. Hupan University was founded by Jack Ma, the richest entrepreneur in China. It seems that the richer and more successful they are, the more eager they are in starting new universities.

Why is there an emergence of neo-boutique universities? The reason seems to be that traditional universities are not meeting the expectation of those successful and future-oriented entrepreneurs. They have given up hope that the existing universities will groom young people to their liking. Instead of complaining, they are starting their own universities. Recruiting high school graduates to their neo-boutique universities, they lead them to equip themselves with practical knowledge and capabilities in artificial intelligence based on data science to advance block chain capabilities in the world of the Internet of Things. The students will finish studying there, and move to the industry to start working from day one.

There is a real challenge that universities today must meet. Perhaps traditional universities with accumulated social capital such as the reputation and other historically based trust can easily meet the challenges coming from the industry. In the real world, people's capabilities are determined not only by an individual talent but also networking and communication. They can afford to be complacent in spite of the challenges coming from the industry. INU cannot. INU has neither the capabilities to teach high school graduates so that they start working professionally in the field from the first day they get employed, nor the reputation nor the network. INU is being sandwiched between the neo-boutique universities with practicality on the left, and the traditional universities with reputation on the right. INU is being squeezed.

How can INU cope with these challenges coming from two different sides? INU found a formula called a set of double-edged strategies. The formula is combination and permutation. Against neo-boutique universities, INU can combat with the combination strategy; and against traditional universities with the permutation strategy.

First, with the strategy of heterogeneous combination, INU can combine humanities and social sciences with natural science and engineering in educating students. Neo-boutique universities cannot afford to teach a wide variety of study subjects, because they are limited in scope to one or a few majors related to each other.

Second, with the strategy of permutation by reverse order, INU can be differentiated from traditional universities with a long history. Usually the logical sequence is for the students in hard science to move to soft science. Can you imagine professors in the humanities picking up electronic engineering or bio science? This permutation by reverse order is exactly what INU is doing in education. Students in soft science can easily get access to the study of hard science at INU through Matrix College.

SUMMARY AND CONCLUSION

When INU became Korea's second national university incorporated by the government in 2013, it was given a new mission of becoming globally competitive along with SNU. Given the long history of SNU and its undisputable legacy and reputation in Korea and worldwide, the only strategic alternative which INU was left to choose was to be different and to become the only university of its kind, instead of targeting the first and the best one. Taking advantage of Songdo's bio cluster, INU chose combination and permutation as a strategic paradigm for the Focused Research University and Matrix College.

Using the combination of sciences which are heterogeneous and the permutation by reverse order, INU has developed creative convergences in research and education. As part of the Focused Research University, INU's annual Global Bio-Convergence Forums have produced a number of insightful topics by non-bio professors, as manifested in their research papers presented. As part of Matrix College, INU's curriculum reflects industry-designed educational programs without interruptions by professors. Both may be the first of their kind, if not the only ones, in the world.

There is still a long way for INU to go to complete the mission of becoming the only university in the world. If and when this mission of becoming the only university is completed, INU may jump to another mission which the INU family desires. Let me conclude this chapter with a paraphrase: that if necessity is the mother of invention, desire is the father of innovation.

REFERENCES

Cho, Dong-Sung, et al., *Innovation of Higher Education: Change-makers at Incheon National University 1*, Seoul: Seoul Selection, 2020.
Cho, Dong-Sung, Yoo, Hye Bae, Song, Sang Houn, Hwang, Seung Hyun, "Biotechnology Manifested in Literature: Past, Present, and Future," 2018 Global Bio-Convergence Forum, November 22, 2018.

Cho, Dong-Sung, Yoo, Hye Bae, Hwang, Seung Hyun, Jung, Chae Kwan, Shin, Nami, "Biotechnology Manifested in Literature: Past, Present, and Future II," 2019 Global Bio-Convergence Forum, November 22, 2019.

Ha, In Hye, "The Imagined Post-human in Eighteenth-Century Britain," 2018 Global Bio-Convergence Forum, November 22, 2018.

Jeon, Kyoungkyu, "A Study on the Improvement of the Effective Physical Stability Control Mechanism of Adolescent Idiopathic Scoliosis by Three-Dimensional Approach," 2019 Global Bio-Convergence Forum, August 20, 2019.

Jeon, Seen Hwa, "The Anthropocene and the Ecological Imagination," 2018 Global Bio-Convergence Forum, November 22, 2018.

Jin, Sung Hun, "Low-Dimensional Semiconductors Enabled Wearable Electronics for Eco-friendly Bio-Sensors Platforms," 2019 Global Bio-Convergence Forum, August 20, 2019.

Kang, Heechan, "An Analysis of Socio-Economic Impact from Change of Emotional and Health Status Caused by PM," 2019 Global Bio-Convergence Forum, August 20, 2019.

Kim, Chang Hee, "New and Renewable Energy of Korea's Shift from FIT to RPS," 2018 Global Bio-Convergence Forum, November 22, 2018.

Kim, Jin Ho, "Basic Study on Architectural Characteristics of Bio-engineering Research Facility," 2019 Global Bio-Convergence Forum, August 20, 2019.

Kim, Sang Lim, "A Developmental Analysis on Children's Death Concepts," 2018 Global Bio-Convergence Forum, November 22, 2018.

Kim, Sun Hee, "Smart Clothing Design for Health Monitoring," 2019 Global Bio-Convergence Forum, August 20, 2019.

Lee, Yonghwa, "'Create' to 'Donate'?: Homo Deus and (Re)Definition of Humanity in Kazuo Ishiguro's *Never Let Me Go*," 2019 Global Bio-Convergence Forum, August 20, 2019.

Park, Tai Hyun, "Biotechnology in Movies," 2018 Global Bio-Convergence Forum, November 22, 2018.

Shin, Yua, "The Role and Status of Official Doctors in Chosun Dynasty," 2018 Global Bio-Convergence Forum, November 22, 2018.

Wikipedia, "Songdo_International_Business_District," https://en.wikipedia.org/wiki/Songdo_International_Business_District, n.d.

Yang, Sung Chil, "Macroscale Brain Map Remodeling at the Cortical Surface," 2019 Global Bio-Convergence Forum, August 20, 2019.

Yang, Sung Gu, "Time-to-Space Conversion in Brain," 2019 Global Bio-Convergence Forum, August 20, 2019.

Yeh, Jung-Yong, "History of Change in Viruses Presented in Culture and Arts," 2018 Global Bio-Convergence Forum, November 22, 2018.

Yeh, Jung-Yong, "Understanding of Viruses: Gene Therapy in Films," 2019 Global Bio-Convergence Forum, August 20, 2019.

Youn, Kwan Hyun, "Interplays between Art and Biomedical Science," 2018 Global Bio-Convergence Forum, November 22, 2018.

7. Human behavior and economic development: culture, psychology and the competitiveness of cities and regions

Robert Huggins and Piers Thompson

INTRODUCTION

Many studies continue to find considerable and persistent differences in economic competitiveness and development across cities and regions (for a review see Huggins and Thompson, 2017). These differences are not always easily explained even when accounting for human capital and knowledge production (Obschonka et al., 2015). This remains the case despite the burgeoning theoretical literature on urban and regional competitiveness and related areas such as economic growth and resilience (Harris, 2017; Martin and Sunley, 2017). In recent years, a new emphasis on behavioral traits has entered the equation in terms of efforts that seek to explain regional and urban differences in economic performance and development, with studies such as Tabellini (2010) finding a connection between culture and institutions and the economic development of regions, whilst others including Huggins and Thompson (2015a, 2016a) find a link between socio-spatial community culture and a noted driver of economic performance, that is, entrepreneurial activity. Similarly, the recent inclusion of personality traits within the rubric of spatial studies of economic performance and development outcomes is a recognition of a growing research stream in psychology that utilizes large personality sets in order to show the distinctiveness and meaningfulness of regional and urban and personality differences (Rentfrow et al., 2013, 2015; Obschonka et al., 2015, 2016).

Based on thinking from behavioral economics, it has been suggested that within cities and regions individual decision-making results from local influences experienced through situations that equate to the dominant cultural traits embedded within the local communities where these influences are formed (Storper, 2013). Behavioral economics concerns the integration of psychological theories of behavior as a means of explaining economic action (Mullainathan and Thaler, 2000; Camerer and Loewenstein, 2004; Borghans et al., 2008; Cartwright, 2014). Such theories have increasingly shown the limits of rational-choice theories in explaining economic as well as social action, and the underlying decision-making processes of individuals in determining such action (Hodgson, 2013). Drawing on Simon's (1955, 1982) notion of "bounded rationality," behavioral economics suggests that the minds of individuals are required to be understood in terms of the environmental context in which they have evolved, resulting in restrictions to human information processing, due to limits in knowledge and computational capacity (Kahneman, 2003).

As a result of these theoretical insights, it is clear that whilst urban and regional competitiveness and development theories are largely rooted in explanations based on the location, agglomeration and organization of firms, industries and capital (Maskell, 1998; Fritsch and Mueller, 2004; Gordon and McCann, 2005), there is move towards a (re)turn to addressing the role of individual and collective behavior in determining urban and regional development outcomes (Francois and Zabojnik, 2005; Jokela, 2009; Obschonka et al., 2013b). A number of concepts relating to the behavior of individuals and groups of individuals have taken an increasingly central role in shaping an understanding of why some places are better able to generate higher rates of development and growth, and avoid the low-road development trajectories and associated higher rates of inequality found in weaker cities and regions (Streeck, 1991; Tabellini, 2010; Tubadji, 2013; Soto-Oñate, 2016).

In parallel with the adoption of ideas from behavioral economics, the more general rise in importance given to cultural values in urban and regional development theory has led to the emergence of a "new sociology of development" that entwines the role of geography with factors relating to individual and collective behavior (Sachs, 2000). As Clark (2015) argues, human behavior is fundamental to the social sciences in terms of understanding what people do, where and why they do it, and the costs and benefits of this behavior. In order, therefore, to understand the aggregate differences in socio-economic activities and performance there is a need to explore how these differences stem from the experiences and actions of individual actors (Ariely, 2008; Storper, 2013).

Fundamentally, within certain strands of the literature – specifically, that within the field of economic geography – there have been calls to better understand the role of microprocesses on macrostructures within cities and regions, as well as the impact of macrostructures on these microprocesses (Peck, 2005; Maskell and Malmberg, 2007; MacKinnon et al., 2009). One of the aims of this chapter, therefore, is to argue that the roots of behavioral differences across cities and regions are co-determined by two key factors combining microprocesses and macrostructure, namely socio-spatial community culture and personality psychology. In essence, it is the interaction of these two factors that forms the behavioral intentions of individuals and the psychocultural behavior of cities and regions. Given this, a further aim of the chapter is to argue that psychocultural behavior is crucial to explaining differences in urban and regional competitiveness. In order to address these issues, the chapter initially seeks to present a conceptualization of the notion of urban and regional competitiveness. It then examines the existing literature to suggest how community culture and personality psychology traits co-determine the psychocultural behavior of cities and regions. Empirical data for Great Britain are then analyzed to examine whether this is the case, whether the distribution of psychocultural behavior varies across urban and regional localities, and whether any particular forms of culture, psychology personality, and psychocultural behavior are associated with competitiveness differentials (the methodological approach and the results of the analysis are presented). In the concluding section, it is proposed that psychocultural behavior impacts urban and regional development by influencing the sources of competitiveness, such as the type and efficacy of institutions and capital generation and deployment within these places.

COMPETITIVENESS

It has been argued that the urban and regional competitiveness discourse can be set within the context of theories concerning regional economic growth (Huggins et al., 2014). Furthermore, it is suggested that the concept of regional competitiveness – which includes cities and urban regions, and models related to its measurement – can be positioned within those theories that attempt to understand and determine the means through which economic development occurs across regions. In general, the competitiveness of regions is understood to refer to the presence of conditions that enable firms to compete in their chosen markets and enable the value these firms create to be captured within a particular region (Begg, 1999; Huggins, 2003).

Regional competitiveness, therefore, is considered to consist of the capability of a particular region to attract and maintain firms with stable or rising market shares in an activity, while maintaining stable or increasing standards of living for those who participate in it (Storper, 1997). Given this, competitiveness may vary across geographic space, as regions develop at different rates depending on the drivers of growth (Audretsch and Keilbach, 2004). As Martin (2005) outlines, concern with competitiveness has filtered down to the regional, urban and local levels, particularly the role of regionally based policy interventions in helping to improve competitiveness. In many advanced nations, these interventions form part of a strategic framework to improve productive and innovative performance.

Regional competitiveness models are usually implicitly constructed in the lineage of endogenous growth frameworks whereby deliberate investments in factors such as human capital and knowledge are considered to be key drivers of growth differentials. Regional competitiveness, therefore, is defined by some scholars as being the difference in the rate of economic development across regions and the capacity and capability of regions to achieve future economic growth relative to other regions at a similar stage of economic development (Huggins et al., 2014). Indeed, the success of regions will clearly be related to their capacity and capability to achieve economic growth, and understanding how and why such growth occurs is central to a number of research streams. Furthermore, competitiveness relates to the ability of an economy to provide its population with sustainable high and rising standards of living and high rates of employment (European Commission, 2001). This emphasis on sustainable competitiveness is particularly marked in work that seeks to measure the competitiveness of urban regions and cities (Kresl, 1995; Ni and Wang, 2017).

As discussed elsewhere, competitiveness may have a number of definitions (Huggins and Thompson, 2017; Harris, 2017) and include both measures based on outcomes and the inputs which generate these outcomes (Aiginger, 2006; Aiginger and Firgo, 2017). The empirical analysis presented in this chapter draws on data from the UK Competitiveness Index (UKCI), which was developed as a composite measure capturing three sets of factors – inputs, outputs and outcomes – across cities and local regions of the United Kingdom (UK) (Huggins, 2003; Huggins and Thompson, 2016b). Competitiveness inputs are principally the factors of production that produce goods and services and drive economic activity and outputs, consisting of the human capital factors at the heart of endogenous growth theories. Inputs are not an end in themselves, but provide the means to achieve outputs and long-term outcomes.

The input factors used in the UKCI reflect those key inputs associated with greater competitiveness, including business start-up rates, number of businesses per head of population, proportion of working-age population with National Vocational Qualification (NVQ) level 4 qualifications or above, and the proportion of businesses classed as knowledge-based. Output and outcome factors are those associated with outcome competitiveness indicating the extent to which a city or region is enjoying the benefits associated with higher standards of living, which it is suggested should be the ultimate aim of economic development (Storper, 1997). The output factors used in the UKCI capture the extent to which inputs are converted into outputs, and include gross value added per head, productivity per hour worked, and employment rates. The outcome factors are more directly associated with the population's welfare in terms of gross weekly pay and unemployment rates.

The methodology used to construct the UKCI is based on the natural log of individual indicators, which reduces the effect of outliers. Indices are created with the UK average taking a value of 100, and within each factor the individual indicators are given equal weighting. Given that there is no theoretical reason to give a greater weighting to any one of the factor indices, the final UKCI measure is the average of the three component indices. To account for the impact of logging the data, the composite scores are "anti-logged" through exponential transformation. This is achieved by calculating the exponential difference between the mean logged and un-logged index of the 50 localities nearest the overall UK mean of 100.

COMMUNITY CULTURE

The concept of culture generally refers to the way in which people behave, often as a result of their background and group affiliation. Guiso et al. (2006, p. 23) define it as "those customary beliefs and values that ethnic, religious and social groups transmit fairly unchanged from generation to generation." Rather than concerning individual behavior, it relates to shared systems of meaning within and across ascribed and acquired social groups (Hofstede, 1980). Van Maanen and Schein (1979) suggest that culture can be defined by the values, beliefs and expectations that members of specific social groups come to share, while Hofstede (1980) refers to it as the collective programming of the mind, which distinguishes one group or category of people from another. Socio-spatial community culture refers to the broader societal traits and relations that underpin places in terms of prevailing mind-sets and the overall way of life within particular places (Huggins and Thompson, 2014a, 2015a, 2016a). Therefore, it principally constitutes the social structure and features of group life within cities and regions that can generally be considered to be beyond the economic life of such places.

Fundamentally, culture consists of the overarching or dominant mind-sets that underlie the way in which cities and regions function; that is, the ways and means by which individuals and groups within communities interact and shape their environment. The decisions of individuals within these cultures, therefore, may have arbitrary coherence as individuals try to ensure they are consistent with personal and collective cultures as well as past decisions (Ariely, 2008; Knott et al., 2008). At a national level, the World Values Survey (WVS) has allowed researchers to investigate differences in culture based on scales such as traditional versus secular-rational, and survival versus self-expression (Inglehart and Welzel, 2010). These cultural dimensions have been found to relate to a wide variety of measures of development (Guiso et al., 2006), both narrowly economic-ally defined as well as in terms of the broader development measures (Pike et al., 2007). In order to examine the relationship between competitiveness and community culture this chapter draws upon the community culture measures developed by Huggins and Thompson (2016a). Within this work, five dimensions of community culture are captured: engagement with work and education; social cohesion; femin-ine and caring activities; adherence to social rules; and collective actions. Each of these is discussed in more detail below.

Engagement with work and education draws upon Weber's (1930) consideration of the impact of "work ethic" on economic outcomes and the importance of education as a cultural feature of places (Tabellini, 2010). Both of these may be associated with self-sufficiency and making an appropriate contribution to society (Brennan et al., 2000; Becker and Woessmann, 2009). Male economic activities rates, and the inverse of the proportion of the population without formal qualifications and school absenteeism rates, are used to capture the underlying culture associated with engaging in these activities (Durand, 1975).

Social cohesion recognizes the literature that has highlighted the importance of social capital in achieving various economic outcomes (Putnam, 1993), such as entrepreneurship (Davidsson and Honig, 2003; Williams et al., 2017) and innovation (Camps and Marques, 2014; Murphy et al., 2016). This may be achieved through aiding knowledge transmission, reducing economic profiteering and encouraging collective actions (Callois and Aubert, 2007). However, Olson (1982) also suggests that social associations linked with the promotion of particular interests may have a detrimental effect and raise inequality. Other empirical studies show that it is the distinction between bridging and bonding social capital that is important, with the former boosting income and the latter having a neutral effect (Hoyman et al., 2016).

Bonding social capital may increase trust and informational flow within a group, but also isolate the group from outside ideas (Granovetter, 1973). As group similarity may help to boost the likelihood of such trust being developed (Easterly and Levine, 1997; Aghion et al., 2004), measures from previous studies used here to measure social cohesion include ethnic similarity, religious similarity, as well as a more direct measure of identification with the wider population: the proportion of the population perceiving themselves as a national of the resident country. It has been suggested that less socially cohesive and diverse communities may benefit from access to new ideas and inward flows of human capital with new ways of deploying available resources (Portes and Landolt, 2000; Florida, 2002; Levie, 2007). To capture these flows of human capital, gross migration rates for the urban and regional local areas and the proportion of migrants born in Great Britain are used as indicators.

Hofstede (1980) defines some national cultures as more masculine or feminine in nature based on measures of greater or lesser competition and individuality, a pattern that others have shown is still present in advanced societies (Shneor et al., 2013). Female involvement in economic activities could be highly influential given that men and women prioritize outcomes of different kinds (Parasuraman et al., 1996). Where roles regarding employment and household production are more traditionally split, as captured by the economic activity of women, a more masculine approach to the economic activity might be expected to dominate. Also, business activities including entrepreneurship and new venture creation are frequently identified with masculine competitive and individualistic cultures (Bennett and Dann, 2000; Bruni et al., 2004). However, such approaches do not necessarily yield the highest levels of broader well-being, in part because of upwardly adjusting reference points (Layard, 2006), although some empirical studies have found positive relationships between economic competitiveness and broader well-being (Huggins and Thompson, 2012). The proportion of female employment that is part-time allows for more flexible working that may allow for broader outcomes to be achieved, and is included as an indicator of feminine cultural attributes (Hundley, 2001). Similarly, caring activities, in terms of the proportion of the population providing caring activities for free, is used as an indicator of femininity.

Social conventions are important in helping to coordinate activities that boost efficiency (Rodríguez-Pose and Storper, 2006; Lorenzen, 2007).

Where adherence to such conventions and rules is relatively low, delinquent behaviors can become the norm (Kearns and Forrest, 2000), hindering economic activities. A knock-on effect is that where an area becomes associated with such behaviors its residents can suffer from a stigma effect, hindering their ability to participate in wider economic and social activities (Atkinson and Kintrea, 2001). However, some studies have suggested that particular activities such as entrepreneurship can be born of frustration (Noorderhaven et al., 2004), and can be positively associated with rule-breaking at a younger age (Obschonka et al., 2013a). The indicators included in this study to capture breaches of rules and accepted behavior are non-sexual violent crimes, crimes by deception, alcohol-related deaths and under-age conceptions, all measured as a proportion of the relevant population.

There is some debate as to whether more individualist cultures or those that promote collective activities best promote economic development (Thomas and Mueller, 2000; Kirkman et al., 2006; Hayton and Cacciotti, 2013; Wennberg et al., 2013). As discussed above in relation to masculinity–femininity, competitiveness may be associated with individualistic behaviors. However, collective approaches can still be successful when directed outwards towards competing with other groups (Greif, 1994; Casson, 1995; Ettlinger, 2003). To capture a preference for collective activities, the indicators used are the proportion of votes cast for left-of-center political parties and trade union membership as a proportion of the workforce.

PERSONALITY PSYCHOLOGY

Personality psychology refers to one of the predominant paradigms in behavioral psychology for understanding and measuring differences in personality traits across individuals (McCrae and Terracciano, 2005; Dodorico McDonald, 2008; Benet-Martinez et al., 2015). Within studies of geographical personality the measures normally considered are those associated with the so-called "Big Five" framework of personality traits, consisting of: (1) openness – the tendency to be open to new aesthetic, cultural or intellectual experiences; (2) conscientiousness – the tendency to be organized, responsible and hardworking; (3) extraversion – an orientation of one's interests and energies towards the outer world of people and things rather than the inner world of subjective experience; characterized by positive affect and sociability; (4) agreeableness – the tendency to act in a cooperative unselfish manner; and (5) neuroticism (cf. emotional stability): neuroticism is a chronic level of emotional instability and proneness to psychological distress, whilst emotional stability is largely the opposite and concerns predictability and stability in emotional reactions, with an absence of rapid mood changes (Costa and McCrae, 1992; Goldberg, 1992; Soldz and Vaillant, 1999; Rammstedt and John, 2007; Credé et al., 2012).

In parallel with recent scholarly work in the field of socio-spatial community culture, researchers of personality psychology have found that in terms of economic prosperity there is a positive link between openness and extraversion, whilst conscientiousness displays a negative association (Rentfrow et al., 2015). Lee (2016) further finds that conscientiousness in cities and regions in England and Wales is positively associated with innovation as captured by patenting activity. Obschonka et al. (2015) include conscientiousness in their entrepreneurial index, which they find is positively linked to entrepreneurial activity. Although the majority of research on personality psychology has examined the impact of individual personality traits on a variety of outcomes, the idiographic perspective suggests that a more holistic view should be taken (Rentfrow et al., 2013). This idiographic perspective refers to understanding behavior through a configuration of differing traits, which at a geographical level facilitates an investigation of the extent to which particular configurations of traits occur with some regularity in specific regions (Rentfrow et al., 2013). Certain configurations of traits have been found to be good predictors of developmental outcomes such as: achievement at school (Asendorpf and van Aken, 1999; Hart et al., 2003); the development of social support networks (Caspi, 2000); older-age health such as the prevalence or avoidance of strokes and heart disease (Chapman and Goldberg, 2011); as well as the likelihood of having spells in unemployment (Caspi, 2000).

Rentfrow et al. (2013) use a cluster analysis approach to identify three psychological profiles of regions – friendly and conventional, relaxed and creative, temperamental and uninhibited – covering the 48 contiguous United States (US) states. The friendly and conventional profile is low on neuroticism and openness, but high on extraversion, agreeableness and conscientiousness. The relaxed and creative states have low extraversion, agreeableness and neuroticism, but are high on openness. The final set of states described as temperamental and uninhibited are low on agreeableness and conscientiousness, and high on neuroticism. These areas display strong differences in terms of a variety of political, economic, social and health outcomes. Economically, the friendly and conventional states are those which are the least successful.

More generally, personality psychology traits are found to play an important role not only independently, but also in terms of the combinations formed. Whereas community culture is a concept that manifests itself at the community level (Beugelsdijk and Maseland, 2011), other characteristics at an individual level may have an impact at the aggregate level due to their unequal distribution across places. At the individual level this chapter draws upon the Big Five personality measures used in Rentfrow et al. (2015). The personality trait data used in the empirical analysis were captured through the British Broadcasting Corporation's (BBC) Lab UK website. These data were used by Rentfrow et al. (2015) to map the distribution of personality traits across Great Britain. A total sample of 417 246 adults aged over 18 was obtained. At the local authority district level the number of participants varies from just 29 in the Isles of Scilly to 6200 in Birmingham. The mean number of respondents in each local authority was 1098 and the median 883. Rentfrow et al. (2015) show that the local authority subsamples are correlated with the underlying populations in terms of ethnic background, and median age.

The instrument used to collect the data is the Big Five Inventory (John and Srivastava, 1999; Hamby et al., 2016). This consists of 44 short statements associated with the prototypical traits of the five personality traits measured on five-point Likert scales. Principal components analysis (PCA) with a varimax rotation is used to generate the five underlying measures. The components display reasonable internal consistency, with Chronbach's alpha ranging from 0.77 for agreeableness to 0.86 for extraversion (Obschonka et al., 2015). As in previous studies the mean values are taken to represent the local authority district personality values (Rentfrow et al., 2008; Renfrow et al., 2015; Obschonka et al., 2016).

As with community culture, particular personality traits may be more positively related to economic activities than others. Barrick et al. (2003) conduct a meta-analysis of the relationship between occupational choice and personality traits. They find that jobs requiring social interaction and avoiding routinization from machines are linked with extraversion. Artistic occupations that need to be expressive and non-conformist and original are linked to greater openness. This fits with the finding that openness and extraversion, in particular, are perceived to be beneficial in terms of achieving informational exchange (Rentfrow et al., 2015). Investigative occupations requiring curiosity, precision and methodological natures are positively associated with conscientiousness, emotional stability (lower neuroticism) and openness. Conscientiousness is also associated with conventional jobs that require data manipulation, but the avoidance of artistic tendencies (Barrick et al., 2003). Interestingly, this implies that whilst creativity is often associated with innovation, the need for precision and methodological approaches may explain why Lee (2016) finds innovation to be positively associated with conscientiousness and a lack of significant relationships with openness and extraversion.

Other studies have identified an entrepreneurship culture based on personality traits where there are high levels of extraversion, conscientiousness and openness, whilst agreeableness and neuroticism are low (Obschonka et al., 2013b). This means that certain cities and regions with more of these traits may be better placed to host certain economic activities. Industries and occupations that dominate may produce feedback effects influencing personality within a particular city or region through informal and formal rules, which in less competitive cities and regions may support established industries over new start-ups (Grabher, 1993), limit entrepreneurial role models who may create the social legitimization for entrepreneurship (Wyrwich, 2015; Kibler et al., 2014), and produce the intergenerational transmission of values associated with particular work experiences (Luster et al., 1989). These differences may be long-lasting, and in the case of the UK, for example, create personality patterns unsuited to entrepreneurial endeavors in cities and regions that were once the dominant locations for large-scale heavy industry (Stuetzer et al., 2016).

PSYCHOCULTURAL BEHAVIOR

Although personality psychology represents a potentially powerful means of explaining the uneven development of cities and regions, it is important to highlight that personality traits in the form of the Big Five are defined without reference to any context, that is, situation or socio-spatial community culture (Almlund et al., 2011). Indeed, a long-term perspective on development should acknowledge that the genetic (encompassing personality psychology) evolution of humans and their cultural evolution are ultimately interactive; that is, positive and negative interactions between cultural and biological evolution may occur and give rise to cultural–genetic co-evolution (Van den Bergh and Stagl, 2003). Such co-evolutionary forces can be related to theories of generation and collective memory, or what Lippmann and Aldrich (2016) refer to "generational units," in the form of meaningful collectives that move through time with high degrees of self-awareness.

In this sense, the interaction between culture and psychology forms part of the complex adaptive systems that are considered to explain economic and social outcomes, partly as a result of the individuals who inhabit such systems. If genetic and cultural factors are co-evolutionary, this suggests the need to give more emphasis to temporal dimensions – current behavior, or behavior in the middle or distant future – when considering urban and regional development outcomes; that is, spatio-temporal dimensions.

Studies frequently treat individual aspects of community culture and personality traits as independent, although this approach is criticized by some scholars (Klotz and Neubaum, 2016). Studying personality traits, Rentfrow et al. (2013) argue that it is the combinations of personality traits that are important, and an idiographic perspective should be taken. Further, there are suggestions that the two can influence one another (Rentfrow et al., 2009). For example, particular types of individual may be attracted to community cultures where their personality traits are most compatible (Rentfrow et al., 2013) or, alternatively, community cultures may generate social norms that influence attitudes and behaviors (Hofstede, 2001; Hofstede and McCrae, 2004). Similarly, the prevailing personality traits of residents of a city or region will have an influence on how community culture evolves (Florida, 2002).

To capture the combinations of community culture and personality traits that form together in cities and regions across Great Britain, a principal components approach can be used to integrate the community culture and personality psychology data discussed above. A varimax approach is applied to generate uncorrelated measures suitable for inclusion in multivariate analysis. The scores were produced using the Anderson–Rubin approach, which is best suited when non-correlated factor scores are required (Tabachnick and Fidell, 2007). Three combined measures capturing different psychocultural behavior are formed: inclusive amenability, individual commitment and diverse extraversion. The results of the principal component analysis are reported in Table 7.1, and can be summarized as follows:

Inclusive amenability:

- high in agreeableness, social cohesion, feminine and caring activities, and adherence to social rules;
- low in openness.

Individual commitment:

- high in conscientiousness, engagement with education and adherence to social rules;
- low in collective activities.

Diverse extraversion:

- high in extraversion and openness;
- low in neuroticism.

Table 7.1   Principal components analysis: rotated component matrix of socio-spatial community culture and personality psychology variables

	Psycho-cultural behavior: inclusive amenability	Psycho-cultural behavior: individual commitment	Psycho-cultural behavior: diverse extraversion	Extracted variance
Extraversion	−0.299	0.068	0.807	0.745
Agreeableness	0.833	−0.059	0.129	0.713
Conscientiousness	0.679	0.548	0.145	0.781
Neuroticism	−0.269	−0.276	−0.824	0.827
Openness	−0.570	−0.222	0.509	0.633
Engagement with education	0.112	0.832	−0.014	0.705
Social cohesion	0.838	−0.066	−0.322	0.810
Femininity and caring	0.757	0.194	−0.153	0.634
Adherence to social rules	0.584	0.577	0.085	0.682
Collective activities	0.080	−0.877	−0.194	0.813
Unrotated				
Eigenvalues	3.865	2.352	1.125	
Percentage of variance	38.7	23.5	11.3	
Rotated				
Eigenvalues	3.275	2.270	1.798	
Percentage of variance	32.8	22.7	18.0	
Average scores				
Cluster 1 Open atomistic	−2.100	−0.279	0.619	
Cluster 2 Closed collectively reliant	0.218	−1.173	−0.237	
Cluster 3 Closed individually responsible	0.268	0.626	0.006	

METHODOLOGICAL APPROACH

This chapter examines how urban and regional competitiveness are associated with community culture, personality psychology traits and psychocultural behavior. This section outlines the methods used to empirically examine these relationships, using the measures of competiveness, community culture, personality psychology and psychocultural behavior outlined in the previous sections. The data used are all captured at the local authority district level across Great Britain. This level of aggregation is based on administrative responsibility rather than economic activities, which is not ideal, but provides access to a much wider variety of data than alternatives such as travel-to-work areas. There are 380 local authority district areas in Great Britain covering various cities and regions, and the analysis undertaken here uses data from 374. The City of London and Isle of Scilly are excluded due to their atypical nature and data availability. These extremely small local authority districts, in terms of both geographical area and population, are quite unlike most other parts of Great Britain. The City of London is at the center of London's dominant financial sector, whilst the Isles of Scilly are remote from the mainland and reliant on tourism for much of their employment. Four Scottish areas – Highland, Orkney Islands, Eilean Siar and Shetland Islands – are also excluded due to a lack of complete data for each.

In order to identify the relationships between community culture, personality traits and psychocultural behavior with competitiveness, a multivariate approach is adopted with the study utilizing regression analysis, with the general form of the estimated equation taking the form outlined below:

$$COMP_{X,i} = \alpha_0 + \boldsymbol{\beta}\ \mathbf{CULT}_i + \gamma \cdot \mathbf{X}_i + \varepsilon_i \qquad (7.1)$$

The dependent variable ($COMP_{X,i}$) is a measure of competitiveness drawn from the UK Competitiveness Index. Regressions are run for the full UKCI, but also the input, output and outcome factor indices. These will be regressed on a vector of community culture or personality variables, $CULT_i$. As there may be close relationships between community culture and the personality measures, a number of different specifications are run. These include examining the groups of community culture variables (Model A) and personality traits (Model B) separately as well as a specification with all measures included (Model C). However, as discussed above, particular community culture and personality traits may evolve in a complementary fashion. The final group of regressions use the psychocultural behavior measures to capture these combinations of community culture and personality traits (Model D). To account for the other influences on competitiveness, a vector of other controls (X_i) is included in the equation as outlined.

In order to control for unobserved factors at a regional level, a dummy is included to represent the local authority area falling in one of the core regions (London, South East England and the East of England). Although the study has captured informal influences on competitiveness through community culture and personality, it is also recognized that formal institutions have a role to play in promoting entrepreneurship and innovation by ensuring contractual obligations are met (Knack and Keefer, 1995; Mauro, 1995; Mo, 2001; Rodríguez-Pose and Di Cataldo, 2014; Huggins and Thompson, 2014b). Charron et al. (2014) develop regional measures of the quality of government for European Union (EU) regions based on the World Bank's Governance Indicators national measures (Kaufmann et al., 2009) and a citizen survey gathered at the regional level (Charron et al., 2011). The citizen survey captured ratings of three public services – education, health care and law enforcement – in terms of their quality, impartiality and corruption. It is not possible to utilize social surveys at the local level in Great Britain. Therefore, in order to extend Charron et al.'s (2011) approach, the study uses a number of complementary sources: satisfaction surveys of the police (Home Office Statistics and Scottish Policing Performance Framework), general practitioners (GPs) (NHS England, National Survey for Wales, 2013–14 – Health – experience of GP services; and Scottish Health and Care Experience Survey), measures of the quality of institutions such as complaints against the police (Her Majesty's Inspectorate of Constabulary and Scottish Policing Performance Framework), average primary school class size (Department for Education, Schools Census results and Summary Statistics for Schools in Scotland) and the proportion of schools rated as good or above (Office for Standards in Education, Children's Services and Skills (Ofsted), Estyn and School Estate Statistics).[1]

---

[1]   For the police and health measures, these are captured at the police force and health team level, each of which includes a number of local authorities. Likewise, the education measures are captured at the unitary authority and county level. This means, unfortunately, that not all variation in the quality of these institutions is captured between local authorities. However, as these largely represent the level at which decisions relating to the operation of these institutions take place it is probable that more of the variation will be between these police forces, health teams and counties than within them.

Industrial specialization and concentration are often suggested to be related to economic performance, although it has been argued that this is a weakness in some contexts. Where firms are concentrated in a particular industry, they may enjoy increasing returns from labor market pooling, industry-specific non-traded inputs at lower cost, and greater variety and knowledge spillovers (Krugman, 1991). Alternatively, Jacobs (1969) suggests that diversity allows the cross-fertilization of industries. To capture this, a measure based on Theil's (1972) diversity entropy index is used to analyze levels of industrial diversity, which is drawn from Fotopoulos (2014):

$$H_l = \sum_i (p_{li}/p_l) \ln(p_l/p_{li})$$

where p_{li} is the proportion of all employment in Britain found in industry i in locality l (E_{li}):

$$p_{li} = E_{li}/\sum_l \sum_i E_{li}$$

p_l is the share of all employment in Britain found in locality l:

$$p_l = \sum_i p_{li}$$

A value of 0 indicates the presence of just one industry in the locality; higher values represent more diverse industrial employment. In order to bound the diversity value within an interval [0, 1] H_l is divided by the natural log of the number of industries considered. The division of 15 industries employed by Fotopoulos (2014) is applied. Data on employment by industry are drawn from the Business Register and Employment Survey for 2013 (BRES).

To consider differences in the industrial structure, and that of Britain as a whole, an industrial specialization measure from Fotopoulos (2014) is formulated as follows:

$$SPEC_l = 1/2 \sum_i (E_{li}/E_l - E_{ni}/E_n)$$

where E_l is all employment in the locality, E_{ni} is all employment in Britain within industry i and E_n is all employment in Britain. The index has a value of 0 when the locality has the same industrial structure as that found in Britain as a whole. It takes a value of 1 when only one industry is present in the locality.

To capture the openness and connections of cities and regions, two measures are included to represent transport infrastructure in close proximity, which might reduce any reliance on local markets and provide additional agglomeration economies (Mejia-Dorantes et al., 2012; Albarran et al., 2013). Rail connections are captured by the gross number of journeys starting and ending in the locality's stations scaled by population (Department of Transport/Office of Rail Regulation). International transport connections are captured by being within 25 miles of a major airport (serving at least 4 million passengers in 2008).

To capture the benefits provided by agglomeration, population density (as of 2013) and population growth (2007 to 2013) are included to measure influences on aggregate demand (Davidsson, 1995). These data are drawn from the Nomis mid-year population estimates. Population density will also capture the urban–rural nature of the locality, which can provide benefits in terms of a larger, more specialized labor supply (Baker et al., 2005) and exchange of information and knowledge (Vernon, 1960; Delgado et al., 2010), but may also be associated with increased costs and congestion (Capello and Camagni, 2000). The last control included is the proportion of the population owning their own home, which is used to capture a potentially important source of collateral for entrepreneurs seeking loans to finance their new ventures (Mason, 2015; Fotopoulos, 2014).

RESULTS

Prior to undertaking the regression analysis, Tables 7.2–7.4 provide the correlation matrices for the UKCI variables and the control variables with the measures for community culture (Table 7.2), personality traits (Table 7.3) and psychocultural behavior (Table 7.4). Starting with the community culture variables there is a positive relationship between the overall UKCI and engagement with work and education, whilst a negative correlation is found with social cohesion, feminine and caring activities, adherence to social rules and collective actions. This would appear to indicate that competitiveness is greater in those areas that follow the typical masculine (Bruni et al., 2004), employment-orientated (Weber, 1930), atomistic (Kirkman et al., 2006), unconstrained by rules (Noorderhaven et al., 2004) but networked (Huggins and Thompson, 2015b) culture. This holds for most of the component indices although the strength of these relationships varies a little. In particular, adherence to social rules has no negative relationship with the UKCI Input index.

Table 7.3 finds overall competitiveness to be associated with greater extraversion, openness and emotional stability (low neuroticism), and lower agreeableness and conscientiousness. This is consistent with those studies that have found a positive relationship between economic performance and more open and extravert areas (Rentfrow et al., 2015). However, some studies, particularly at the individual level, have also suggested that the combination of personality traits may be important, not just individual traits, for outcomes such as success in education (Asendorpf and van Aken, 1999; Hart et al., 2003) and the development of social networks (Caspi, 2000). This means that although US states classed by Rentfrow et al. (2013) as friendly and conventional are high in extraversion and emotional stability, they are low in openness, high in agreeableness and exhibit poorer economic performance.

When the combined psychocultural behavior measures are used (Table 7.4), a positive relationship is found with individual commitment and diverse extraversion, and a negative relationship with inclusive amenability. This suggests that inclusive amenable psychocultural behavior – which is high with regard to more tightly bonded, friendly, caring, hardworking and rule-abiding characteristics – is less likely to promote competitiveness (although this is not to say that broader measures of well-being might not be promoted). Diverse extraversion, on the other hand, is the form of behavior which appears to have the strongest positive relationship with competitiveness, with its extravert, emotionally stable and more open profile. Based on previous studies this might be expected, whereby an environment with higher levels of these characteristics generates individuals suited to artistic and investigative occupations that may be expected to promote innovative activities.

It is interesting to find that conscientiousness alone in Table 7.3 was negatively related to competitiveness, given the findings of Lee (2016) which suggested that it was the personality trait most strongly related to innovation. However, whilst the inclusive amenable behavior is negatively related to competitiveness, the individual commitment profile, which also has high conscientiousness, displays a positive relationship. As with inclusive amenability, there is higher adherence to social rules, but where they differ is that for cities and regions displaying high levels of individual commitment, feminine and caring attitudes and collective activities are less pronounced, whilst engagement with work and education is higher, implying a much more self-sufficient perspective (Weber, 1930).

Table 7.2 Correlation matrix for community culture measures

	1. UKCI Input Index	2	3	4	5	6	7	8	9	10	11	12	13	14	15	16
2. UKCI Output Index	0.813 (0.000)															
3. UKCI Outcome Index	0.638 (0.000)	0.663 (0.000)														
4. UKCI	0.963 (0.000)	0.926 (0.000)	0.749 (0.000)													
5. Engagement with work and education	0.215 (0.000)	0.070 (0.175)	0.114 (0.027)	0.178 (0.001)												
6. Social cohesion	-0.616 (0.000)	-0.574 (0.000)	-0.513 (0.000)	-0.638 (0.000)	0.078 (0.132)											
7. Feminine and caring activities	-0.369 (0.000)	-0.444 (0.000)	-0.376 (0.000)	-0.422 (0.000)	0.211 (0.000)	0.686 (0.000)										
8. Adherence to social rules	-0.033 (0.529)	-0.200 (0.000)	-0.174 (0.001)	-0.106 (0.040)	0.453 (0.000)	0.444 (0.000)	0.568 (0.000)									
9. Collective actions	-0.384 (0.000)	-0.264 (0.000)	-0.213 (0.000)	-0.359 (0.000)	-0.544 (0.000)	0.205 (0.000)	-0.121 (0.020)	-0.449 (0.000)								
10. Institutions	0.293 (0.000)	0.255 (0.000)	0.274 (0.000)	0.303 (0.000)	0.246 (0.000)	-0.289 (0.000)	-0.207 (0.000)	-0.047 (0.361)	-0.453 (0.000)							
11. Diversity index	-0.371 (0.000)	-0.306 (0.000)	-0.318 (0.000)	-0.367 (0.000)	0.274 (0.000)	0.516 (0.000)	0.375 (0.000)	0.322 (0.000)	0.036 (0.485)	-0.188 (0.000)						
12. Specialization index	-0.029 (0.573)	0.106 (0.041)	0.128 (0.013)	0.032 (0.540)	-0.074 (0.151)	-0.006 (0.908)	-0.037 (0.470)	0.002 (0.965)	0.120 (0.020)	-0.144 (0.005)	-0.072 (0.166)					

	1	2	3	4	5	6	7	8	9	10	11	12	13	14	15	16
13. Proximity to a major airport	0.347 (0.000)	0.270 (0.000)	0.325 (0.000)	0.344 (0.000)	0.088 (0.088)	-0.353 (0.000)	-0.324 (0.000)	-0.267 (0.000)	0.069 (0.181)	0.075 (0.149)	-0.158 (0.002)	-0.089 (0.084)				
14. Rail usage	0.659 (0.000)	0.666 (0.000)	0.455 (0.000)	0.672 (0.000)	-0.067 (0.199)	-0.532 (0.000)	-0.419 (0.000)	-0.367 (0.000)	-0.111 (0.032)	0.285 (0.000)	-0.443 (0.000)	0.071 (0.169)	0.272 (0.000)			
15. Population growth	0.372 (0.000)	0.364 (0.000)	0.444 (0.000)	0.420 (0.000)	0.063 (0.222)	-0.688 (0.000)	-0.451 (0.000)	-0.279 (0.000)	-0.246 (0.000)	0.265 (0.000)	-0.287 (0.000)	-0.033 (0.530)	0.248 (0.000)	0.304 (0.000)		
16. Population density	0.497 (0.000)	0.543 (0.000)	0.447 (0.000)	0.541 (0.000)	-0.194 (0.000)	-0.799 (0.000)	-0.667 (0.000)	-0.605 (0.000)	0.005 (0.925)	0.268 (0.000)	-0.505 (0.000)	0.066 (0.204)	0.327 (0.000)	0.578 (0.000)	0.508 (0.000)	
17. Home ownership	-0.269 (0.000)	-0.440 (0.000)	-0.431 (0.000)	-0.375 (0.000)	0.224 (0.000)	0.639 (0.000)	0.699 (0.000)	0.705 (0.000)	-0.179 (0.000)	-0.211 (0.000)	0.372 (0.000)	0.027 (0.609)	-0.362 (0.000)	-0.431 (0.000)	-0.603 (0.000)	-0.714 (0.000)

Note: p-values in parentheses.

Table 7.3   Correlation matrix for personality psychology measures

	1. UKCI Input Index	2	3	4	5	6	7	8	9	10	11	12	13	14	15	16
2. UKCI Output Index	0.813 (0.000)															
3. UKCI Outcome Index	0.638 (0.000)	0.663 (0.000)														
4. UKCI	0.963 (0.000)	0.926 (0.000)	0.749 (0.000)													
5. Extraversion	0.598 (0.000)	0.400 (0.000)	0.387 (0.000)	0.548 (0.000)												
6. Agreeableness	-0.405 (0.000)	-0.423 (0.000)	-0.353 (0.000)	-0.435 (0.000)	-0.214 (0.000)											
7. Conscientiousness	-0.093 (0.073)	-0.171 (0.001)	-0.180 (0.000)	-0.133 (0.010)	-0.087 (0.091)	0.551 (0.000)										
8. Neuroticism	-0.398 (0.000)	-0.221 (0.000)	-0.207 (0.000)	-0.346 (0.000)	-0.491 (0.000)	-0.269 (0.000)	-0.434 (0.000)									
9. Openness	0.535 (0.000)	0.425 (0.000)	0.308 (0.000)	0.505 (0.000)	0.462 (0.000)	-0.419 (0.000)	-0.440 (0.000)	-0.113 (0.029)								
10. Institutions	0.293 (0.000)	0.255 (0.000)	0.274 (0.000)	0.303 (0.000)	0.236 (0.000)	-0.235 (0.000)	0.008 (0.884)	-0.094 (0.071)	0.107 (0.039)							
11. Diversity index	-0.371 (0.000)	-0.306 (0.000)	-0.318 (0.000)	-0.367 (0.000)	-0.334 (0.000)	0.349 (0.000)	0.375 (0.000)	0.067 (0.194)	-0.477 (0.000)	-0.188 (0.000)						
12. Specialization index	-0.029 (0.573)	0.106 (0.041)	0.128 (0.013)	0.032 (0.540)	-0.108 (0.037)	-0.028 (0.589)	-0.079 (0.128)	0.080 (0.122)	0.056 (0.278)	-0.144 (0.005)	-0.072 (0.166)					

	1	2	3	4	5	6	7	8	9	10	11	12	13	14	15	16
13. Proximity to a major airport	0.347	0.270	0.325	0.344	0.276	-0.246	-0.166	-0.013	0.200	0.075	-0.158	-0.089				
	(0.000)	(0.000)	(0.000)	(0.000)	(0.000)	(0.000)	(0.001)	(0.806)	(0.000)	(0.149)	(0.002)	(0.084)				
14. Rail usage	0.659	0.666	0.455	0.672	0.363	-0.398	-0.270	-0.112	0.448	0.285	-0.443	0.071	0.272			
	(0.000)	(0.000)	(0.000)	(0.000)	(0.000)	(0.000)	(0.000)	(0.030)	(0.000)	(0.000)	(0.000)	(0.169)	(0.000)			
15. Population growth	0.372	0.364	0.444	0.420	0.216	-0.362	-0.264	-0.008	0.301	0.265	-0.287	-0.033	0.248	0.304		
	(0.000)	(0.000)	(0.000)	(0.000)	(0.000)	(0.000)	(0.000)	(0.879)	(0.000)	(0.000)	(0.000)	(0.530)	(0.000)	(0.000)		
16. Population density	0.497	0.543	0.447	0.541	0.395	-0.574	-0.549	0.097	0.616	0.268	-0.505	0.066	0.327	0.578	0.508	
	(0.000)	(0.000)	(0.000)	(0.000)	(0.000)	(0.000)	(0.000)	(0.062)	(0.000)	(0.000)	(0.000)	(0.204)	(0.000)	(0.000)	(0.000)	
17. Home ownership	-0.269	-0.440	-0.431	-0.375	-0.200	0.465	0.558	-0.220	-0.309	-0.211	0.372	0.027	-0.362	-0.431	-0.603	-0.714
	(0.000)	(0.000)	(0.000)	(0.000)	(0.000)	(0.000)	(0.000)	(0.000)	(0.000)	(0.000)	(0.000)	(0.609)	(0.000)	(0.000)	(0.000)	(0.000)

Note: p-values in parentheses.

127

Table 7.4 *Correlation matrix for psychocultural behavior measures*

	1. UKCI Input Index	2	3	4	5	6	7	8	9	10	11	12	13	14
2. UKCI Output Index	0.813 (0.000)													
3. UKCI Outcome Index	0.638 (0.000)	0.663 (0.000)												
4. UKCI	0.963 (0.000)	0.926 (0.000)	0.749 (0.000)											
5. Inclusive amenability	-0.499 (0.000)	-0.527 (0.000)	-0.456 (0.000)	-0.542 (0.000)										
6. Individual commitment	0.309 (0.000)	0.173 (0.001)	0.165 (0.001)	0.278 (0.000)	0.011 (0.833)									
7. Diverse extraversion	0.551 (0.000)	0.347 (0.000)	0.303 (0.000)	0.490 (0.000)	-0.009 (0.867)	0.006 (0.915)								
8. Institutions	0.293 (0.000)	0.255 (0.000)	0.274 (0.000)	0.303 (0.000)	-0.319 (0.000)	0.370 (0.000)	0.108 (0.036)							
9. Diversity index	-0.371 (0.000)	-0.306 (0.000)	-0.318 (0.000)	-0.367 (0.000)	0.472 (0.000)	0.157 (0.002)	-0.301 (0.000)	-0.188 (0.000)						
10. Specialization index	-0.029 (0.573)	0.106 (0.041)	0.128 (0.013)	0.032 (0.540)	-0.022 (0.678)	-0.092 (0.074)	-0.067 (0.199)	-0.144 (0.005)	-0.072 (0.166)					
11. Proximity to a major airport	0.347 (0.000)	0.270 (0.000)	0.325 (0.000)	0.344 (0.000)	-0.342 (0.000)	-0.009 (0.861)	0.144 (0.005)	0.075 (0.149)	-0.158 (0.002)	-0.089 (0.084)				
12. Rail usage	0.659 (0.000)	0.666 (0.000)	0.455 (0.000)	0.672 (0.000)	-0.518 (0.000)	-0.013 (0.809)	0.295 (0.000)	0.285 (0.000)	-0.443 (0.000)	0.071 (0.169)	0.272 (0.000)			

	1	2	3	4	5	6	7	8	9	10	11	12	13	14
13. Population growth	0.372 (0.000)	0.364 (0.000)	0.444 (0.000)	0.420 (0.000)	-0.587 (0.000)	0.168 (0.001)	0.130 (0.012)	0.265 (0.000)	-0.287 (0.000)	-0.033 (0.530)	0.248 (0.000)	0.304 (0.000)		
14. Population density	0.497 (0.000)	0.543 (0.000)	0.447 (0.000)	0.541 (0.000)	-0.810 (0.000)	-0.150 (0.004)	0.237 (0.000)	0.268 (0.000)	-0.505 (0.000)	0.066 (0.204)	0.327 (0.000)	0.578 (0.000)	0.508 (0.000)	
15. Home ownership	-0.269 (0.000)	-0.440 (0.000)	-0.431 (0.000)	-0.375 (0.000)	0.706 (0.000)	0.258 (0.000)	-0.012 (0.813)	-0.211 (0.000)	0.372 (0.000)	0.027 (0.609)	-0.362 (0.000)	-0.431 (0.000)	-0.603 (0.000)	-0.714 (0.000)

Note: p-values in parentheses.

The other relationships indicate that cities and regions with stronger formal institutions, more concentrated industrial structures, good transport links, population growth and urban natures, but lower home ownership are more competitive. It is clear that some control variables have strong relationships with the community culture, personality trait and psychocultural behavior variables. For example, population growth and population density are negatively associated with social cohesion, whilst home ownership is positively associated.

Moving to the multivariate analysis, to reduce potential problems of collinearity three specifications are run for each regression model. The first contains the cultural or personality variables and controls for location in a core region and formal institutions. The second introduces those variables associated with industrial structure and transport infrastructure. The third introduces the variables relating to the population and home ownership. The variance inflation factors are below the conventional cut-off of 10 for all specifications, but social cohesion has a variance inflation factor of 5.998 when all community culture and personality trait variables are included in the third specification with the full set of controls (Model C3). Even with both the community culture and personality trait variables included when the second specification is used that excludes the population and home ownership measures (Model C2), the variance inflation factor drops to 4.15.

Table 7.5 presents the regression analysis for overall competitiveness as captured by the UKCI. All of the regressions reject the null of collective insignificance according to the F-test results. The variance explained by the regressions varies depending on the competitiveness measure used, but those incorporating personality traits appear to perform most strongly. In terms of overall competitiveness, the variance explained varies from 50 percent when using the community culture variables and minimal controls (Table 7.5, Model A1) to 74 percent when community culture, personality traits and a full set of controls are included (Table 7.5, Model C3).

Models A1 to A3 and C1 to C3 include the community culture variables. The coefficients for engagement with work and education are positive and significant in all specifications run, regardless of whether the personality traits are included in the estimations (Models C1 to C3) or not (Models A1 to A3). This implies that cultures with a strong work ethic remain important even in advanced cities and regions where knowledge and networking have gone some way to superseding more basic and routine tasks (Weber, 1930; Tabellini, 2010). The other community culture variable that remains significant in all specifications is social cohesion, where a negative relationship is found. This supports

Table 7.5 Regressions for the competitiveness of British cities and regions (local authority areas)

	Model A1	Model A2	Model A3	Model B1	Model B2	Model B3	Model C1	Model C2	Model C3	Model D1	Model D2	Model D3
Core region	**7.421**	3.194	3.186	**10.921**	**8.542**	**7.169**	**7.659**	**4.483**	**3.509**	**5.076**	**3.325**	**3.101**
	(0.000)	(0.067)	(0.082)	(0.000)	(0.000)	(0.000)	(0.000)	(0.005)	(0.034)	(0.002)	(0.021)	(0.040)
Institutions	-3.395	-4.278	-4.932	-3.857	-4.584	-4.560	**-5.552**	**-5.477**	**-5.354**	**-6.060**	**-6.666**	**-6.994**
	(0.283)	(0.102)	(0.061)	(0.169)	(0.059)	(0.061)	(0.044)	(0.022)	(0.025)	(0.023)	(0.004)	(0.003)
Diversity index		-0.753	2.163		**28.380**	**29.952**		20.559	21.495		20.473	19.172
		(0.953)	(0.866)		(0.021)	(0.015)		(0.084)	(0.069)		(0.082)	(0.104)
Specialization index		2.356	1.919		7.793	8.096		5.825	7.108		8.481	9.639
		(0.664)	(0.725)		(0.136)	(0.122)		(0.239)	(0.152)		(0.084)	(0.052)
Proximity to a major airport		**3.556**	**3.405**		**3.742**	**3.075**		**2.542**	**2.294**		**2.693**	**2.337**
		(0.002)	(0.003)		(0.000)	(0.004)		(0.017)	(0.030)		(0.007)	(0.021)
Rail usage		**0.151**	**0.145**		**0.121**	**0.115**		**0.123**	**0.121**		**0.121**	**0.120**
		(0.000)	(0.000)		(0.000)	(0.000)		(0.000)	(0.000)		(0.000)	(0.000)
Population growth			-0.341			0.291			-0.316			-0.247
			(0.154)			(0.147)			(0.142)			(0.218)
Population density			0.001			0.000			0.000			0.000
			(0.144)			(0.394)			(0.620)			(0.391)
Home ownership			-23.816			-11.123			-48.943			-28.797
			(0.171)			(0.442)			(0.002)			(0.043)

131

Table 7.5 (continued)

	Model A1	Model A2	Model A3	Model B1	Model B2	Model B3	Model C1	Model C2	Model C3	Model D1	Model D2	Model D3
Community culture												
Engagement with work and education	**2.606**	**1.851**	**1.850**				**3.099**	**2.143**	**2.030**			
	(0.001)	(0.007)	(0.008)				(0.000)	(0.001)	(0.002)			
Social cohesion	**-8.488**	**-5.589**	**-5.223**				**-3.865**	**-3.088**	**-3.295**			
	(0.000)	(0.000)	(0.000)				(0.000)	(0.001)	(0.003)			
Feminine and caring activities	**-1.863**	**-1.602**	-1.143				-1.474	-1.238	-0.610			
	(0.049)	(0.039)	(0.157)				(0.074)	(0.082)	(0.406)			
Adherence to social rules	1.370	**3.502**	**4.326**				0.080	**2.045**	**2.950**			
	(0.141)	(0.000)	(0.000)				(0.923)	(0.006)	(0.000)			
Collective actions	-0.512	-1.194	-1.497				0.346	-0.601	-1.143			
	(0.633)	(0.186)	(0.104)				(0.730)	(0.500)	(0.205)			

Notes: p-values in parentheses; emboldened values significant at 5% level.

those studies that have found access to new ideas and people to be key factors for competitiveness-generating activities such as entrepreneurship and innovation (Levie, 2007; Huggins and Thompson, 2016a).

Other elements of community culture do not display a consistently significant relationship. For example, feminine and caring activities are found to have a negative relationship with competitiveness in models A1 and A2, but this disappears when controlling for population characteristics and home ownership. In a similar fashion, whilst adherence to social rules is not initially significant in model A1, a positive relationship is found when controlling for industry structure and transport infrastructure. Table 7.2 indicated that adherence to social rules tends to be weaker in places with stronger transport connections, which are likely to be cities and larger urban areas. However, after taking into account the benefit these receive from their transport links, adherence to social rules does have a positive effect, potentially associated with the support this provides in terms of aiding coordination (Rodríguez-Pose and Storper, 2006; Lorenzen, 2007).

With regard to the personality traits included in models B1 to B3 and models C1 to C3, four traits consistently show a significant relationship to competitiveness. Extraversion and openness are positively linked to competitiveness, whilst neuroticism and agreeableness display a negative relationship. These results largely support the findings from the descriptive analysis and previous studies, where greater levels of openness and extraversion aid creative and networking activities (Caspi, 2000; Barrick et al., 2003). These activities are also supported by lower levels of neuroticism (emotional stability). However, contrary to the results produced by Lee's (2016) investigation of innovation, conscientiousness is only significantly related to competitiveness in model B3 after controlling for population growth, population density and home ownership. Agreeableness is negatively associated with competitiveness, indicating that in Britain at least it appears that a city of region's ability to continue to compete and provide a high standard of living is often associated with psychologies where personal conflict is more readily accepted. However, this does not preclude a positive relationship with broader measures of well-being, with other studies finding that competitiveness is positively associated with alternative broader measures of well-being (Huggins and Thompson, 2012).

Given the results relating to community culture and personality trait variables discussed above, it is of little surprise to find that the most competitive localities are those that display higher levels of diverse extravert and individually committed psychocultural behaviors. The

inclusive amenability psychocultural behavior profile is negatively associated with competitiveness, implying that cities and regions with behavior that might be regarded as socially "nicer" are likely to enjoy this
benefit at the cost of economic rewards if competitiveness is eroded.

Formal institutions, surprisingly, do not display a positive relationship,
but rather a negative relationship with competitiveness, albeit frequently
only significant at the 10 percent level. This might reflect Rodríguez-
Pose and Storper's (2006) argument that culture and institutions are
substitutes, and the former strengthens to account for weaknesses in the
latter.

In terms of the component factor indices of the UKCI, due to space
constraints the full results are not presented here, but it is instructive to
note that there are some subtle differences to overall competitiveness.
The regressions for input competitiveness perform similarly to those for
overall competitiveness in terms of percentage of variance explained,
with the community culture and personality traits variables showing
significant relationships, being the same as for overall competitiveness.
Positive links are found with engagement with work and education,
extraversion and openness. Negative links are found with: social
cohesion, agreeableness and neuroticism. However, when the community
culture variables are not included in the regressions, among the personality traits variables conscientiousness also has a positive link with input
competitiveness. This makes sense given that many high-growth and
innovative businesses may be attracted to cities and regions with a labor
supply displaying a strong work ethic and prepared to work methodically
to complete investigative tasks (Barrick et al., 2003). This is likely to be
self-supporting, with the jobs created encouraging like-minded highly
skilled individuals to move to such places. As such, the positive relationship with the individually committed psychocultural behavior remains.

Compared to the regressions for overall competitiveness, the regressions for output competitiveness perform less strongly, with community
culture and personality traits in combination only explaining 63 percent
of the variance. Engagement with work and education, and to a degree
social cohesion, are the community cultural aspects that are found to play
less of a role; and for personality traits, extraversion and conscientiousness are not significant. As with social cohesion, openness is more
weakly related to output competitiveness. Instead, it seems that a more
individualistic competitive but emotionally stable personality is what is
required to turn inputs into high-value production.

The regressions relating to outcome competitiveness are the weakest,
performing with only 48 percent of variance explained when all variables
are included. With regard to how outputs are converted into incomes for

the residents of the localities – the UKCI Outcome Index – again a slightly different pattern is present to that for overall competitiveness. Although agreeableness retains a negative relationship with outcome competitiveness, as does neuroticism, at the community level there is less evidence that collective actions have a negative effect, and when other controls are excluded a positive relationship is found. Key factors, however, are a culture of engagement with work and education. Also, what appears to be consistent throughout is that friendlier localities do not succeed in terms of input, output or outcome competitiveness, suggesting that any benefits in terms of welfare are likely to have to overcome a large potential deficit from that obtained through economic outputs. Only the diverse extraversion psychocultural behavior is positively associated with outcome competitiveness, which given the results for the individual personality traits and community culture variables suggests that emotional stability is a key rooted determinant of competitivness.

CONCLUSION

This chapter has argued that the underlying community culture and aggregate personality psychology found in particular cities and regions are determining factors of the level of economic competitiveness found in these places. Furthermore, the chapter has empirically found a range of strong and significant relationships between a number of dominant cultural and psychology traits within cities and regions of Great Britain and the competitiveness of these territorial areas. In particular, it appears to be the case that the interplay between culture and psychology in the form of the psychocultural behavior of cities and regions helps to shape their long-term competitiveness trajectories. Cities and regions that have relatively atomized behavioral environments with high levels of individual commitment tend to enjoy competitiveness benefits. Similarly, places with high rates of cultural diversity and extravert individuals have relatively high levels of competitiveness.

On the other hand, cities and regions that tend to be culturally socially inclusive, with a significant number of people with amenable and agreeable personality traits, experience relatively low rates of competitiveness. To a large extent, the findings make intuitive sense with, for example, the individual commitment found in competitive cities and regions being a manifestation of a "personal competitiveness" that subsequently becomes visible at an aggregated spatial level. Clearly, however, the relationship between psychocultural human behavior and urban and regional competitiveness is unlikely to be a direct one. It is more likely that behavior initially impacts other sources of competitive-ness such as the form and efficiency of local institutions as well as the capability and capacity to generate and mobilize the types of capital required for high rates of economic competitiveness.

As previously noted, at the highest level it can be argued that the key tenets of urban and regional competitiveness theories – in the form of knowledge, innovation and entrepreneurship – are strongly associated with endogenous growth frameworks, and represent the more down-stream explanations of urban and regional development. However, it is increasingly suggested that positive urban and regional growth and development also requires high-quality institutions, in the form of growth-enabling rules and incentives, alongside the types of capital suggested by regional competitiveness theory. Therefore, as shown by Figure 7.1, a more midstream means of explaining urban and regional competitiveness and development is to conceptualize cities and regions as growth systems within which the interaction between available capital assets and the institutional infrastructure is the major determinant (Hug-gins, 2016).

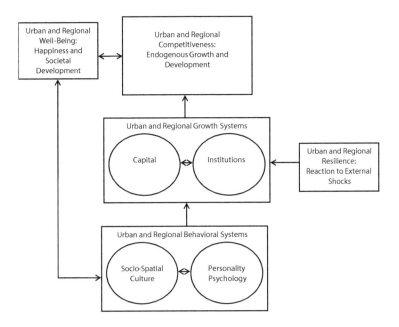

Figure 7.1   Connecting contemporary theories of urban and regional competitiveness and development

Such a systems-based approach to connecting endogenous capital accumulation and institutional theories of urban and regional competitiveness and development potentially offers a means of delineating a framework to better understand how investment in capital assets, especially intangible assets, is related to the institutions underlying the economic functioning of cities and regions. In the past, both capital accumulation and institutional theories of growth and development have been criticized by some scholars for their lack of explanatory power (Glaeser et al., 2004; Chang, 2011), which is perhaps a result of each theory being viewed somewhat in isolation. A meshing of these theoretical approaches, however, indicates that regional growth is a highly endogenous, recursive and evolutionary process whereby the interaction between capital and institutions at a number of different, yet interdependent, levels of organizational arrangement may offer more explanatory power (Huggins, 2016).

Within this framework, it is proposed here that the economic growth systems of cities regions are shaped and influenced by deeper-rooted upstream determinants stemming from the human behavioral traits of these places. Whilst institutions can be considered to be the rules of the game governing growth processes, cultural and psychological traits encompass the extent to which such rules are adhered to, as well as the way in which they foster future institutional change.

It is concluded that in the field of urban and regional competitiveness and development research there is a need for further theoretical integration, particularly through the deployment of a behavioral conceptual lens. Behavioral economic geography – encompassing culture, psychology and the agency of individuals – potentially provides new insights into the persistence of the long-term unevenness of competitiveness across regions. In particular, psychocultural behavioral patterns, and their evolution, provide a basis for understanding the type and nature of human agency that exists within cities and regions, and the institutions such agency generates. Furthermore, behavioral-based frameworks incorporating cultural and psychological aspects help us to understand why particular agents within a city or region, especially entrepreneurial agents, may possess a proclivity towards fostering the forms of innovation that propel competitiveness, as well as how the interaction between cultural and psychology factors result in city and regional behavioral systems with a higher or lower tendency to sustain long-term economic growth. Finally, although the focus of urban and regional competitiveness narratives concerns explanations of economic outcomes, there is scope to consider further theoretical connections with wider development goals beyond economic growth, such as those related to social development, well-being and the sustainable development of cities and regions.

REFERENCES

Aghion, P., A. Alesina and F. Trebbi, "Endogenous political institutions," *Quarterly Journal of Economics*, Vol. 119, No. 2, pp. 565–612, 2004.

Aiginger, K., "Competitiveness: from a dangerous obsession to a welfare creating ability with positive externalities," *Journal of Industry, Competition and Trade*, Vol. 6, No. 2, pp. 161–177, 2006.

Aiginger, K. and M. Firgo, "Regional competitiveness: connecting an old concept with new goals," in R. Huggins and P. Thompson (eds), *Handbook of Regions and Competitiveness: Contemporary Theories and Perspectives on Economic Development*, Cheltenham, UK and Northampton, MA, USA: Edward Elgar Publishing, pp. 155–191, 2017.

Albarran, P., R. Carrasco and A. Holl, "Domestic transport infrastructure and firms' export market participation," *Small Business Economics*, Vol. 40, No. 4, pp. 879–898, 2013.

Almlund, M., A.L. Duckworth, J.J. Heckman and T.D. Kautz, "Personality psychology and economics," No. w16822, National Bureau of Economic Research, 2011.

Ariely, D., *Predictably Irrational: The Hidden Forces that Shape our Decisions*, New York: Harper, 2008.

Asendorpf, J.B. and M.A.G. van Aken, "Resilient, overcontrolled, and under-controlled personality prototypes in childhood: replicability predictive power, and the trait-type issue," *Journal of Personality and Social Psychology*, Vol. 77, No. 4, pp. 815–832, 1999.

Atkinson, R. and K. Kintrea, "Disentangling area effects: evidence from deprived and non-deprived neighbourhoods," *Urban Studies*, Vol. 38, No. 12, pp. 2277–2298, 2001.

Audretsch, D.B. and M. Keilbach, "Entrepreneurship capital and economic performance," *Regional Studies*, Vol. 38, No. 8, pp. 949–959, 2004.

Baker, T., E. Gedajlovic and M. Lubatkin, "A framework for comparing entrepreneurship processes across nations," *Journal of International Business Studies*, Vol. 36, No. 5, pp. 492–504, 2005.

Barrick, M.R., M.K. Mount and R. Gupta, "Meta-analysis of the relationship between the Five Factor model of personality and Holland's occupational types," *Personnel Psychology*, Vol. 56, pp. 45–74, 2003.

Becker, S.O. and L. Woessmann, "Was Weber wrong? A human capital theory of Protestant economic history," *Quarterly Journal of Economics*, Vol. 124, No. 2, pp. 531–596, 2009.

Begg, I., "Cities and competitiveness," *Urban Studies*, Vol. 36, Nos 5–6, pp. 795–810, 1999.

Benet-Martinez, V., M.B. Donnellan, W. Fleeson, R.C. Fraley, S.D. Gosling, et al., "Six visions for the future of personality psychology," in M. Mikulincer, P.R. Shaver, M.L. Cooper and R.J. Larsen (eds), *APA Handbook of Personality* and Social Psychology: Personality Processes and Individual Differences, Vol. 4, Washington, DC: American Psychology Association, pp. 665–690, 2015.

Bennett, R. and S. Dann, "The changing experience of Australian female entrepreneurs," *Gender, Work and Organization*, Vol. 7, No. 2, pp. 75–82, 2000.

Beugelsdijk, S. and R. Maseland, *Culture in Economics: History, Methodological Reflections and Contemporary Applications*, Cambridge: Cambridge University Press, 2011.

Borghans, L., A. Lee Duckworth, J.J. Heckman and B. ter Weel, "The economics and psychology of personality traits," *Journal of Human Resources*, Vol. 43, No. 4, pp. 972–1059, 2008.

Brennan, A., J. Rhodes and P. Tyler, "The nature of local area social exclusion in England and the role of the labour market," *Oxford Review of Economic Policy*, Vol. 16, No. 1, pp. 129–146, 2000.

Bruni, A., S. Gherardi and B. Poggio, "Doing gender, doing entrepreneurship: an ethnographic account of intertwined practices," *Gender, Work and Organization*, Vol. 11, No. 4, pp. 407–429, 2004.

Callois, J.M. and F. Aubert, "Towards indicators of social capital for regional development issues: the case of French rural areas," *Regional Studies*, Vol. 41, No. 6, pp. 809–821, 2007.

Camerer, C.F. and G. Loewenstein, "Behavioral economics: past, present, future," in C.F. Camerer, G. Loewenstein and M. Rabin (eds), *Advances in Behavioral Economics*, Woodstock, UK and Princeton, NJ, USA: Princeton University Press, pp. 3–52, 2004.

Camps, S. and P. Marques, "Exploring how social capital facilitates innovation: the role of innovation enablers," *Technological Forecasting and Social Change*, Vol. 88, pp. 325–348, 2014.

Capello, R. and R. Camagni, "Beyond optimal city size: an evaluation of alternative urban growth patterns," *Urban Studies*, Vol. 37, No. 9, pp. 1479–1496, 2000.

Cartwright, E., *Behavioural Economics*, 2nd edition, Abingdon: Routledge, 2014.

Caspi, A., "The child is father of the man: personality continuities from childhood to adulthood," *Journal of Personality and Social Psychology*, Vol. 78, No. 1, pp. 158–172, 2000.

Casson, M., *Entrepreneurship and Business Culture: Studies in the Economics of Trust Volume 1*, Aldershot, UK and Brookfield, VT, USA: Edward Elgar Publishing, 1995.

Chang, H.J., "Institutions and economic development: theory, policy and history," *Journal of Institutional Economics*, Vol. 7, pp. 473–498, 2011.

Chapman, B.P. and L.R. Goldberg, "Replicability and 40 year predictive power of childhood ARC types," *Journal of Personality and Social Psychology*, Vol. 101, No. 3, pp. 593–606, 2011.

Charron, N., L. Dijkstra and V. Lapuente, "Regional governance matters: quality of Government with European Union member states," *Regional Studies*, Vol. 48, No. 1, pp. 68–90, 2014.

Charron, N., V. Lapuente and B. Rothstein, *Measuring Quality of Government and Sub-National Variation*, Brussels: European Commission Directorate-General Regional Policy Directorate Policy Development, 2011.

Clark, G.L., "Behavior, cognition and context," mimeo, Smith School of Enterprise and the Environment, Oxford University, Oxford, 2015.

Costa Jr, P.T. and R.R. McCrae, *Revised NEO Personality Inventory (NEO-PI-R) and NEO Five-factor Inventory (NEO-FFI) Professional Manual*, Odessa, FL: Psychological Assessment Resources, 1992.

Credé, M., P.O. Harms, S. Niehorster and A. Gaye-Valentine, "An evaluation of the consequences of using short measures of the Big Five personality traits," *Journal of Personality and Social Psychology*, Vol. 102, No. 4, pp. 874–888, 2012.

Davidsson, P., "Culture, structure and regional levels of entrepreneurship," *Entrepreneurship and Regional Development*, Vol. 7, No. 1, pp. 41–62, 1995.

Davidsson, P. and B. Honig, "The role of social and human capital among nascent entrepreneurs," *Journal of Business Venturing*, Vol. 18, No. 3, pp. 301–331, 2003.

Delgado, M., M.E. Porter and S. Stern, "Clusters and entrepreneurship," *Journal of Economic Geography*, Vol. 10, No. 4, pp. 495–518, 2010.

Dodorico McDonald, J., "Measuring personality constructs: the advantages and disadvantages of self-reports, informant reports and behavioural assessments," *Enquire*, Vol. 1, No. 1, pp. 75–94, 2008.

Durand, J.D., *The Labor Force in Economic Development: A Comparison of International Census Data, 1946–1996*, Princeton, NJ: Princeton University Press, 1975.

Easterly, W. and R. Levine, "Africa's growth tragedy: politics and ethnic divisions," *Quarterly Journal of Economics*, Vol. 112, No. 4, pp. 1203–1250, 1997.

Ettlinger, N., "Cultural economic geography and a relational and microspace approach to trusts, rationalities, networks, and change in collaborative workplaces," *Journal of Economic Geography*, Vol. 3, No. 1, pp. 1–28, 2003.

European Commission, *European Competitiveness Report 2001*, Luxembourg: Publications Office of the European Union, 2001.

Florida, R., *The Rise of the Creative Class*, New York: Basic Books, 2002.

Fotopoulos, G., "On the spatial stickiness of UK new firm formation rates," *Journal of Economic Geography*, Vol. 14, No. 3, pp. 651–679, 2014.

Francois, P. and J. Zabojnik, "Trust, social capital, and economic development," *Journal of the European Economic Association*, Vol. 3, No. 1, pp. 51–94, 2005.

Fritsch, M. and P. Mueller, "Effects of new business formation on regional development over time," *Regional Studies*, Vol. 38, No. 8, pp. 961–975, 2004.

Glaeser, E.L., R. La Porta, F. Lopez-De-Silanes and A. Shleifer (2004), "Do institutions cause growth?," *Journal of Economic Growth*, Vol. 9, No. 3, pp. 271–303, 2004.

Goldberg, L.R.,"The development of markers for the Big-Five factor structure," *Psychological Assessment*, Vol. 4, No. 1, pp. 26–42, 1992.

Gordon, I.R. and P. McCann, "Innovation, agglomeration, and regional development," *Journal of Economic Geography*, Vol. 5, No. 5, pp. 523–543, 2005.

Grabher, G., "The weakness of strong ties: the lock-in of regional development in the Ruhr area," in G. Grabher (ed.), *The Embedded Firm: On the Socioeconomics of Interfirm Relations*, London: Routledge, pp. 255–278, 1993.

Granovetter, M., "The strength of weak ties," *American Journal of Sociology*, Vol. 78, No. 6, pp. 1360–1380, 1973.

Greif, A., "Cultural beliefs and the organization of society: a historical and theoretical reflection on collectivist and individualist societies," *Journal of Political Economy*, Vol. 102, No. 5, pp. 912–950, 1994.

Guiso, L., P. Sapienza and L. Zingales, "Does culture affect economic outcomes?," *Journal of Economic Perspectives*, Vol. 20, No. 2, pp. 23–48, 2006.

Hamby, T., W. Taylor, A.K. Snowden and R.A. Peterson, "A meta-analysis of the reliability of free and for-pay Big Five scales," *Journal of Psychology: Interdisciplinary and Applied*, Vol. 150, No. 4, pp. 422–430, 2016.

Harris, R., "Regional competitiveness and economic growth: the evolution of explanatory models," in R. Huggins and P. Thompson (eds), *Handbook of Regions and Competiveness: Contemporary Theories and Perspectives on Economic Development*, Cheltenham, UK and Northampton, MA, USA: Edward Elgar Publishing, pp. 80–116, 2017.

Hart, D., R. Atkins and S. Fegley, "Personality and development in childhood: a person-centred approach," *Monographs of the Society for Research in Child Development*, Vol. 68, No. 1, pp. i–122, 2003.

Hayton, J.C. and G. Cacciotti, "Is there an entrepreneurial culture? A review of empirical research," *Entrepreneurship and Regional Development*, Vol. 25, Nos 9–10, pp. 708–731, 2013.

Hodgson, G.M., *From Pleasure Machines to Moral Communities: An Evolutionary Economics without Homo Economicus*, Chicago, IL: University of Chicago Press, 2013.

Hofstede, G., *Culture's Consequences: Internal Differences in Work Related Values*, Beverly Hills, CA: SAGE Publications, 1980.

Hofstede, G., *Culture's Consequences: Comparing Values, Behaviors, Institutions and Organizations across Nations*, 2nd edition, Thousand Oaks, CA: SAGE Publications, 2001.

Hofstede, G. and R.R. McCrae, "Personality and culture revisited: linking traits and dimensions of culture," *Cross-Cultural Research*, Vol. 38, No. 1, pp. 52–88, 2004.

Hoyman, M., J. McCall, L. Paarlberg and J. Brennan, "Considering the role of social capital for economic development outcomes in US counties," *Economic Development Quarterly*, Vol. 30, No. 4, pp. 342–357, 2016.

Huggins, R., "Creating a UK Competitiveness Index: regional and local benchmarking," *Regional Studies*, Vol. 37, No. 1, pp. 89–96, 2003.

Huggins, R., "Capital, institutions and urban growth systems," *Cambridge Journal of Regions, Economy and Society*, Vol. 9, No. 2, pp. 443–463, 2016.

Huggins, R., H. Izushi, D. Prokop and P. Thompson, *The Global Competitiveness of Regions*, Abingdon, UK and New York, USA: Routledge, 2014.

Huggins, R. and P. Thompson, "Well-being and competitiveness: are the two linked at a place-based level?," *Cambridge Journal of Regions, Economy and Society*, Vol. 5, No. 1, pp. 45–60, 2012.

Huggins, R. and P. Thompson, "Culture, entrepreneurship and uneven development: a spatial analysis," *Entrepreneurship and Regional Development*, Vol. 26, Nos 9–10, pp. 726–752, 2014a.

142	*Towards a competitive, sustainable modern city*

Huggins, R. and P. Thompson, "Entrepreneurial urban development: culture, institutions and economic evolution," *Leadership and Policy Quarterly*, Vol. 3, No. 4, pp. 161–184, 2014b.

Huggins, R. and P. Thompson, "Culture and place-based development: a socio-economic analysis," *Regional Studies*, Vol. 49, No. 1, pp. 130–159, 2015a.

Huggins, R. and P. Thompson, "Entrepreneurship, innovation and regional growth: a network theory," *Small Business Economics*, Vol. 45, No. 1, pp. 103–128, 2015b.

Huggins, R. and P. Thompson, "Socio-spatial culture and entrepreneurship: some theoretical and empirical observations," *Economic Geography*, Vol. 92, No. 3, pp. 269–300, 2016a.

Huggins, R. and P. Thompson, *UK Competitiveness Index 2016*, Cardiff: Cardiff University, 2016b.

Huggins, R. and P. Thompson, "Introducing regional competitiveness and development: contemporary theories and perspectives," in R. Huggins and P. Thompson (eds), *Handbook of Regions and Competitiveness: Contemporary Theories and Perspectives on Economic Development*, Cheltenham, UK and Northampton, MA, USA: Edward Elgar Publishing, pp. 1–31, 2017.

Hundley, G., "What and when are the self-employed more satisfied with their work," *Industrial Relations*, Vol. 40, No. 2, pp. 293–316, 2001.

Inglehart, R. and C. Welzel, "Changing mass priorities: the link between modernization and democracy," *Perspectives on Politics*, Vol. 8, No. 2, pp. 551–567, 2010.

Jacobs, J., *The Economy of Cities*, New York: Random House, 1969.

John, O.P. and S. Srivastava, "The Big Five trait taxonomy: history, measurement, and theoretical perspectives," in O.P. John and L.A. Pervin (eds), *Handbook of Personality: Theory and Research*, New York: Guilford Press, pp. 102–138, 1999.

Jokela, M., "Personality predicts migration within and between US states," *Journal of Research in Personality*, Vol. 43, pp. 79–83, 2009.

Kahneman, D., "Maps of bounded rationality: psychology for behavioral economics," *American Economic Review*, Vol. 93, No. 5, pp. 1449–1475, 2003.

Kaufmann, D., A. Kraay and M. Mastruzzi, "Governance Matters VIII: Aggregate and individual governance indicators for 1996–2008," Policy Research Paper 4978. Washington, DC: World Bank, 2009.

Kearns, A. and R. Forrest, "Social cohesion and multilevel urban governance," *Urban Studies*, Vol. 37, Nos 5–6, pp. 995–1017, 2000.

Kibler, E., T. Kautonen and M. Fink, "Regional social legitimacy of entrepreneurship: implications for entrepreneurial intention and start-up behaviour," *Regional Studies*, Vol. 48, No. 6, pp. 995–1015, 2014.

Kirkman, B.L., K.B. Lowe and C.B. Gibson, "A quarter century of 'Culture's Consequences': a review of empirical research incorporating Hofstede's cultural values framework," *Journal of International Business Studies*, Vol. 37, No. 3, pp. 285–320, 2006.

Klotz, A.C. and D.O. Neubaum, "Research on the dark side of personality traits in entrepreneurship: observations from an organizational behavior perspective," *Entrepreneurship Theory and Practice*, Vol. 40, No. 1, pp. 7–17, 2016.

Knack, S. and P. Keefer, "Institutions and economic performance: cross country tests using alternative institutional measures," *Economics and Politics*, Vol. 7, No. 3, pp. 207–227, 1995.

Knott, D., S. Muers and S. Aldridge, *Achieving Cultural Change: A Policy Framework*, London: Strategy Unit, 2008.

Kresl, P.K., "The determinants of urban competitiveness: a survey," in P. Kresl and G. Gappert (eds), *North American Cities and the Global Economy*, Thousand Oaks, CA: SAGE Publications, pp. 45–68, 1995.

Krugman, P., *Geography and Trade*, Cambridge, MA: MIT Press, 1991.

Layard, R., "Happiness and public policy: a challenge to the profession," *Economic Journal*, Vol. 116, No. 510, C24–C33, 2006.

Lee, N., "Psychology and the geography of innovation," *Economic Geography*, Vol. 93, No. 2, pp. 106–130, 2016.

Levie, J., "Immigration, in-migration, ethnicity and entrepreneurship in the United Kingdom," *Small Business Economics*, Vol. 28, Nos 2–3, pp. 143–170, 2007.

Lippmann, S. and H. Aldrich, "A rolling stone gathers momentum: generational units, collective memory, and entrepreneurship," *Academy of Management Review*, Vol. 41, No. 4, pp. 658–675, 2016.

Lorenzen, M., "Social capital and localised learning: proximity and place in technological and institutional dynamics," *Urban Studies*, Vol. 44, No. 4, pp. 799–817, 2007.

Luster, T., K. Rhoades and B. Haas, "The relation between parental values and parenting behaviour: a test of the Kohn hypothesis," *Journal of Marriage and Family*, Vol. 51, No. 1, pp. 139–147, 1989.

MacKinnon, D., A. Cumbers, A. Pike, K. Birch and R. McMaster, "Evolution in economic geography: institutions, political economy, and adaptation," *Economic Geography*, Vol. 85, No. 2, pp. 129–150, 2009.

Martin, R., *Thinking About Regional Competitiveness: Critical Issues*, Nottingham: East Midlands Development Agency, 2005.

Martin, R. and P. Sunley, "Competitiveness and regional economic resilience," in R. Huggins and P. Thompson (eds), *Handbook of Regions and Competitiveness: Contemporary Theories and Perspectives on Economic Development*, Cheltenham, UK and Northampton, MA, USA: Edward Elgar Publishing, 2017.

Maskell, P., *Competitiveness, Localised Learning and Regional Development: Specialisation and Prosperity in Small Open Economies*, London: Routledge, 1998.

Maskell, P. and A. Malmberg, "Myopia, knowledge development and cluster evolution," *Journal of Economic Geography*, Vol. 7, No. 5, pp. 603–618, 2007.

Mason, C., "Spatial variations in enterprise," in R. Burrows (ed.), *Deciphering the Enterprise Culture*, London: Routledge, pp. 74–106, 2015.

Mauro, P., "Corruption and growth," *Quarterly Journal of Economics*, Vol. 110, No. 3, pp. 681–712, 1995.

McCrae, R.R. and A. Terracciano, "Personality profiles of cultures: aggregate personality traits," *Journal of Personality and Social Psychology*, Vol. 89, No. 3, pp. 407–425, 2005.

Mejia-Dorantes, L., A. Paez and J.M. Vassallo, "Transportation infrastructure impacts on firm location: the effect of a new metro line in the suburbs of Madrid," *Journal of Transport Geography*, Vol. 22, pp. 236–250, 2012.

Mo, P.H., "Corruption and economic growth," *Journal of Comparative Economics*, Vol. 29, No. 1, pp. 66–79, 2001.

Mullainathan, S. and R.H. Thaler, "Behavioral economics," NBER Working Paper Series, No. 7948, 2000.

Murphy, L., R. Huggins and P. Thompson, "Social capital and innovation: a comparative analysis of regional policies," *Environment and Planning C*, Vol. 34, No. 6, pp. 1025–1057, 2016.

Ni, P. and Y. Wang, "Urban sustainable competitiveness: a comparative analysis of 500 cities around the world," in R. Huggins and P. Thompson (eds), *Handbook of Regions and Competitiveness: Contemporary Theories and Perspectives on Economic Development*, Cheltenham, UK and Norhampton, MA, USA: Edward Elgar Publishing, 2017.

Noorderhaven, N., R. Thurik, S. Wennekers and A. Van Stel, "The role of dissatisfaction and per capita income in explaining self-employment across 15 European countries," *Entrepreneurship Theory and Practice*, Vol. 28, No. 5, pp. 447–466, 2004.

Obschonka, M., H. Andersson, R.K. Silbereisen and M. Sverke, "Rule-breaking, crime, and entrepreneurship: a replication extension study with 37-year longitudinal data," *Journal of Vocational Behavior*, Vol. 83, No. 3, pp. 386–396, 2013a.

Obschonka, M., E. Schmitt-Rodermund, S.D. Gosling and R.K. Silbereisen, "The regional distribution and correlates of an entrepreneurship-prone personality profile in the United States, Germany, and the United Kingdom: a socio-ecological perspective," *Journal of Personality and Social Psychology*, Vol. 105, No. 1, pp. 104–122, 2013b.

Obschonka, M., M. Stuetzer, D.B. Audretsch, P.J. Rentfrow, J. Potter and S.D. Gosling, "Macropsychological factors predict regional economic resilience during a major economic crisis," *Social Psychological and Personality Science*, Vol. 7, No. 2, pp. 95–104, 2016.

Obschonka, M., M. Stuetzer, S.D. Gosling, P.J. Rentfrow, M.E. Lamb, et al., "Entrepreneurial regions: do macro-psychological cultural characteristics of regions help solve the 'knowledge paradox' of economics?," *PLoS ONE*, Vol. 10, No. 6, doi: 10.1371/journal.pone.0129332, 2015.

Olson, M., *Rise and Decline of Nations*, New Haven, CT: Yale University Press, 1982.

Parasuraman, S., Y.S. Purohit, V.M. Godshalk and N.J. Beutell, "Work and family variables, entrepreneurial career success, and psychological well-being," *Journal of Vocational Behavior*, Vol. 48, No. 3, pp. 275–300, 1996.

Peck, J., "Economic sociologies in space," *Economic Geography*, Vol. 81, No. 2, pp. 129–178, 2005.

Pike, A., A. Rodríguez-Pose and J. Tomaney, "What kind of local and regional development and for whom?," *Regional Studies*, Vol. 41, No. 9, pp. 1253–1269, 2007.

Portes, A. and P. Landolt, "Social capital: promise and pitfalls of its role in development," *Journal of Latin American Studies*, Vol. 32, No. 2, pp. 529–547, 2000.

Putnam, R., *Making Democracy Work: Civic Traditions in Modern Italy*, Princeton, NJ: Princeton University Press, 1993.

Rammstedt, B. and O.P. John, "Measuring personality in one minute or less: a 10-item short version of the Big Five Inventory in English and German," *Journal of Research in Personality*, Vol. 41, No. 1, pp. 203–212, 2007.

Rentfrow, P.J., S.D. Gosling, M. Jokela, D.J. Stillwell, M. Kosinski and J. Potter, "Divided we stand: three psychological regions of the United States and their political, economic, social and health correlates," *Journal of Personality and Social Psychology*, Vol. 105, No. 6, pp. 996–1012, 2013.

Rentfrow, P.J., S.D. Gosling and J. Potter, "A theory of the emergence, persistence, and expression of geographical variation in psychological characteristics," *Perspectives on Psychological Science*, Vol. 3, No. 5, pp. 339–369, 2008.

Rentfrow, P.J., M. Jokela and M.E. Lamb, "Regional personality differences in Great Britain," *PLoS ONE*, Vol. 10, No. 3, doi: 10.1371/journal.pone.0122245, 2015.

Rentfrow, P.J., J.T. Jost, S.D. Gosling and J. Potter, "Statewide differences in personality predict voting patterns in 1996–2004 US presidential elections," in J.T. Jost, A.C. Kay and H. Thorisdottir (eds), *Social and Psychological Bases of Ideology and System Justification*, Oxford: Oxford University Press, pp. 314–350, 2009.

Rodríguez-Pose, A. and M. Di Cataldo, "Quality of government and innovative performance in the regions of Europe," *Journal of Economic Geography*, Vol. 15, No. 4, pp. 673–706, 2014.

Rodríguez-Pose, A. and M. Storper, "Better rules or stronger communities? On the social foundations of institutional change and its economic effects," *Economic Geography*, Vol. 82, No. 1, pp. 1–25, 2006.

Sachs, J., "Notes on a new sociology of economic development," in L.E. Harrison and S.P. Huntington (eds), *Culture Matters: How Values Shape Human Progress*, New York: Basic Books, pp. 29–43, 2000.

Shneor, R., S. Metin Camgöz and P. Bayhan Karapinar, "The interaction between culture and sex in the formation of entrepreneurial intentions," *Entrepreneurship and Regional Development*, Vol. 25, Nos 9–10, pp. 781–803, 2013.

Simon, H.A., "A behavioral model of rational choice," *Quarterly Journal of Economics*, Vol. 69, No. 1, pp. 99–118, 1955.

Simon, H.A., *Models of Bounded Rationality*, Cambridge, MA: MIT Press, 1982.

Soldz, S. and G.E. Vaillant, "The Big Five personality traits and the life course: a 45-year longitudinal study," *Journal of Research in Personality*, Vol. 33, No. 2, pp. 208–232, 1999.

Soto-Oñate, D., "The historical origins of regional economic inequality in Spain: the cultural legacy of political institutions," in N. Schofield and G. Caballero (eds), *The Political Economy of Governance: Institutions, Political Performance and Elections*, Cham, Switzerland and New York, USA: Springer, pp. 79–111, 2016.

Storper, M., *The Regional World: Territorial Development in a Global Economy*, New York: Guilford, 1997.

Storper, M., *Keys to the City: How Economics, Institutions, Social Interaction and Politics Shape Development*, Oxford, UK and Princeton, NJ, USA: Princeton University Press, 2013.

Streeck, W., "On the institutional conditions of diversified quality production," in E. Metzner and W. Streeck (eds), *Beyond Keynesianism: Socio-Economics of Production and Full Employment*, Aldershot, UK and Brookfield, VT, USA: Edward Elgar Publishing, pp. 21–61, 1991.

Stuetzer, M., M. Obschonka, D.B. Audretsch, M. Wyrwich, P.J. Rentfrow, et al. "Industry structure, entrepreneurship, and culture: an empirical analysis using historical coalfields," *European Economic Review*, Vol. 86, No. 1, pp. 52–72, 2016.

Tabachnick, B.G. and L.S. Fidell, *Using Multivariate Statistics*, 5th edition, Boston, MA: Allyn & Bacon, 2007.

Tabellini, G., "Culture and institutions: economic development in the regions of Europe," *Journal of the European Economic Association*, Vol. 8, No. 4, pp. 677–716, 2010.

Theil, H., *Statistical Decomposition Analysis: With Applications in the Social and Administrative Sciences*, Amsterdam: North-Holland, 1972.

Thomas, A.S. and S.L. Mueller, "A case for comparative entrepreneurship: assessing the relevance of culture," *Journal of International Business Studies*, Vol. 31, No. 2, pp. 287–301, 2000.

Tubadji, A., "Culture-based development – culture and institutions: economic development in the regions of Europe," *Society Systems Science*, Vol. 5, No. 4, pp. 355–391, 2013.

Van den Bergh, J.C. and S. Stagl, "Coevolution of economic behaviour and institutions: towards a theory of institutional change," *Journal of Evolutionary Economics*, Vol. 13, No. 3, pp. 289–317, 2003.

Van Maanen, J. and E.H. Schein, "Toward a theory of organizational socialization," *Research in Organizational Behavior*, Vol. 1, No. 1, pp. 209–264, 1979.

Vernon, R., *Metropolis 1985: Interpretation of the Findings of the New York Metropolitan Region Study*, Cambridge, MA: Harvard University Press, 1960.

Weber, M., *The Protestant Ethic and the Spirit of Capitalism*, London: Routledge, 1930.

Wennberg, K., S. Pathak and E. Autio, "How culture moulds the effects of self-efficacy and fear of failure on entrepreneurship," *Entrepreneurship and Regional Development*, Vol. 25, Nos 9–10, pp. 756–780, 2013.

Williams, N., R. Huggins and P. Thompson, "Social capital and entrepreneurship: does the relationship hold in deprived urban neighbourhoods?," *Growth and Change*, doi: 10.1111/grow.12197, 2017.

Wyrwich, M., "Entrepreneurship and intergenerational transmission of values," *Small Business Economics*, Vol. 45, No. 1, pp. 191–213, 2015.

8. Must a competitive city be a tolerant city?

Peter Karl Kresl

In recent years one of the foci of urban scholars has been on the "modern" city, which links this to three of its most important challenges: competitiveness, sustainability and tolerance. Urban development has always had to be concerned with both competitiveness and its sustainability over decades. As we enter the Fourth Industrial Revolution (I-4), as identified by Klaus Schwab and the World Economic Forum, we enter a world in which technological change is supplemented by connectivity and communication, and the key labor force is no longer blue-collar manufacturing workers but rather a highly educated, highly skilled, younger and also highly mobile labor force. In addition to demanding the best of the "soft" determinants of urban competitiveness – public security, health care, excellent schools, pleasant residential neighborhoods, access to recreation and retail outlets, and to a complex of cultural and entertainment facilities – these younger, skilled and educated workers also demand a degree of tolerance that was often wanting in the pre-I-4 economy, marked as it often was by conflict over jobs by competing immigrant groups of different ethnicities.

Tolerance has been thought of in two distinct ways. Richard Florida and Melanie Faasche do a Global Index of Tolerance each year, and they focus on the openness of the city or the country in which it is situated to immigrants, minorities, newcomers, and gays and lesbians. They argue that this is important for any city that wants to be a generator, a meeting place and a host to innovative and creative people. It is also necessary to link tolerance with talent, and with technology (Florida and Faasche, 2017). Another approach is offered by the World Bank, for which the crucial tolerance element is economic and social exclusion, and the net is cast a bit wider to focus on discrimination against individuals or groups on the basis on religious, cultural or sexual preferences, or categories such as the elderly, the disabled, the homeless and women (World Bank,

2015). This discrimination may be found in access to employment, housing, public services, land and infrastructure.

THE FLORIDA AND FAASCHE APPROACH TO TOLERANCE

The young and educated workers in the I-4 economy understand that they can enhance their productivity if they work in an environment in which the only qualifications for participation are knowledge and skill. They have the option of offering their labor to employers located in any part of the world, or of starting their own firm in a location that is most congenial for them. I-4 employers understand this and they, too, will avoid and seek out the same sorts of places. This phenomenon has been seen in all countries that are actively engaged in the modern economy for the past two or three decades. In this chapter I focus primarily on experiences with tolerance in the United States (US), first with a rather general case and then with some specific cases.

The general example is that of the American South, essentially the states of what was the Confederacy during the US Civil War, 1861–1865. Slavery was, of course, the most significant and enduring institution of the Confederacy. African Americans (blacks) were held as enslaved property, principally by owners of cotton plantations. This enslavement went contemporaneously with the owner class's evaluation of blacks as human beings and their qualities: they were seen as ignorant, uneducable, lacking in initiative, and untrustworthy. This estimation did not end with the victory of the North in 1865, but lingers on today. Another institution of the South is the Southern Baptist Church. Southern Baptists have tended to be hostile to non-Baptists, such as atheists, Catholics and Jews, and so homosexuals, abortion, labor unions, liberals; to a non-Southern Baptist, the list seems to be endless. In other words, while intolerance raises its ugly head in other parts of the US, the South has been the primary center in the US of intolerance.

Richard Florida has studied creativity and tolerance, and in his *The Rise of the Creative Class Revisited* (Florida, 2012) he gives rankings of 361 metropolitan areas (MAs). The cities of the Confederacy comprise 33 percent of these MAs. If we create three groups of 120, 120 and 121 MAs, the South accounts for only 22.5 percent of the top 120 areas in creativity and 25.0 percent in tolerance. In the second third, they comprise 38.3 and 40.0 percent, respectively; and in the third it is 38.3 and 33.9 percent. In other words, the South is under-represented in the most creative and tolerant MAs, and over-represented in the lower two, although in the lowest third the difference is not significant for tolerance. The results actually rank the set of MAs of the South higher than they would be were it not for the fact that many of the MAs in Florida are places that have been populated by "sun birds" from the US North and from Eastern Canada who have brought their higher tolerance values with them. If we omit from the South the retiree centers Orlando, Sarasota, Ft Pierce, Vero Beach, Naples, Daytona Beach and Fort Myers, to get the True South, the impact on tolerance percentage is a reduction at the top by almost 20 percent and an increase in the bottom two by 7.5 percent (Table 8.1).

Table 8.1   The South and creativity and tolerance, 2010, with and without "Sun Bird" cities

	Creativity				Tolerance			
	All South		True South		All South		True South	
Top 1/3	27	22.5	25	22.3	30	25.0	23	20.5
Middle 1/3	46	38.3	41	36.6	48	40.0	48	42.8
Lowest 1/3	46	38.3	46	41.0	33.9	33.9	41	36.6

Source: Based on data from Florida (2012, Table A.2).

This cultural trait has come into conflict with the demands of the modern economy. While the region was largely agricultural, there were several centers of manufacturing activity in cities such as Atlanta, Birmingham and Mobile, in industries such as steel-making and ship-building. This involved, in essence, the traditional lower-skill, blue-collar labor force that was either local in origin or immigrant. There was virtually no conflict between traditional Southern values (intolerance) and the labor force. This began to change in the 1990s as political and economic leaders in many cities began to try to attract a higher-technology production system to the region. In North Carolina, the Research Triangle of the University of North Carolina, North Carolina State University and Duke University sought to attract a highly skilled and educated research labor force, and then workers for the spin-off firms that the Triangle generated in the cities of Chapel Hill, Durham and Raleigh. Charlotte, North Carolina sought to become a major center of financial institutions. Atlanta, Georgia built its modern economy on local assets such as Georgia Tech University, and major cultural institutions such as the Atlanta Symphony and the High Museum of Art. Finally, in South Carolina the automobile industry has established production sites such as

BMW in Spartanburg-Greenville in the western highlands, where there is Clemson University and its automotive research facility, and close to Charleston, with access to two interstate highways and to the port facilities. The Boeing facility close to Charleston, at which some of the 787 aircraft were made, was not allowed to transfer experienced aircraft workers from Everitt, Washington because they were union workers and this was not to be tolerated in South Carolina. Production at this new facility that was staffed with workers new to aircraft manufacture was marked by metal shavings carelessly left near cables (with the possibility of damage to the cables), and tools and a small step ladder being left in various parts of the planes. Production had to be reduced or halted until quality and safety could be assured. Boeing has stated that for Qatar Airlines, the major customer for the 787, all aircraft will come from the Everitt plant.

In all of these instances, the cities and regions involved had to attract a skilled and educated labor force from other parts of the US or from other countries; failure to do this, as with Boeing in South Carolina, led to difficulties. These out-of-region workers were more liberal and tolerant than were the locals, and over time the relevant political entities have all become more tolerant, liberal and democratic. In November 2018, Democrat Stacy Abrams came within 1.4 percent in the popular vote of becoming Georgia's first black or woman governor, in spite of the fact that it was generally recognized that the political establishment had suppressed black voting. This shift to tolerance is true of many other university and technology districts in the "Old South."

It is also true that the Interstate Highway System, television, air travel, modern telecommunications, and easier and cheaper travel have all served to break down the 200 years of intolerance of the states of the old Confederacy through increased interregional personal contact. However, in the rural, agricultural and less connected parts of the region, the old intolerance continues to exert its influence. In his recent book, *This Land*, Christopher Ketcham explores the relationship between a past-bound religion, fundamental Mormonism, which supports antagonism to the state (except for things such as grazing subsidies that benefit them), enthusiasm for gun ownership, claims to ownership of the land, white supremacy, and intolerance (Ketcham, 2019, Part 1).

Much the same is to be found in much of Texas, another state of the Confederacy. In East Texas, cotton was a major crop and slavery was key for the labor force. As one went west, cotton was no longer the major crop, and cattle and other crops and petroleum were predominant. As a consequence, in East Texas intolerance was focused on blacks, but in south-west Texas migration, or original settlement, was dominated by people from Mexico. The Mexicans were actually in Texas before Texas was either settled by whites, or even Texas. They owned land, established towns and cities and had a strong culture. In the 20th century several Latinos have risen to positions of distinction. Henry Cisneros was to become mayor of a major city, San Antonio, and the Secretary of Housing and Urban Development in the Clinton administration. Julian Castro followed in the footsteps of Cisneros, becoming Mayor of San Antonio and was then chosen by President Obama to be Secretary of Housing and Urban Development. His brother Joaquin currently represents the San Antonio area in the US House of Representatives. Both brothers were educated at Stanford University and Harvard Law School. Barbara Jordan was the first African American woman to be elected to the Texas Senate and then to the US House of Representatives. Being African American, she was not able to attend the University of Texas at Austin, and graduated from Texas Southern University and the University of Boston Law School, graduating in 1959, before the civil rights legislation in the 1960s. These three distinguished individuals were all from central Texas, San Antonio and Houston. It is noteworthy that there are no large cities or distinguished universities in East Texas. The Texas experience with tolerance, while not perfect, did differ dramatically from that of the other states of the Confederacy.

The primary high-tech city in Texas is undoubtedly Austin, state capital and seat of the main campus of the University of Texas. In the last half-century, Austin has become the principal center of tolerance and liberalism in the state. The university, and St Edwards University, have attracted faculty and students from all parts of the country and have developed programs in the sciences, computer science, business and management, and the arts that have had a powerful impact on the city and its culture. It has developed its own version of country music, with notables such as Willie Nelson and Janis Joplin, and its own set of venues for performance. In recent years the television program *Austin City Limits* has celebrated this distinctive approach to popular music, and given rise to the ACL Music Festival held each September. This music, plus a notably funky, laid-back lifestyle, has generated the city motto "Keep Austin Weird"; not something you would expect to see in Dallas or Houston, devoted as they are to business and the oil industry. Other notably liberal Texans include Molly Ivens, who was a distinguished reporter for the liberal Austin-based *Texas Observer*, and Ann Richards, Texas State Treasurer and then Governor. No matter where Texas liberals are born, they seem to end up in Austin and then pass their last days there.

If we do a calculation with regard to creativity and to tolerance, as we did with the South, with and without "sun bird" cities, we find that Texas cities as regards creativity are, in the three thirds groupings, 19 percent, 33 percent and 48 percent, somewhat less creative than cities of the South, given the large number of small rural towns in the state. However, with regard to tolerance the Texas cities are 24 percent, 52 percent and 24 percent in the three thirds, or significantly more tolerant than the cities of the True South. Of the five Texas cities that are in the most tolerant 120 cities category, Austin (#34) is the intellectual and tech center of the state, Dallas (#47) is a corporate and financial center, Midland (#70) is an oil center, Laredo (#79) is a border city paired with Nuevo Laredo, and Houston (#116) is a center of oil, shipping and medicine. All but Laredo are dependent upon their attractiveness to the I-4 labor force – younger, educated, skilled and mobile – and would be hindered in their competitiveness with substantially lower tolerance levels. Austin, Dallas and Houston are all cites with major university complexes, almost always centers of liberal tolerance. Laredo is over 95 percent Hispanic or Latino, so the question of tolerance is quite different than it is for other Texas cities, although it is perhaps the state's most economically segregated city. What we find in the states of the Confederacy, then, is a higher level of intolerance than elsewhere in the country; however, in the cities that are actively and aggressively engaged in the modern high-tech, I-4 economy the level of tolerance is among the highest in the country.

THE WORLD BANK APPROACH TO TOLERANCE

The World Bank's notion of tolerance is much broader than that of Florida and Faasche. In fact, while their focus is on immigrants, minorities and gays, that of the World Bank includes these elements as well as children, youth, the aged, the disabled, the homeless, migrants and women. At issue here is whether the city or nation has enacted legislation to guarantee the rights and access to employment, housing, social programs, and so on, or whether they have been assured by means of decisions of the courts. Failing this, these groups will also, and more fundamentally, be excluded from the political processes and governance, in addition to the economy.

For the World Bank, the crucial result of lack of tolerance is a widening of social and economic inequality: "Urban inequality can undermine urbanization's benefits by threatening the sustainability of the growth process and slowing poverty reduction, and it can lead to social divisions, conflict, and rising crime and violence in cities." This generates an inability to develop "inclusive, safe, resilient and sustainable cities" (World Bank, 2015, pp. xv–xvi). All of this causes a reduction in the competitiveness of the urban area: city, metropolitan statistical area, or region.

While the World Bank was writing specifically about cities in East Asia and the Pacific region, many cities in the US have introduced policies that have created such exclusion and segregation through a variety of policies and structural initiatives. "Red-lining" drew a line around a part of the city that was meant to contain spatially low-income and minority populations through the polities of financial institutions and other lending agencies that make it impossible for these populations to obtain mortgages on houses or even to rent apartments in areas that were declared to be "white." Many areas of cities are zoned single-family housing only, because multi-story apartment buildings were thought to be attractive to minorities and lower-income individuals or families. Structures such as major highways and rail lines were used to provide dividing "walls" between white and higher-income neighborhoods and those with minority and lower-income areas. Americans have spoken for generations of low-income and minority people being from the "wrong side of the tracks." In many cities, such as Washington, DC and Atlanta, metro lines have been kept out of high-income areas, such as Georgetown in DC, because of the fear of the consequences of improved access by low-income and minority residents of the larger city. The Metropolitan Atlanta Regional Transportation Authority (MARTA) is, on the streets, referred to as "Moving Africans Rapidly Through Atlanta," with white travelers using their cars to travel on publicly funded highways and roads. Currently, Atlanta has the greatest income inequality of any large city in the US (Berube, 2018, Table 1). Inadequate public funding of education, housing, employment opportunities, safe public spaces and non-discrimination policies only entrench these inequalities of quality of living and of social and economic conditions. These conditions exist in many if not most of the other countries of the industrialized world, but this does not provide an excuse for any nation.

TOLERANCE AND COMPETITIVENESS

What is of concern here is the impact these inequalities and indications of lack of tolerance and diversity have on the comparative competitiveness of the countries – or for the purpose of this chapter, the cities – in which they are allowed to exist, if not be actively promoted. This issue is taken on directly by Bruno Lanvin and Paul Evans in their *Global Talent Competitiveness Report* for INSEAD. Initiated in 2013, the 2018 report focuses on "Diversity for Competitiveness," in which they examine "the full potential of diversity as a pillar of innovation sustainability, and ultimately competitiveness" (Lanvin and Evans, 2018, p. 3). They identify three types of diversity. First, cognitive diversity – a diversity of knowledge, experience and perspectives or ways of tackling problems. These are acquired through education or experience. Second, identity diversity – what one is born with: gender, ethnicity, religion, sexual orientation, nationality and age. Creativity comes when individuals differently endowed with these characteristics work together as a team. Third, preference diversity – differences in fundamental interests and values that are inherent in each of us as individuals. While a city does not want to encourage a work force of clones who hold the same values, extreme preference diversity can lead to wasted time and energy and "unproductive and unresolved conflict." The authors caution that "there is a price to all three types of diversity. It is not easy to work in a diverse team or organization. It requires a high level of social and collaborative skills, and it means finding ways to overcome the unconscious biases that we all hold" (Lanvin and Evans, 2018, p. 4). One of the five "messages" they offer (on p. 10) is that benefitting from diversity "requires bold and visionary leadership – in the absence of such leadership similar people tend to cluster together in the shape of tribes, cliques, and cohorts." While this clustering can give support to new entrants, the end result is often a deleterious ghetto or *banlieu*.

A final classification of aspects of tolerance that arise from the process of urbanization is offered by the International Bank for Reconstruction and Development. Economic exclusion considers access to, or exclusion from, well-paying jobs, with reference to workers who are discriminated against for any of the reasons already noted. Spatial exclusion constrains discriminants from access to good housing, land and public services, such as potable water and sanitation. Social exclusion refers to individuals and groups being kept from the political process and governance, in addition to access to the modern economy. Individuals may be trapped in isolated villages, or subjected to limitation of movement, such as the Chinese hukou residence permit system. This creates a multifaceted structure of intolerance from which an individual finds it exceedingly difficult to escape (IBRD, 2017).

One of the sources referred to by Lanvin and Evans is a study done for the National Bureau of Economic Research by Gianmarco Ottaviano and Giovanni Peri. Their most relevant finding is that "higher wages and higher rents for US natives are significantly correlated with higher diversity … a more multicultural urban environment makes US-born citizens more productive" (Ottaviano and Peri, 2004, p. 22). One of the important factors in this result is that, given different education, natural endowments and experiences, very important reciprocal learning will take place. Of course, higher wages and rents are also the consequence of having an economy that has a comparatively high level of competitiveness. These positive elements are more powerful at the level of the city than at that of the nation. Richard Florida notes that while gay marriage is now accepted in most parts of the country, with the exception of relatively backward states such as Alabama, substantial wage and opportunity differences between men and women and between whites and other racial and ethnic groups still exist throughout the US. He quotes Vivek Wadhwa as saying: "more than 50% of Silicon Valley is foreign born. Less than 5% women, almost no blacks or Hispanics, sadly. A lot needs to be fixed" (Florida, 2012, p. 59). Florida concludes that is it is just as important for cities to have low barriers to entry for people as it is to have low barriers to entry for new firms.

Increased immigration can be a positive factor in two different ways. First, it can afford an inflow of skilled I-4 workers. Florida concludes that it is just as important for cities to have low barriers to entry for people as it is to have low barriers to entry to new firms.

Second, immigrants have a positive impact on the economy, whatever their level of education. We see the essential workers in food and other services, and so many health sector workers, from physicians to nurses to support staff during this COVID-19 crisis. Furthermore, their expenditures are extremely important for some communities and cities are sustaining aggregate demand for goods and services provided by them and by other participants in the economy.

The experience of Silicon Valley affords a brilliant example of this impact. In her recent book *The Code*, Margaret O'Mara describes the impact of open borders:

> Immigrants had been getting the job done for some time in Silicon Valley, from European-born refugees like Andy Grove and Charles Simonyi to the Asian American and Latina women who assembled microchips in fab plant clean rooms. But the wave of immigration that began in the 1970s had a scale and impact that the Valley had never seen … From San Mateo to Sunnyvale to Fremont, bedroom suburbs whose populations had been nearly entirely white now became dynamic and diverse communities of high-achieving, highly educated immigrants from India, China, Hong Kong and Taiwan. They started newspapers, opened businesses, built houses of worship and schools and arts centers … And they worked in – and became founders of – technology companies. By 1990, foreign-born engineers made up 35 per cent [*sic*] of the

Valley's engineering workforce. The numbers spiked higher still after the 1990 creation of the H-1B visa program, which allowed technical workers a path to permanent residency. (O'Mara, 2019, pp. 283–284)

The impact of openness or closedness to flows of migrants has clear impacts on the ability of a city to attract and to retain talented, young and mobile workers. There are many classic contrasting cities in the rest of the world that have suffered or benefitted from their acceptance of flows of immigrants of ethnicity, religion or race that is other than that of the host nation, as well as unacceptable gender identity when it comes to their competitiveness. Brief examination of just two of these cities will be sufficient to make this point: Jakarta in Indonesia, and Kuala Lumpur in Malaysia.

Jakarta is one of the least tolerant of cities in East Asia. The city is near the bottom of the Florida and Faasche Index of Tolerance, and only 8 percent of its population are in the creative class (Florida and Faasche, 2017). Eighty-three percent of the population are Muslim and 12 percent are Christian. In a recent election, it was widely debated whether a Christian could indeed be a leader in a Muslim government. There have been movements in several sectors of the society to ban gays and effeminate-appearing men from employment in universities or government. These policies will make Jakarta continue to be unattractive to the skilled and talented I-4 workers who all aspiring urban economies should be seeking (*The Economist*, 2019).

On the other hand, Kuala Lumpur has a population that is 38 percent Malay, 43 percent Chinese and 10 percent Indian. This mixture of nationalities is reflected in the city's architecture, food, music and clothing. It is a conservative culture with regard to cultural performances, some of which are seen to be offensive to local standards. Nonetheless, it has made a solid commitment to encouraging participation of women in the economy and in the broader society. Women's labor participation rate is 54 percent; still below the 80 percent for men, but impressive in relation to other Asian societies (International Monetary Fund, 2018, pp. 61–62). Under the New Economic Policy of 1971, and then Vision 2020 of Prime Minister Mahthir in 1991, the city has made progress in creating a modern economy, although political scandals have hindered successful accomplishment of the plans' objectives. In spite of this, Florida and Faasche rank Kuala Lumpur below Tokyo, Singapore, Seoul and Hong Kong with regard to per capita income, and above Shanghai and Beijing; in their Global City Index, Kuala Lumpur is ranked lower than only these six cities (Florida and Faasche, 2017).

Another increasingly powerful negative impact of aversion to immigration is its impact on a nation's demography. A population pyramid consists of a vertical line with population age values from birth to over 100 years, and on the horizontal in one direction the number of females and in the other that of males (Kresl and Ietri, 2010, Ch. 2). This gives us the percentage of the population of each sex for each year of age. For a society to be viable in the long run, the base should be broader than it is at the top: a healthy society should have more individuals who are younger and fewer who are older. The dynamic is that the younger generate the workers for the economy of tomorrow, and when working they contribute taxes to health and retirement programs to sustain the elderly in their needs, just as today's elderly contributed when they were younger and working. If the base shrinks over time, this deprives the economy of a labor force and a sustainable society for the elderly. Unfortunately, in many of the developed world's economies the population pyramid is narrow at the top. This is the case with Italy, Russia, China, Korea, Japan, the United Kingdom, France, and most of the others.

It is also the case now in the United States. A birth rate per woman of 2.1 is what is required for the population to reproduce itself, and recently the US has fallen to about 1.7. What has sustained the US over the years is its welcoming of immigrants. The current anti-immigrant policy of President Trump is putting the US into the birth-deficient category. While native-born Americans have a birth rate that is insufficient and declining, recent immigrants usually have several children in the family, and this has pushed the US above the critical level of 2.1.

In many societies there is an often irrational rejection of immigrants. Flows have increased in recent years due to violence in their countries of origin, but rejecting them outright through national policy only hurts the economy in the longer run. This policy in countries such as Hungary and Italy is causing the above-mentioned consequences, as well as the de-population of the countryside and the abandonment of many small towns.

Thus intolerance extends its negative impacts beyond the work force and the sustainability of retirement and health programs, to the very survival of many towns and regions of the country. Such economies are hardly sustainable or competitive.

IN CONCLUSION

In the I-4 economy that looks to tomorrow, in which connectivity and communication are of increasing importance relative to technology, it has been both argued and demonstrated that competitiveness and sustainability are dependent upon the "softer" elements of competitiveness, including, very prominently, diversity and tolerance. This is, and will continue increasingly to be, an economy of high mobility, of flexibility and adaptability, of variety, and of public policy that is both responsive and supportive. It is no longer the case that young people become educated and then move back to their home city or to the largest city that is close to home; rather, students travel across the country to get the specific education and experience they seek, and upon graduation seek employment in the most desirable place in the country or internationally. The burden now is on the leaders of cities, large and small, to sell themselves to the companies that will offer jobs to this emerging work force, and to provide a living space that will be attractive to this labor force.

This chapter has shown that diversity and tolerance to all lifestyles, personal preferences, belief systems – religious and political, and ethnic and national origins, are essential characteristics of the successful I-4 economy city or metropolitan area. Both national and city governments can contribute to a positive situation for the local economy. Depending on the national political system, national governments can do much to support education, legal rights for various minority groups, open immigration systems, financial and regulatory support for new firms, and creative employment structures. Cities, in turn, can support the provision of the various amenities and living situations that are attractive to the I-4 economy labor force: zoning, availability of suitable housing, local transportation, local schools, cultural and recreational facilities, and an appealing urban architecture. If a city is passive in this regard, the desirable workers will opt for employment in other cities that are more congenial to them. Now more than ever, city officials must work actively to create an urban space that will enable the city to participate actively and successfully in the I-4 economy.

REFERENCES

Berube, Alan, "City and Metropolitan income inequality data reveal ups and downs through 2016," Washington, DC: Brookings Institution, February 5, 2018.

The Economist, "The rise of intolerance," www.economist.com, August 20, 2019.

Florida, Richard, *The Rise of the Creative Class Revisited*, New York: Basic Books, 2012.

Florida, Richard and Melanie Faasche, *The Rise of the Urban Creative Class in Southeast Asia*, Toronto: Martin Prosperity Institute, 2017.

International Bank for Reconstruction and Development (IBRD), *East Asia and Pacific Cities: Expanding Opportunities for the Urban Poor*, Washington, DC: IBRD, 2017.

International Monetary Fund, *Malaysia: 2018 Article IV Consultation with Malaysia*, Washington, DC: International Monetary Fund, March 7, 2018.

Ketcham, Christopher, *This Land*, New York: Viking, 2019.

Kresl, Peter Karl and Daniele Ietri, *The Aging Population and the Competitiveness of Cities: Benefits to the Urban Economy*, Cheltenham, UK and Northampton, MA, USA: Edward Elgar Publishing, 2010.

Lanvin, Bruno and Paul Evans, *Global Talent Competitiveness Report: Diversity for Competitiveness*, Paris: INSEAD, 2018.

O'Mara, Margaret, *The Code*, New York: Penguin Press, 2019.

Ottaviano, Gianmarco and Giovanni Peri, "The economic value of cultural diversity: the evidence from US cities," Working Paper 10904, Cambridge, MA: National Bureau of Economic Research, 2004.

World Bank, *East Asia's Changing Urban Landscape*, Washington, DC: World Bank, 2015.

9. Ecological environment competitiveness in emerging economies: a case of urban India

Shaleen Singhal and Meenakshi Kumar

INTRODUCTION

The rapid pace of economic growth and urbanization in city-regions around the world is known to be detrimental to ecology and environment. Such degradation lowers the economic attractiveness of urban areas despite realizing short-term economic benefits. City-regions also present opportunities to reduce environmental risks and safeguard ecosystems through focus on resilient and resource-efficient urban development (Lee, 2015). Enhancing the efficiency of available ecological resources, in particular, the efficiency of urban forests can have a positive effect on multiple ecological services such as water supply regulation and air quality for improving the quality of life and competitiveness. Such opportunities facilitate enhanced quality of life and conservation of natural resources, thereby influencing the economic competitiveness of city-regions. Resource efficiency is explained as the ratio of per unit out of a resource to input (Auzi et al., 2014) and is associated with compact and high-density urban forms (Dempsey et al., 2010). The ecology and environment-based urban development approaches such as the eco-city, compact city and urban resiliency lay emphasis on land use and land cover patterns for more sustainable cities and city-regions (Hu, 2015). These approaches aid competitiveness by: (1) promoting higher land-use efficiency in the form of ecological efficiency and economic efficiency; and (2) building resilience, the ability of a city or city-region to absorb and recover from external stress such as natural disasters. Such approaches also raise the significance of urban regeneration strategies, such as the restoration of urban land and ecosystems and promotion of urban agriculture for enhancing productivity and competitiveness (Habitat III, 2016; Singhal et al., 2013). Land-use efficiency is an important socio-economic indicator that affects ecosystem health of a region (Costanza, 2012). The ecology-based approach to competitiveness emphasizes achieving ecological efficiency, economic efficiency and resilience, and increasing access to ecosystem benefits.

Progressive city-regions around the world are striving to enhance their ecological competitiveness through more efficient use of ecological resources and increased resilience. The unsustainable patterns of consumption and production, steered under the disguise of raising standards of living, pose threats to the environment and ecological health of challenged city-regions in developing economies (Jayanti and Gowda, 2014). Mega city-regions in India, China and Brazil are facing high levels of carbon emissions, high concentration of particulate matter and scarcity of water due to depleting natural resources. Cities in countries such as Peru and Russia, despite access to a rich natural resources base, forest resources and protected areas, exhibit poor environmental performance mainly due to weak implementation of environment-related regulations and policies (WEF, 2013). Improving ecological efficiency calls for conservation and management of existing resources in cities from emerging economies characterized by high urban density and high rates of biodiversity loss (Abbu et al., 2015). Balanced urban development reduces dependence on ecological resources and has the potential to assist in ecosystem recovery. For example, the protected mangrove forests in Navi Mumbai have shown an increase in population of Lesser Flamingoes, an indication of recovery of the forest ecosystem, attributed to reduced dependency on wood fuel of the nearby villages which are now a part of the urban area (Nagendra et al., 2013). The conservation and management strategies for protected areas in urban settings, and regulation of economic activities in ecologically sensitive urban areas, can contribute to enhancing ecological competitiveness. Protected areas, in city-regions, are the geographic spaces aim for long-term protection and management of existing natural resources to halt habitat loss and degradation (Srivastava and Tyagi, 2016).

In the context of urban land-use planning, economic efficiency relates to the increase in productivity of land through strategies such as restoring the degraded land and ecosystem, an important component of the Convention for Biological Diversity, 2002, for facilitating increase in ecological connectivity (Jongman, 2016) and increase in green cover to enhance resilience (OECD, 2012). An example of restoring landscape connectivity is the eco-regional plan for Northern Great Plains in the United States of America that aims at extensive restoration of habitat across protected areas and outer areas for increasing spatial connectivity to supports species movement (Keenleyside et al., 2012). Considering the high anthropogenic pressures on ecological resources and the high value of ecological services in developing countries, protective strategies through locally appropriate solutions (Hostetler et al., 2011; Keenleyside et al., 2012) are critical for increasing the resilience at multiple scales. Identifying critical land areas which can improve ecosystem resilience can help in insuring cities and city-regions against external disturbances. This insurance value is more likely to yield long-term economic benefits through environmental cost savings while reducing dependency or degrading remote and non-urban ecosystems. Hence, investment in land and ecosystem restoration to reduce risk and increase insurance capacity is an important strategy for increasing competitiveness and resilience (Costanza, 2012; Green et al., 2016). For example, as a response to flood hazards in Mahanadi Delta, the State Government of Odisha invested in nature-based solutions to restore the degraded land (Lee, 2015).

This chapter presents the status of development towards ecological environment competitiveness in India. It first provides an outline of various national policies and top-down strategies of increasing protected areas, increasing restored land and ecosystems, and notification of ecologically sensitive areas, that tend to draw attention towards the ecological dimension for urban and regional development in India. The next section focuses on conservation and management of forest resources in select city-regions in India and outlines key strategies aimed to raise the ecological profile of city-regions. The "Discussion" section presents a tiered framework for strengthening the urban ecological competitiveness of cities and city-regions, and emphasizes governance, knowledge platforms and finance for operationalizing the framework.

TOWARDS ECOLOGICAL ENVIRONMENT COMPETITIVENESS IN INDIA

India was among the first few countries that included protection and management of the environment in the National Constitution (MoEFCC, 2015). However, the country's urban environmental and ecological performance remains poor, mainly due to weak implementation of policies and regulations (WEF, 2013). India has set an enabling policy landscape for conservation and management of urban ecological resources through strategies aimed at increasing protected areas, managing protected areas by designating ecologically sensitive zones and restoring degraded land and ecosystems (Kapoor et al., 2009; Ravi and Priyadarsanan, 2015). The policies such as the National Mission on

Green India, 2014 and the Wildlife Action Plan 2002–2016 aimed at improving environmental services and supporting the country's commitment to the United Nations (UN) 2030 Agenda for Sustainable Development and the Convention on Biological Diversity (CBD) 2002 (MoEFCC, 2019, 2015; NITI Aayog, 2018). National-level strategies for building ecological competitiveness aim at protection of ecological resources, regulating activities in ecologically sensitive areas, and restoring degraded land and ecosystems to improve the productivity of land for increasing ecological, economic efficiency and resilience in city-regions.

Increasing Protected Areas for Ecological Efficiency

Urban ecosystems are impacted by the consumption patterns and planning approaches that influence the quality of life and protected area in the city and its catchment region (Keenleyside et al., 2012). In India, the National Wildlife Action Plan 2002–2016 has been a key policy aimed at effective conservation and management of protected areas and biodiversity conservation. Under this policy initiative, areas outside the protected area network also are to be protected to avoid habitat fragmentation (Kapoor et al., 2009). This policy assigns responsibility to the state governments to identify and designate ecologically sensitive zones around the protected areas and to regulate anthropogenic activities in such areas. As a result, between 1988 and 2012 (see Table 9.1), India recorded an increase of 89 percent in the number of national parks and an increase of 38 percent in the number of wildlife sanctuaries (Wildlife Institute of India, 2012).

Table 9.1   Change in land under protected areas in India

Category	1988			2012			% increase		Increase in net area (km)
	No.	Area (km)	%	No.	Area (km)	%	No.	Area	
National parks	54	21 003	0.64	102	39 888.11	1.21	89	90	18 885
Wildlife sanctuaries	372	88 649	2.7	515	119 838.63	3.65	38	35	31 190
Community reserves	–	–	–	4	20.69	<0.01	–	–	20.69
Conservation reserves	–	–	–	48	1 384.59	0.04	–	–	1 384.59
Protected areas	426	109 652	3.34	669	161 132.02	4.90	57	47	51 480.28

Source: Wildlife Institute of India (2012).

Among various states, Delhi launched the Biodiversity Parks program to restore degraded land and ecosystems, and the state of Gujarat so far has the maximum number of notified ecologically sensitive areas in the country.

Notifying Ecologically Sensitive Areas (ESAs) for Building Resilience

Ecological sensitivity is explained as the possibility of permanent and irreparable loss of extant life-forms from the world (Srivastava and Tyagi, 2016). Ecologically Sensitive Areas/Zones (ESA/ESZ) act as shock absorbers for increasing resilience in a region. In city-regions of India, the percentage of notified ESAs is greater in suburban areas and less in the core areas of cities. This can be attributed to the fact that green spaces are found to be better protected in the core of cities, such as in Bengaluru and Pune (Nagendra et al., 2013). The Environment (Protection) Act 1986 empowers the Central Government of India to take measures necessary for conservation of ecological resources in the country. The Act provides power to the Central Government to restrict activities in ecologically sensitive areas based on considerations such as biological diversity in an area and proximity to protected areas. The National Wild Life Action Plan 2002–2016 and the Environment Impact Assessment Notification 2006 also incorporated provisions for ecologically sensitive areas (Kapoor et al., 2009; MoEFCC, 2019). The identification of ESAs is done by the state governments, and proposals are notified by the Central Government. Once notified, the host state has responsibility to prepare an Ecologically Sensitive Zone plan that provides details of prohibited, restricted and permissible activities in the notified area. For example, prohibition of industrial activities such as mining was an important factor for conserving the forest network in the National Capital Region of Delhi (Government of Rajasthan, 1992). Likewise, regulating tourism in the ESA of Matheran in Mumbai Metropolitan Region has been an important factor in managing water scarcity in the region (MMRDA, 2019). Such context-specific strategies assist in regulating ecosystem services such as water supply, and protect self-sustaining and regenerative natural resources for ecological competitiveness.

Increasing Productivity of Degraded Land and Ecosystems

Land degradation affects the provision of ecosystem services, resulting in a decline of economic returns from land that influences the economic efficiency of the resource base (TERI, 2018). City-regions in India are largely dependent on catchment areas outside city boundaries for the provision of certain ecosystem services such as the supply of water, that are adversely affected due to contamination and degradation in catchment areas (Habitat III, 2016). Strategies for implementing restoration include increasing the landscape connectivity and enhancing ecological services for economic and ecological efficiency in cities and city-regions (Keenleyside et al., 2012). In India, policy initiatives such as the National Afforestation program aim at sustainability and management of forest resources, and at increasing and improving forest and tree cover through rehabilitation of degraded forests. Likewise, the Green India Mission aims to increase the forest cover in urban and peri-urban areas. Complementing such national policy initiatives, many cities such as Delhi have their own city-level policies for restoring degraded ecosystems, indicating ecological and economic efficiency of land as an important agenda across multiple levels of governance (ICFRE, 2008).

CONSERVATION AND MANAGEMENT OF FOREST RESOURCES FOR ECOLOGICAL ENVIRONMENT COMPETITIVENESS IN SELECT METROPOLITAN REGIONS

Availability of forested land in urban regions is an important indicator for competitiveness as it measures the stock of renewable resources available for economic growth (Brabec and Lewis, 2012). Forest land use in urban areas has the highest greenhouse gas emissions due to land use and land cover changes. Restoring degraded forest land and increasing the forest cover in city-regions for enhancing carbon sinks in natural ecosystems is also part of the call for action against climate change by the Intergovernmental Panel for Climate Change (IPCC) (DeFries et al., 2007). While there are no international standards for a minimum per capita requirement of urban forest cover, experts from developed countries propose 140 m² urban/suburban forest area per capita for maintaining ecological balance and provisioning of ecosystem services for human well-being (Singh et al., 2010). Among developed countries, the Greater Paris region has 80 m² of urban forest per inhabitant (Konijnendijk, 2003), and the city of Tokyo has a forest area of 21 630 ha. In India, metropolitan cities of Delhi (5.5 km²) and Bengaluru (17.79 km²) are rich in forest resources (Govindarajulu, 2014). The "forest area," or "recorded forest area," in India refers to the geographic areas recorded as forest that comprise reserved forests and protected forests (as per the

Indian Forest Act, 1927). "Forest cover" refers to all land areas of more than 1 hectare with a tree canopy density of more than 10 percent.

Among major causes, mining is one of the most critical economic activities that continues to cause land degradation in urban forested areas in India (Bhaskar, 2012; TERI, 2018). Over the years, the Forest Survey of India has recorded an increase in forest cover in many cities and metropolitan regions (Table 9.2) of which Delhi has recorded the highest increase (3 km^2) in forest cover from 2017 to 2019. Among smaller metro cities, Ahmedabad (2 km^2) and Coimbatore (9 km^2) have shown increase in forest cover; whereas cities such as Gandhinagar, Chennai, Nagpur and Surat indicate a decrease in forest cover. The decrease in scrub land area has been recorded only in the cities of Delhi, Ahmedabad and Surat; whereas the other metropolitan cities indicate an increase. Table 9.2 presents a comparison of forest cover per 10 000 population and forest cover per unit built-up area for five selected metropolitan regions in India: Delhi, Mumbai, Bengaluru, Surat and Chennai. Three large metropolitan regions and two smaller metropolitan regions have been selected based on strategies for forest resources in the Regional Master Plans.

Table 9.2   Relative efficiency of forest resources in selected metropolitan regions in India

Metro-politan region	Geo-graphic area (sqm)	Area under forest cover (km)	% of GA	Popu-lation/ 10 000 (2021)	Forest cover per 10 000 popu-lation	Relative efficiency forest cover per 10 000 popu-lation	Built-up area	Forest area/ built-up area	Relative efficiency forest cover for built-up area
Mumbai	4 311	833	19.32	2 651.90	31.41	0.47	697.01	119.51	1.00
Chennai	1 189	24	2.01	1 119.70	2.14	0.03	426.00	5.63	0.05
Surat	4 418	92	2.08	663.30	13.87	0.21	288.70	31.87	0.27
Delhi	54 980	2 064	3.75	6 413.80	32.18	0.48	2 635.00	78.33	0.66
Bengaluru	8 006	831	10.38	1 250.00	66.48	1.00	723.00	114.94	0.96

Sources: BMRDA (2016), CMDA (2013), MMRDA (2019), NCRPB (2013) and SUDA (2017).

In some of the major metropolitan regions in India the core cities (such as Mumbai, Delhi, Bengaluru and Chennai) have nearly half of their population living in the metropolitan area. The forest area in these cities constitutes less than 10 percent of the geographic area, with the exception of Mumbai Metropolitan Region (19 percent). In smaller metropolitan regions of Surat and Coimbatore, the majority of the population live in the core city area and the forest cover available is more than 10 percent of the geographic area of the respective metropolitan region. There is huge variation in per capita availability of forest resources between the five metropolitan regions. The availability of forest resources per 10 000 population ranges from as low as 2 percent in Chennai to as high as 32 percent in Delhi and 31 percent in Mumbai. The forest cover per 10 000 population is highest in the Bengaluru region and lowest in the Chennai metropolitan area. The relative efficiency of forest cover compared to the built-up area is highest in the Mumbai metropolitan region and lowest for the Chennai metropolitan area. The Chennai metropolitan region clearly indicates the most inefficient use of forest resources, followed by Surat metropolitan area. Bengaluru has a rich forest resource use based on both population statistics and built-up area, thus indicating a higher potential to enhance ecological competitiveness in the cities of Bengaluru and Delhi. At district level (Table 9.3), Alwar, Bharatpur, Delhi NCT and Surat city have shown a decrease in scrub land area between 2017 and 2019. Of these, Alwar district in the state of Rajasthan is covered under the Aravali Notification 1992, which recognizes the Aravalli range as an ecologically sensitive area (Government of Rajasthan, 1992).

Most districts in the metropolitan regions have recorded an increase in forest cover (Table 9.3) with an increase of 35 km^2 in Thane district of Mumbai metropolitan region and 53.45 km^2 in Bengaluru district. Districts such as Chennai city and Kancheepuram district in Chennai metropolitan area and Gaziabad in Delhi National Capital Region (NCR) have shown a marginal decrease in forest cover.

CITY-REGION STRATEGIES FOR URBAN ECOLOGICAL COMPETITIVENESS

An analysis of selected metropolitan region master plans (Mumbai, Delhi, Bengaluru, Chennai and Surat) and district plans (Mumbai, Delhi, Bengaluru, Chennai, Surat and Coimbatore) indicates that regions in India address urban ecological competitiveness aspects through key strategies relating to prohibiting mining activities, regulating ecotourism, increasing habitat connectivity, biodiversity conservation and increasing forest cover at the district, city and city-region levels. These bottom-up strategies are in different ways interlinked with the top-down strategies identified for strengthening urban ecological competitiveness in India.

Table 9.3   Change in forest cover and scrub cover in selected districts of metropolitan regions in India

	Region	Geo-graphic area (km)	Area under forest (2019)	% of geo-graphic area	Change in forest cover (2017–2019)	Area under scrub (2019)	Area under scrub (2017)	Change in scrub (2017–2019)
1	Mumbai metropolitan region							
	Thane	9 558	2 998.09	31.37	35.09	261.07	228.00	33.07
	Mumbai city	157	3.00	1.19	0	0	0.00	0.00
	Mumbai suburban	446	139.86	31.36	−0.14	0.43	0.00	0.43
	Raigad district	7 152	2 939.46	41.10	22.46	77.60	71.00	6.60
2	Delhi NCR							
	Delhi NCT	1 483	195.44	13.18	3.03	0.30	0.67	−0.37
	Ghaziabad	1 179	25.22	2.14	−0.78	0	0	0.00
	Noida	1 282	20.00	1.56	0	0	0	0.00
	Meerut	2 559	68.41	2.67	0.41	0	0	0.00
	Muzzafarnagar	4 008	66.11	1.65	26.11	0	0	0.00
	Alwar	8 380	1 196.60	14.28	−0.34	245.66	246.00	−0.34
	Bharatpur	5 066	230.27	4.55	1.27	77.93	79.00	−1.07
	Karnal	2 520	32.24	1.28	0.24	0.76	1.00	−0.24
	Faridabad	741	79.94	10.79	−0.06	17.76	17.00	0.76
	Gurgaon	1 258	116.18	9.24	−0.82	17.00	17.00	0.00
	Jhajjar	1 834	25.93	1.41	1.93	4.00	4.00	0.00
3	Chennai metropolitan area							
	Chennai city	175	12.84	7.34	−1.16	0	0.00	0.00
	Kanchipuram district	4 483	307.78	6.87	−2.22	35.75	34.00	1.75
	Tiruvallur district	3 394	285.67	8.42	−1.33	49.43	50.00	−0.57
4	Bangalore							
	Ramanagara	3 516	664.69	18.90	53.69	170.09	170.00	0.09
	Bangalore urban	2 196	287.43	13.09	53.43	8.00	8.00	0.00
5	Surat							
	Surat city	4 549	500.06	10.99	−14.94	81.94	90.00	−8.06
6	Coimbatore							
	Coimbatore	4 732	1 984.64	41.94	9.64	7.01	1.00	6.01
	Erode	5 760	2 294.46	39.83	−12.54	36.73	32.00	4.73
	Tiruppur	5 187	844.43	16.28	39.43	8.78	8.00	0.78
	The Nilgiris	2 565	1 731.01	67.49	12.01	6.85	4.00	2.85

Sources: Compiled from FSI (2017, 2019).

Prohibiting Mining Activities

Mining is an important economic activity that continues to cause land degradation and fragmentation in urban forested areas (Keenleyside et al., 2012). Hence, prohibiting mining of important mineral resources in forested areas is vital for meeting various policy goals and maintaining the ecological efficiency. Prohibiting mining activities is an important aspect of notified ecologically sensitive areas. For example, mining was the major industrial activity in Alwar before it was banned in the 1990s; however, the Alwar Eco Sensitive Zone Plan in Delhi region now prohibits mining activities in the district (NCRPB, 2013). The over-exploitation of resources through mining in the Aravalli Range has led to large-scale fragmentation of forest ecosystem in the Delhi region.

Regulating Ecotourism

Over the last decade ecotourism around protected areas has witnessed a growth of 6 percent in India. However, the current mass tourism approach is detrimental for the environment and for urban ecological competitiveness (Poyyamoli, 2018), and there are calls for regulating tourism activities around protected areas in designated ESAs. As an example, the Matheran eco-sensitive zone plan that spans parts of Raigad and Thane districts in Mumbai metropolitan region aims to regulate tourism in the region. The plan limits and regulates development and construction of resorts and guest-houses in the eco-sensitive zone. The plan has an established ecotourism regulating strategy based on the availability of water in the region and on the carrying capacity of the eco-sensitive region (MMRDA, 2019). Other examples where ecotourism policies have been implemented include Periyar Tiger Reserve, Thekkady community-based ecotourism in partnership with the forest department, Kerala and the Kumbalangi community-based ecotourism village near Kochi, Kerela (Poyyamoli, 2018).

Increasing Habitat Connectivity

Many protected areas in India are intercepted by linear infrastructures such as roads and transmission lines thereby causing habitat fragmentation. Some examples of barriers to connectivity include National Highway (NH) 72 and 74 which cross Rajaji National Park (WII, 2016). The problems of maintaining connectivity and biodiversity conservation along such linear infrastructures can be addressed through comprehensive green infrastructure strategies that facilitate an increase in the ecological connectivity in urban and suburban regions (WII, 2016). To maintain the habitat connectivity in ecologically sensitive zones, some city-regions have designated species movement corridors in their regional plan. For example, the Coimbatore region has a designated 1 km wide elephant corridor around the reserved forest area in the districts of Erode, Tiruppur and Nilgiris. The Erode sub-region has a policy aimed at increasing the (ecological) competitiveness and resilience of the region that includes conservation and the management of forest resources (SPA, 2018). Likewise, the existing protected area network in Alwar district that includes the Sariska Tiger Reserve is highly fragmented. For this purpose, the protected zone had been increased by 234 km^2 and a designated Tiger corridor leading up to Jaipur in Rajasthan had been assigned in the region (Government of Rajasthan, 1992). These district-level initiatives indicate the recognition of the need for protection of ecological resources to promote urban ecological competiveness and resilience. However, these are disjointed approaches that need to be streamlined and applied to other districts to increase their connectivity and resilience, and to maximize their ecological benefits for enhanced competitiveness.

Biodiversity Conservation and Ecological Restoration

In India, a key objective of designating protected areas and ecologically sensitive areas is biodiversity conservation (MoEFCC, 2019). Bio-diversity conservation in cities and city-regions helps in maintaining important ecosystem processes to ensure the provision of ecosystem services. However, success of the biodiversity conservation measures depends on the development status of the respective region. In the urban context, a key challenge relating to the biodiversity conservation is to protect fringe areas from encroachment and to increase connectivity. Under the Biodiversity Act 2002, the state government is expected to notify areas of biodiversity importance as Biodiversity Heritage Sites (BHSs) and can frame rules for the management and conservation of such sites (MoEFCC, 2015). In India there are 12 notified Biodiversity Heritage Sites; however, these sites do not propose restrictions on development activities in the notified area. Some initiatives relating to biodiversity conservation include the Sanjay Gandhi National Park in Mumbai and the Sundar Nursery project for biodiversity conservation in Delhi (Mayes et al., 2004). For Delhi, the Biodiversity Parks programme in collaboration with the Centre for Environmental Management of Degraded Ecosystems, University of Delhi, funded by the Delhi Devel-opment Authority (DDA), was formulated for restoring degraded and barren forest areas in the region. Under this programme, the Aravalli Biodiversity Park had been developed over an area of 2.8km², and is referred to as an urban (green) infrastructure for Delhi (CEMDE, 2018; Dhasmana, 2016). Similarly, in the city of Gurugram, the Aravalli Biodiversity Park that forms part of the extended forest network from Delhi lies in the state of Haryana (part of Delhi NCR) and is owned by the Municipal Corporation of Gurugram (Dhasmana, 2016).

Increasing Forest Cover

Urban forest systems can provide many environmental and ecological benefits and help in maintaining biodiversity to increase the ecological efficiency of city-regions (Chaudhry et al., 2011). Proximity to urban forests (and other green areas) is also known to have a positive effect on property prices (Singh et al., 2010). Change (increase) in forest cover has been indicated in the literature as an important indicator for urban competiveness (Hu, 2015). Table 9.2 indicates that most districts in selected city-regions in India show an increase in forest cover recently (between 2017 and 2019). This can be attributed to policies and investments such as the National Green Mission and the National Afforestation Programme (NAP) that have led to an overall increase in forest and tree cover by 21.4 percent at the national level (ICFRE, 2008). At the state level, the State Government of Telangana launched the Telangana Ku Haritha Haram program with the aim to increase the forest and tree cover in the state from 24 percent to 33 percent (EPTRI, 2015). The Ama Jungle Yojana of the Government of Odisha is implementing a scheme to create 5000 ha of new forest cover in six years (2016/17 to 2021/22) (Government of Odisha, 2019).

DISCUSSION

Based on the top-down and bottom-up strategies for urban ecological competitiveness described above, this section proposes a broad framework for strengthening urban ecological competitiveness in the country. This chapter raises the significance of ecological competitiveness complementing the existing emphasis on the economic dimension of urban competitiveness. The need for greater attention to ecological efficiency, building resilience and economic efficiency, is highlighted in the context of city-regions exposed to pressures of urbanization in emerging economies. The importance is indicated of a multi-scalar approach for strengthening the existing governance mechanism through specific top-down strategies for city-regions that are challenged to address the ecological dimension of competitiveness. The variance in availability and management of ecological resources in city-regions in India indicates the need for an integrated approach. In this context, a tiered framework for strengthening the ecology-based urban competitiveness is presented in Figure 9.1.

In this tiered framework, Tier 2 presents three dimensions of ecological competitiveness relating to ecological efficiency, economic efficiency and resilience of cities and city-regions. Tier 3 mentions three key outcomes targeted from the top-down national policy initiatives that relate to three dimensions presented in Tier 2. Tier 4 outlines five key strategies that are advocated to be promoted by cities and city-regions to strengthen their ecological competitiveness. City-regions in India exhibit varying levels of maturity in achieving ecological efficiency. The relative efficiency of forest resources is high in the cities of Delhi and Bengaluru where the availability of forest resources is high. Likewise, the relative efficiency of forest resources is low in the cities of Chennai and Mumbai where availability of forest resources is low. To fast-track an increase in ecological efficiency in cities in emerging economies would require proper institutional systems for the conservation and management of resources and ecosystem services. The three key overarching strategies required to operationalize the tiered framework for strengthening urban ecological competitiveness, with emphasis on governance, knowledge platforms and finance, are presented below.

Governance for Urban Ecological Competitiveness

An enabling policy and regulatory environment is essential to facilitate the country's pathway towards enhancing the ecological competitiveness of its cities and city-regions. Urban competitiveness and urban governance are interrelated, and the pursuit of ecology-based urban competitiveness in India necessitates strengthening the effectiveness of multi-level governance through effective coordination between the Central Government, state governments, and urban and regional local institutions. The concomitant awareness-generation of beneficiary communities, and sensitization and capacity enhancement of the professionals from key stakeholder institutions, is imperative. Streamlined horizontal coordination across engaged institutions at the city, region and state level will facilitate the desired implementation of overarching policy initiatives, regulations and sectoral strategies such as those relating to forestry and water resources. With respect to forest resources in India, there are examples of top-down policy initiatives such as the National Afforestation Programme, and bottom-up district and city-region-level examples

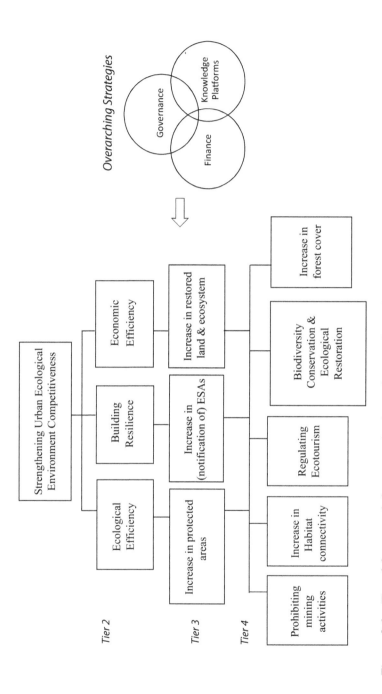

Figure 9.1 Tiered framework for strengthening urban ecological competitiveness of cities and city-regions in India

such as notified Ecologically Sensitive Zones in Matheran and Coimbatore, which highlight the initiatives taken for achieving ecological efficiency. Likewise, Delhi's Biodiversity Parks program, and Telangana's program to increase forest cover, highlight the importance of restoring degraded ecosystems to increase land productivity and economic efficiency. However, these are disjointed approaches in select states which call for a broader policy integration on top-down and bottom-up strategies to enhance ecological competitiveness through multiple levels of governance in India. The value of this multi-scalar approach in examining and addressing such urban ecological competitiveness aspects is to create economies of scale. There is also an urgent need to enlarge the pool of experts and city managers who are noticeably sensitized towards the ecological dimension of development in cities and city-regions. The higher education institutions have a significant role to play in creating such social capital.

Knowledge Platforms for Urban Ecological Competitiveness

To strengthen the ecological dimension for urban competitiveness, a comprehensive research-led approach needs to be promoted for effective formulation and implementation of policies, strategies and action plans in India. Knowledge exchange partnerships between striving city-regions from emerging economies and performing city-regions from mature economies, focusing on ecological dimensions, will enrich the existing policy and praxis discourse. Furthermore, the requirement to strengthen the capacity and engagement of, and result-oriented partnerships between, public sector institutions, the business sector, research institutions and community-based organizations needs to be addressed through innovative ecology-based planning and assessment tools, technology advancement and advanced training opportunities for professionals. In India, there is an urgent need to streamline and extend the existing database relating to the availability and management of ecological resources, for informed planning and decision-making. An academy of urban ecological competitiveness led by a consortium of national research and public sector institutions in partnership with leading international institutions will accelerate the agenda for India.

Financing for Urban Ecological Competitiveness

According to the Economic Survey of India, 2016, an investment of US$2.5 trillion will be needed between 2015 and 2030 for strengthening resilience and (natural) disaster management in the country; and US$206 billion would be required between 2015 and 2030 for implementing adaptation actions in key areas such as forestry, water resources and ecosystems. India's National Action Plan on Climate Change in 2008 provides the broad policy for climate change action; however, it lacks a policy framework for engaging the financial sector proactively. Financial sustainability through tools such as environmental taxes, insurances, green bonds and promotion of sustainable patterns of consumption needs to be enhanced to achieve this, through spreading awareness and address-ing the behavioral aspects of all engaged stakeholders. Innovative finan-cing and business models, such as green bonds and private sector investment in ecosystem restoration, are necessary for large-scale implementation of nature-based solutions (Keenleyside et al., 2012). Monitoring and sharing information among regions is critical to actively engage in promoting the ecological competitiveness of urban regions in India.

REFERENCES

Abbu, N., Bhagavatula, L., Rao-Ghorpade, A., et al., "Urban Green Growth Strategies for Indian Cities," *ICLEI-Local Governments for Sustainability, South Asia*, Vol. 1, 2015.

Auzi, A., Geipele, S., and Geipele, I., "New Indicator System for Evaluation of Land Use Efficiency," *Proceedings of the 2014 International Conference on Industrial Engineering and Operations Management, Bali, Indonesia*, 2014, pp. 2285–2293.

Bangalore Metropolitan Region Development Authority (BMRDA), "Final Report Revised of Structure Plan – 2031 Bangalore Metropolitan Region," 2016.

Bhaskar, P., "Urbanization and Changing Green Spaces in Indian Cities (Case Study – City of Pune)," *International Journal of Geology*, Vol. 2, No. 2, 2012, pp. 148–156.

Brabec, E., and Lewis, G.M.D., "Defining the Pattern of the Sustainable Urban Region – Development of Regional Measurement Methods," Advances in Architecture Series, 2012.

Centre for Environmental Management of Degraded Ecosystems (CEMDE), *Biodiversity Parks: Examples of Innovation and Best Practices for Biodiversity Conservation*, Centre for Environmental Management of Degraded Eco-systems, University of Delhi, 2018.

Chaudhry, P., Bagra, K., and Singh, B., "Urban Greenery Status of Some Indian Cities: A Short Communication," *International Journal of Environmental Scientific Development*, Vol. 2, No. 2, 2011, pp. 98–101.

Chennai Metropolitan Development Authority (CMDA), *Second Master Plan For Chennai Metropolitan Area, 2026*, Vol. 2, Chennai: Chennai Metropolitan Development Authority, 2013.

Costanza, R., "Ecosystem Health and Ecological Engineering," *Ecological Engineering*, Vol. 45, 2012, pp. 24–29.

DeFries, R., Achard, F., Brown, S., Martin, H., Daniel, M., et al., "Earth Observations for Estimating Greenhouse Gas Emissions from Deforestation in Developing Countries," *Environmental Science and Policy*, Vol. 10, No. 4, 2007, pp. 385–394.

Dempsey, N., Porta, S., Jenks, M., and Jones, C., "Elements of Urban Form," in Jenks, M., and Jones, C. (eds), *Dimensions of the Sustainable Cities*, London: Springer, 2010.

Dhasmana, V., "Healing Touch – Aravalli Biodiversity Park, Gurgaon," *Landscape Architecture*, 2016.

Environment Protection Training and Research Institute (EPTRI), *State Action Plan on Climate Change for Telangana State*, Ministry of Environment, Forests and Climate Change Government of India, 2015.

Forest Survey of India (FSI), *State Forest Report of India*, Forest Survey of India, 2017.

Forest Survey of India (FSI), *State Forest Report of India*, Forest Survey of India, 2019.

Government of Odisha, *Highlights of Odisha Forestry Sector 2019*, Forest and Environment Department, Bhubhaneshwar, India, 2019.

Government of Rajasthan, *Environmental Master Plan Alwar District, for Areas Covered under Aravali, Notification dated 7th May 1992*, Jaipur: Government of Rajasthan, 1992.

Govindarajulu, D., "Urban Green Space Planning for Climate Adaptation in Indian Cities," *Urban Climate*, Vol. 10, No. P1, 2014, pp. 35–41.

Green, T., Kronenberg, J., Andersson, E., Elmqvist, T., and Gomez-Baggethun, E., "Insurance Value of Green Infrastructure in and Around Cities," *Ecosystems*, Vol. 19, 2016, pp. 1051–1063.

Habitat III, *Urban Ecology and Resilience*, Policy Papers: Policy Paper 8, United Nations Conference on Housing and Sustainable Urban Development, Habitat III, New York: United Nations, 2016.

Hostetler, M., Allen, W., and Meurk, C., "Conserving Urban Biodiversity? Creating Green Infrastructure is Only the First Step," *Landscape Urban Planning*, Vol. 100, No. 4, 2011, pp. 369–371.

Hu, R., "Sustainability and Competitiveness in Australian Cities," *Sustainability*, Vol. 7, No. 2, 2015, pp. 1840–1860.

Indian Council of Forestry Research and Education (ICFRE), "Mid Term Evaluation of the National Afforestation Program (NAP) Schemes Implemented through Forest Development Agencies (FDAs)," submitted to National Afforestation and Eco-Development Board (NAEB), Ministry of Environment and Forests (MoEF), Government of India, Dehradun, India, 2008.

Jayanti, R.K., and Gowda, M.V.R., "Sustainability Dilemmas in Emerging Economies," *IIMB Management Review*, Vol. 26, No. 2, 2014, pp. 130–142.

Jongman, R.H.G., "Connectivity and Ecological Networks," *Landscape Institute Technical Informantion Note 01*, 2016, pp. 366–376.

Kapoor, M., Kohli, K., and Menon, M., *India's Notified Ecologically Sensitive Areas (ESAs) The Story so far … ,* New Delhi: Kalpavriksh and WWF-India, 2009.

Keenleyside, K., Dudley, N., Cairns, S., Hall, C., and Stolton, S., "Ecological Restoration for Protected Areas Principles, Guidelines and Best Practices," Guidelines Series No. 18, Prepared by the IUCN WCPA Ecological Restoration Taskforce, Gland, Switzerland: IUCN, 2012.

Konijnendijk, C.C., "A Decade of Urban Forestry in Europe," *Forest Policy and Economics*, Vol. 5, 2003, pp. 175–186.

Lee, S., "Resource Efficiency for Green and Resilient Urban Development in the Asia-Pacific Region – The Case of Water," prepared for United Nations Economic and Social Commission for Asia and the Pacific, 2015.

Mayes, R., Bhale, P., and Bhatti, I., *Sanjay Gandhi National Park, A Concise Report*, London: University of East London, 2004.

Ministry of Environment, Forest and Climate Change (MoEFCC), Government of India, *First Biennial Update Report to the United Nations Framework Convention on Climate Change*, 2015.

MoEFCC, *Implementation of India's National Biodiversity Action Plan: An Overview*, Ministry of Environment, Forest and Climate Change, Government of India, 2019.

Mumbai Metropolitan Region Development Authority (MMRDA), *Zonal Master Plan for Matheran Eco-Sensitive Zone (MESZ) 2016–2036*, Provisions for Zonal Master Plan for Matheran Eco-Sensitive Zone, Mumbai: Mumbai Metropolitan Region Development Authority, 2019.

Nagendra, H., Sudhira, H.S., Katti, M., and Schewenius, M., "Sub-regional Assessment of India: Effects of Urbanization on Land Use, Biodiversity and Ecosystem Services," *Urbanization, Biodiversity and Ecosystems Services: Challenges and Opportunities. A Global Assessment*, 2013.

National Capital Region Planning Board (NCRPB), *Regional Plan 2021 National Capital Region*, Ministry of Urban Development, Government of India, 2013.

NITI Aayog, *SDG INDIA INDEX: 2018 Baseline Report*, 2018.

Organisation for Economic Co-operation and Development (OECD), *Monitoring Land Cover Change*, 2012.

Poyyamoli, G., "Ecotourism Policy in India: Rhetoric and Reality," *Grassroots Journal of Natural Resources*, Vol. 1, No. 1, 2018, pp. 46–61.

Ravi, R., and Priyadarsanan, D.R., "Needs for Policy on Landscape Restoration in India," *Current Science*, Vol. 108, No. 7, 2015, pp. 1208–1209.

School of Planning and Architecture (SPA) Bhopal, *Coimbatore Regional Plan 2038*, 2018.

Singh, V.S., Pandey, D.N., and Chaudhry, P., "Urban Forests and Open Green Spaces: Lessons for Jaipur, Rajasthan, India," Rajasthan State Pollution Control Board Occasional Paper No. 1, Jaipur, India, 2010.

Singhal, S., Stanley, M., and Berry, J., "Application of a Hierarchical Model for City Competitiveness in Cities of India," *Cities*, Vol. 31, 2013, pp. 114–122.

Srivastava, R., and Tyagi, R., "Wildlife Corridors in India," *Environmental Law Review*, Vol. 18, No. 3, 2016, pp. 205–223.

Surat Urban Development Authority (SUDA), *Surat Development Plan, 2035*, 2017.

The Energy and Resources Institute (TERI), *Economics of Desertification, Land Degradation and Drought in India Macroeconomic Assessment of the Costs of*

Land Degradation in India, Prepared for Ministry of Environment, Forest and Climate Change, New Delhi, Vol. 1, 2018.

Wildlife Institute of India (WII), *Action Plan for Implementing the Programme of Work on Protected Areas of the Convention on Biological Diversity Protected Area Information*, Submitted to the Secretariat of the Convention on Biological Diversity, Dehradun, 2012, pp. 1–10.

Wildlife Institute of India (WII). *Eco-friendly Measures to Mitigate Impacts of Linear Infrastructure on Wildlife*, Dehradun: Wildlife Institute of India, Vol. 1, No. 1, 2016, pp. 1–168.

World Economic Forum (WEF), *Assessing the Sustainable Competitiveness of Nations, The Global Competitiveness Report*, 2013.

10. Metropolitan development and geographical deconcentration in Mexico, 1980–2015

Jaime Sobrino

The territorial distribution of the population and its activities is characterized by temporary patterns of concentration and dispersion. These trends are the product of processes that occur over time, where at some point demographic, economic and territorial factors push towards geographical concentration, while at another time the interrelationship of these factors, together with political and environmental ones, lead to a relative dispersion, which can be in the form of centripetal forces and centrifugal forces. These territorial patterns are presented at different geographical scales: (1) global, with territorial units being the countries; (2) supraregional, with a group of countries again being observation units; (3) national, where territorial units are subnational spaces, or major administrative divisions; (4) regional-metropolitan, where regional units are minor administrative divisions; and (5) metropolitan-urban, where territorial units under review are urbanized space areas.

The purpose of this chapter is to discuss the concepts of geographical deconcentration of population and employment for the context of Latin American metropolises, and to provide empirical evidence on the processes of demographic deconcentration in Mexico in the period 1980–2015, in the interaction of national and regional-metropolitan geographical scales, trying to establish the links that are generated between the two scales. To accomplish the objective, bibliographic references of spatial economic theory are used, especially that made for Latin America, and statistical information from the National Institute of Statistics and Geography (INEGI) of Mexico and the United Nations. The time horizon for the study is from 1980 to 2010. The first year marks part of Mexico's demographic and economic evolution: starting, on the one hand, the late phase of the demographic transition model, characterized by a decrease in fertility rates; and on the other hand, the end of the

179

strategy of economic growth underpinned by import substitution, to look towards opening up economies to global markets.

DRIVERS OF TERRITORIAL DECONCENTRATION

In the context of globalization, urban and regional studies have mentioned that the search for territorial convergence remains a pending issue, while the divergence between territories has occurred from processes of concentration of economic activities, as well as the existence of stages of metropolitanism, or the cycle of urbanization, within urban agglomerations, which result in the de-population of central areas, relative decentralization of industrial and commercial activities, and propensity for the concentration of modern service units (Pacione, 2009, pp. 80–88; Suarez-Villa, 1988). In this context, the intensity of internal migration during the early years of the 21st century has been decreasing (Anderson, 2015, pp. 402–424; Rodríguez, 2018).

The contemporary regional economy redefines the concept of the region towards a more virtual and less territorial connotation (Boisier, 1994; Hiernaux, 1991; Ramírez, 1992), while the dichotomy between interregional convergence or divergence in the face of changes in the international economic environment prevails (McCann, 2013, pp. 303–329). Within the framework of the new international division of labor, territorial deconcentration policies and local government actions play a central role in the competition for investment attraction. The actions of local governments to promote the development and reconfiguration of economic spaces have been shaped as major topics in urban studies since the last decade of the 20th century (Malecki, 1997, pp. 1–2; Nallari et al., 2012, pp. 1–12).

The new economic geography takes as a starting point the contributions of the pioneering models of localization of economic activities, and seeks their abstraction and mathematical formalization (Fujita and Krugman, 2003; Krugman, 1991). For this paradigm, industrial localization is understood from the interaction between transport costs and economies of scale, producing a pattern of high industrial concentration in a few cities that had initial advantages for localization, and where these advantages translate into increasing returns of scale for established large enterprises. Industrial localization is analyzed as a persistent center–periphery relationship and the tendency to sharpen territorial disparities.

On the other hand, the urban development cycle is a process of change, in which cities experience different rates of population growth over time, depending on their population size. This model was proposed by geographers Hermanus Geyer and Thomas Kontuly (1993), and is called differential urbanization. The initial phase of the cycle, called concentration and primacy, is characterized by the main city experiencing the highest population growth in the whole country. The second phase, of regressive polarization, occurs when the decline in the rate of population growth of the primate city is combined with the higher relative growth of the intermediate cities, causing a territorial deconcentration of the population. The third phase, of counter-development, occurs when small towns have the greatest population dynamism. Finally, in the fourth phase, of neoconcentration, large cities take command as the urban areas with the highest population growth, but these cities are not necessarily the same ones that led to the first phase (Figure 10.1).

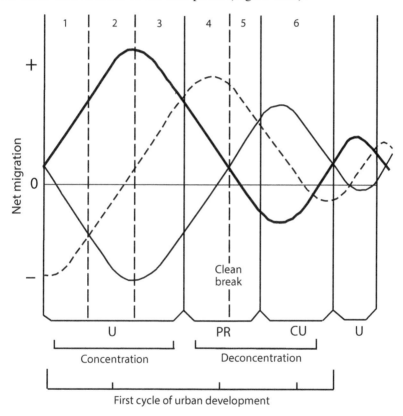

Source: Geyer and Kontuly (1993, p. 163).

Figure 10.1 Phases of differential urbanization

According to this model, the volume and destination of internal migration flows are the explanatory variables of differential urbanization. The migratory movements, of the rural–urban typology, are responsible for the first phase of concentration and primacy. Subsequently, the destination of rural–urban migration diversifies, while urban–urban migration appears from the primate city to the cities of its metropolitan region; this population mobility promotes the second phase of concentration polarization. For its part, the counter-development, the third phase of differential urbanization, is the effect of urban–urban migration, especially from larger to smaller centers, even with return migration. Finally, the fourth phase of neoconcentration means a reaccommodation in the geography of economic activity, intervening competitive advantages related to the scale, which drive the reorientation of migration flows to urban areas with better economic performance.

Latin America's big cities have experienced profound mutations since the last decades of the last century. From the post-war period until the 1980s, Latin American metropolises led the economic expansion of their respective countries; expanded and renewed their productive capacities; registered significant social and urban advances; concentrated the opening up of new education and health opportunities; and became destinations for internal migration flows. However, this dynamism faced structural problems of relative capacity for labor absorption, housing availability, and management and planning of urban and metropolitan development. Financial, technical and institutional capacities to plan and manage large cities were insufficient to cope with their explosive growth, and driven by a migration of citizens often expelled from their birthplaces, with little preparation to meet the challenges of the new habitat. On the other hand, the metropolitan management was unsuccessful in managing metropolitan development, modifying its structure, making it more suitable to absorb this explosive growth and solve its structural limitations in terms of roadways, services and operation.

These metropolitan mutations have been described from various perspectives in the literature (Aguilar and Escamilla, 1999; De Mattos, 2010; Duhau, 2016; Rodríguez, 2019). From a demographic perspective, the following stand out: (1) deconcentration, with its concentrated deconcentration counterpoint; (2) large-scale suburban expansion in line with metropolitan diffusion and fragmentation processes; (3) the social diversification of the periphery caused directly by new mobility; (4) housing renewal and recovery of residential migratory attractiveness of central areas, in some cases in association with gentrification or similar changes; (5) changes in volume and intensity of segregation; and (6) increase in daily mobility. These issues are related with the first and the second demographic transition (Ordorica, 2006).

TERRITORIAL PATTERNS AT REGIONAL SCALE

Based on United Nations data, Mexico's population in 2015 was 122 million people, the 12th most populous country in the world and the second most populous in Latin America and the Caribbean, below Brazil. This population accounted for 1.65 percent of the global total. On the other hand, its gross domestic product (GDP) stood at $1.2 trillion, at 2010 constant prices, and it was the 15th country according to wealth generation and, again, the second in Latin America and the Caribbean. This amount represented 1.62 percent of the global GDP. Its GDP per capita was US$10 037, slightly lower than the global average of US$10 208.

The total area of Mexico is about 2 million square kilometers, being the 13th-largest country in the world by surface area, and third in Latin America. The country's political constitution divides this area into 32 states or federal entities, each with its own government and resources. The areas of these range from just under 1500 to about 247 000 square kilometers, corresponding to Mexico City and Chihuahua, respectively; while population size in 2015 ranged from 710 000 to 16.2 million people, in Colima and the state of Mexico, respectively. These major administrative divisions are used to analyze territorial patterns at the regional level.

In terms of population growth, degree of urbanization, economic structure and geographical position, the 32 federal entities can be divided into five regions: (1) North Frontier (six states); (2) North (six states); (3) West (five states); (4) Center (seven states); and (5) South and Southeast (eight states). Figure 10.2 shows these regions and the location of major cities, while Table 10.1 shows the analysis indicators.

The five states in the North Frontier region are the largest and together represent 41 percent of the national territory. The second-largest region is the South and Southeast with 24 percent of the country's surface area. At the opposite pole, the Center region has the lowest surface area and occupies only 5 percent of the total area. The North Frontier and North regions have predominantly a warm and desert climate, while the South and Southeast region is predominantly warm and humid. A temperate climate predominates in the West and Center regions, and this has been one of the fundamental elements that has influenced the geography of the population and activities in the country.

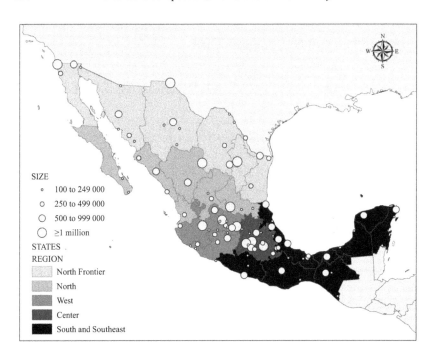

Figure 10.2   A map of Mexico and its regions

Table 10.1   Mexico: regional indicators, 1980–2015

Variable	Mexico	Regions				South and South-east
		North Frontier	North	West	Center	
Surface in sq km	1 956 338	795 022	415 799	177 916	98 942	468 659
Share	100.0	40.6	21.3	9.1	5.1	24.0
Main cities 2010	95	16	20	15	16	28
Population 1980 (thousands)	66 847	10 692	6 784	11 113	23 534	14 724
Population 2000 (thousands)	97 483	16 643	8 983	16 458	32 936	22 464
Population 2015 (thousands)	119 531	21 239	10 911	20 307	39 349	27 725
Annual growth rate 1980–2000	1.90	2.24	1.41	1.98	1.69	2.13
Annual growth rate 2000–2015	1.37	1.64	1.31	1.41	1.19	1.41

Variable		Regions				South and South-east
	Mexico	North Frontier	North	West	Center	
Share 1980	100.0	16.0	10.1	16.6	35.2	22.0
Share 2015	100.0	17.8	9.1	17.0	32.9	23.2
Population density 2015 (hab/sqkm)	61	27	26	114	398	59
GDP 1980 (at 2010 billion dollars)	537.8	105.8	40.2	72.8	186.9	132.1
GDP 2000 (at 2010 billion dollars)	915.2	204.8	64.3	125.6	312.9	207.6
GDP 2015 (at 2010 billion dollars)	1 223.1	283.6	95.3	181.1	422.3	240.8
Annual growth rate 1980–2000	2.69	3.35	2.37	2.77	2.61	2.29
Annual growth rate 2000–2015	1.95	2.20	2.66	2.47	2.02	0.99
Share 1980	100.0	22.4	7.0	13.7	34.2	22.7
Share 2015	100.0	23.2	7.8	14.8	34.5	19.7
GDP per capita 2015 (dollars)	10 233	13 353	8 735	8 920	10 731	8 685

Mexico's urban system in 2010 consisted of 59 metropolitan areas and 325 cities, each with a population of 15 000 and more, which together accounted for 81.2 million inhabitants, representing a 72.3 percent urbanization degree. The largest urban agglomeration was Mexico City, with 20.1 million inhabitants, with 17.9 percent of the national population, and ranking as the fourth-largest agglomeration on the planet, only below Tokyo, Delhi and Shanghai. In addition to Mexico City there were ten other metropolitan areas with more than 1 million inhabitants (Guadalajara, Monterrey, Puebla, Toluca, Tijuana, León, Ciudad Juárez, Torreón, Querétaro and San Luis Potosí). The main urban system was complemented by 84 cities with a population between 100 000 and 999 000 inhabitants, forming the group of intermediate cities. In these 95 urban areas, there lived 71.9 million people, representing 64 percent of the country's total population.

Of these 95 cities, 28 were located in the South and Southeast region, the largest concentration of urban areas, although none of them had more than 1 million inhabitants. The region with the second-highest number of cities was the North with 20, and only one of them had more than

1 million inhabitants (San Luis Potosí). In contrast, the North Frontier, West and Center regions had the fewest urban agglomerations, but each had three metropolitan areas of more than 1 million inhabitants.

Mexico's population between 1980 and 2015 increased from 66.8 million to 119.5 million inhabitants, with an annual growth rate of 1.6 percent; this annual growth rate between 1980 and 2000 was 1.9 percent, and 1.4 percent in 2000–2015. The decrease in demographic dynamism is explained by the pattern of Mexico during these years that started and consolidated the last phase in the demographic transition model, which is characterized by the decrease in fertility. In 1980 the overall fertility rate was 4.9, and it was 2.2 in 2015.

The regions of the country had different population dynamics during the period 1980–2015. In absolute terms, the country increased its population by just under 53 million people, with the Center region having the most absolute growth, with almost 16 million people, followed by the South and Southeast with 13 million. Conversely, the lowest absolute growth occurred in the North region with 4 million, and West with 9 million. Relative growth showed another scenario: in Mexico the population between 1980 and 2015 increased by 79 percent, with the North Frontier region having the highest population dynamism by nearly doubling its population, while the South and Southeast region increased by 88 percent and 83 percent in the West region. In contrast, the North region grew by 61 percent and the Center by 67 percent.

The Center region is the one with the highest concentration of demographics, and where Mexico City is located, as well as the fourth and fifth most populated urban agglomerations in the country, Puebla and Toluca. Its lower population dynamism meant a geographical pattern of demographic deconcentration mainly in favor of the West and South and Southeast regions. In 1980 the Center region concentrated 35.2 percent of the country's population, while in 2015 its share fell to 32.9 percent; this means that demographic deconcentration, or internal migration, from this region to the rest of the national territory was just over 2.7 million people. Another region with low population dynamism was the North: internal migration originating from it totaled 1.2 million people, and these were mainly aimed at the North Frontier region, the territory that also received a significant number of population migrants from the South and Southeast region.

The geography of the population in Mexico between 1980 and 2015 showed a pattern of geographical deconcentration of about 4 million people, equivalent to 3.3 percent of the country's total population in 2015. While this geographical redistribution of the population was not so significant on this geographical scale, it was when there was a change in scale. For example, of the country's 95 major cities in 2010, a total of 15 tripled their population, six of which were the South and Southeast region, three from the North Frontier and West regions, two from the Center region, and one from the North region. At the opposite pole, eight urban agglomerations grew by less than 50 percent, one of them being Mexico City.

Mexico's GDP increased from \$538 billion in 1980 to \$1.2 trillion in 2015, at constant prices in 2010, with a rate of growth of 2.4 percent. The dynamics during the period 1980–2000 were 2.7 percent, and 2.0 percent in the period 2000–2015. The country's economic growth was slightly higher than the demographic growth. GDP per capita reached \$10 233 in 2015, slightly below the global average.

The regions of the country showed different performances in their economic activity. The region with the most dynamism was the North Frontier, largely due to the expansion of its export manufacturing industry. The second-largest growing region was the West, due to the expansion of its manufacturing base in the automotive and electronics sectors. The North region had a marginal increase in its participation; while the Center region showed a growth rate similar to the national total; and the South and Southeast region was the lowest in economic performance mainly due to the stagnation of the oil activity.

The Center region is the area in the country with the highest concentration of population and economic activity. In 1980, it produced 34.8 percent of the country's GDP, while in 2015 its share declined to 34.5 percent, a loss of just three-tenths of a percentage point. Its pace of growth was the same as the national total, or in other words, its economic expansion continued to lead to what happened in the national total.

The information presented in Table 10.1 does not allow detailed study of the change in the geography of economic activity, or productive decentralization. To do so, data from the activity sector were used, especially agriculture, manufacturing and high-order services. This information is only available and comparable for the period 2003–2015, the period in which the study will be made (Table 10.2).

Agricultural production has been one of the industries hit hardest by the North American Free Trade Agreement (NAFTA), to the benefit of farmers of the United States. In the national context, the West region has the highest generation of GDP in this activity, and its growth rate exceeded the national total, so its share increased from 24.6 to 26 percent. At the opposite pole, the Center region provides the lowest share of GDP in this sector and its growth rate was lower than the national total, so its share fell from 14.5 to 13.9 percent. Other dynamic regions in the agricultural sector were the North Frontier and North, while the South and Southeast region grew below the national total.

Table 10.2   Mexico: sector changes by regions, 2003–2015

Variable	México	North Frontier	North	West	Center	South and Southeast
Share on agriculture GDP 2003	100.0	20.4	17.3	24.6	14.5	23.2
Share on agriculture GDP 2015	100.0	21.6	18.0	26.0	13.9	20.5
Share on manufacturing GDP 2003	100.0	34.8	5.3	15.8	32.4	11.7
Share on manufacturing GDP 2015	100.0	36.8	6.1	19.2	28.0	9.9
Share on high-order services GDP 2003	100.0	18.7	3.6	8.5	60.9	8.2
Share on high-order services GDP 2015	100.0	20.4	3.8	8.9	58.7	8.1

Source: Author's calculations with data from INEGI and United Nations.

Manufacturing has been supported by export dynamics. In 2015, Mexico's exports of goods and services stood at $424 billion, being the country with the 18th-highest value of exports, amounting to 1.9 percent of global trade. However, the boom in manufacturing exports has not been in line with the GDP growth of the manufacturing sector in the country, due to the significant import of manufactured goods for final, intermediate and capital consumption. The most industrialized region in the country is the North Frontier, and its pace of growth between 2003 and 2015 surpassed the national total, so its share increased from 34.8 to 36.8 percent. The Center region produced half of the country's GDP in the sector in the 1980s, and between 2003 and 2015 it continued the decentralization process, losing participation from 32.4 to 28 percent. As in the case of the agricultural sector, the North and West regions had greater manufacturing dynamism relative to the national total; while the South and Southeast region grew at a slower pace and its share fell from 11.7 to 9.9 percent.

Finally, higher-order services, including producer services, corporate offices and business support services, have a high concentration around the Center region and especially towards Mexico City. Between 2003 and 2015 there was some decentralization to the North Frontier region. The

Center region lost participation in the national total, from 60.9 to 58.7 percent, while the North Frontier region raised its contribution from 18.7 to 20.4 percent.

METROPOLITAN REGIONS

The urban or metropolitan region refers either to an area containing a large metropolitan area and smaller surrounding urban areas, within a radius that has generally been delimited up to 150 kilometers, or to a number of urban areas of intermediate size or with a population of more than 1 million, without much dominance on the part of any of them. In this settlement configuration there are interrelationships and interdependencies that result in population redistribution and economic activities, productive specialization of each population center and complex social processes (Meltzer, 1984, p. 163). There are three major models for the shaping of urban regions (Champion, 2001; Pacione, 2009, pp. 88–91): (1) by diffusion, where the nodal center of the region develops centripetal diffuser forces towards the rest of its regional sub-system of cities, but also centrifugal forces to other urban areas outside its regional area of influence; (2) by incorporation, where the urban expansion of the regional node adds to its area of influence smaller population centers that were self-sufficient localities in terms of employment and services; and (3) by merger, that is, the functional union of centers of previously independent populations and of similar size, which is caused by the improvement in transport systems between them.

There are eight metropolitan regions in Mexico (Figure 10.3). These regions included 430 municipalities; they had a combined population in 2010 of 58.5 million inhabitants, 52 percent of the country's total, and generated a GDP of $827 billion, 68 percent of national wealth in 2015. These data show the emergence in Mexico of a pattern of population concentration and economic activities around metropolitan regions. One way to analyze the regional distribution of population and economic activities is through the concepts of centripetal forces and centrifugal forces. The former takes families and businesses to locate themselves in or near the center of a region, while centrifugal forces encourage population deconcentration and decentralization of economic activities to other regions.

The metropolitan region of the Center has by far the greatest complexity and population and economic concentration. Its evolution until 1980 was based on the use of centripetal forces, but from then on it began the generation of centrifugal forces. The formation of this region is radially

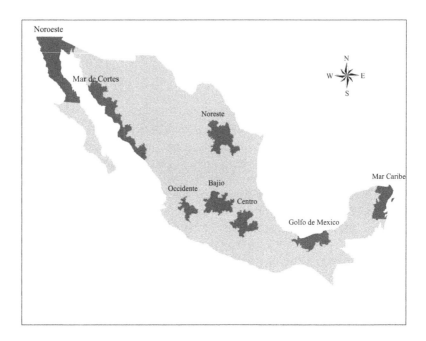

Figure 10.3   Mexico: metropolitan regions, 2010

through the main road axes of the country. Its GDP per inhabitant was 1.3 times higher than the national total, which speaks of the use of agglomeration economies for the location of economic activities. The urban sub-system showed the increased presence of cities specialized in producer services, consumer services and industry. This region has in recent years experienced productive restructuring from industry to services, which have concentrated in Mexico City, especially those aimed at producers, and this metropolis has begun a process of deindustrialization and centripetal and centrifugal diffusion for manufacturing growth to and outside other locations in the sub-system.

   The second urban region according to its conformation, population size and complexity is Bajío. This is rather linear, along a highway that crosses it from northwest to southeast, complemented by two transverse axes. The central places of this region are León and Querétaro. The distribution of economic activity over the region indicates that the highest-ranking localities specialized in manufacturing, indicating the potential use of agglomeration economies, while lower-ranking localities oriented towards either trade or agricultural production; this agricultural and livestock production is used as inputs to the industrial plants of the highest-ranking locations.

The Monterrey metropolitan area is the central place of the Northeast region. This region is the third according to population size and the first according to GDP per inhabitant. This region is formed with two north–south and east–west axes. The significant GDP per capita is the result of the concentration of manufacturing companies. The metropolitan area of Guadalajara is the second most populous city in the country, and the central place of the fourth-largest urban region, the West. The conformation of this region is axial, with Guadalajara as the central place and two axes: north–south and east–west. Its GDP per capita was 1.2 times higher than the national average, so there are no large advantages of agglomeration economies, and it specializes in industry and trade.

The region with the fifth-largest population in 2010 was the Sea of Cortes, in the northwest of the country, with central locations in Culiacán and Hermosillo. Its conformation is linear, along the coast of the Sea of Cortez (or Gulf of California) and is crossed by a road axis that departs from Los Mochis. In this territory, localization economies are used for agricultural production and electricity generation; it is worth mentioning that it is home to the most productive agricultural irrigation districts in the country. The next urban region by population size in 2010 was the Northwest, whose central location is occupied by Tijuana. This region is integrated into the urban region of San Diego in the United States, also with the megalopolitan formation that begins in Los Angeles, in such a way that it is constituted in a bi-national concentration. The economic structure of this region excels in trade and the *maquiladora* export industry.

Finally, the Gulf of Mexico and Caribbean Sea regions are located in the southeast of the national territory; their formation has been contingent on an economic activity: the extraction and refining of oil in the first, and tourism in the second. In the urban region of the Gulf of Mexico there are four cities that function as central places (Coatzacoalcos, Minatitlán, Villahermosa and Ciudad del Carmen), while in the Caribbean Sea there are two (Cancun and Playa del Carmen). GDP per capita in 2008 in both regions was 1.4 times higher than the country average. It is worth mentioning that the urban region of the Caribbean was the country's territory with the greatest population dynamism in the period 1980–2010; in 1980 its population was 173 000, while in 2010 it totaled 1.1 million, which means an annual average growth rate of 6.5 percent.

Two reflections can be made on the urban regions of the country. The first has to do with the form of internal organization, where it is appreciated that the urban regions of the Northeast and the West correspond to the concept of a city-region, that is, territories where there is a large city which concentrates the bulk of the population and economic activities of the region, and which imprints a monocentric character. The Northwest region, because of its geographical position, is more suited to the region-bridge typology, because by being at the convergence of two markets it has positioned itself as a production channel, taking advantage of the shadow prices provided by the border, as well as the movement of goods, services and people between the two countries; the metropolitan area of Tijuana had a positive immigration net balance throughout the 20th century (Sobrino, 2010), much of which had the original intention of migrating to the United States.

The urban regions of the Centro and Bajío are closer to the polycentric typology, since they are territories with a high population density and where there are several urban areas of different sizes. Perhaps the difference from the ideal typology is that economic activities within the region are organized hierarchically according to their distribution in the larger city, which speaks more of centripetal diffuser effects from the node to its regional crown of localities, and less of the use of particular economies in each locality. This typology also includes the urban regions of the Sea of Cortez, Gulf of Mexico and the Caribbean Sea, although its formation is linear (along the coast) and its functional relationships are defined by specific economic activities: agricultural the first, oil in the second and tourism in the third.

The second reflection has to do with the transmission of economic performance from the node of the urban region to its area of influence, a situation that could well be classified as cooperation for competitiveness, and which is presented in the Center, Bajío, Northwest, Northeast and Caribbean Sea regions. On the contrary, in the Western, Sea of Cortez and Gulf of Mexico regions there is a lack of diffusion of benefits from the center to the periphery.

The formation of urban regions in Mexico is an emerging territorial modality in terms of spatial distribution of population, location of economic activities and juxtaposition of urban labor markets. The top places in each urban region preferably concentrate the competitive advantages for their economic performance, with a lean transfer of profits to their subsidiary locations. A public policy challenge will be to recognize, in the first instance, the existence of this type of territorial organization; and second, to seek policy guidelines to promote the economic growth of such functional territorial units.

SIGNS OF DEMOGRAPHIC AND OCCUPATIONAL DECONCENTRATION

To assess population deconcentration in Mexico between 1980 and 2015, and to provide evidence on possible concentrated deconcentration, the country's territorial units were divided into five groups: (1) central city of Mexico City; (2) inner periphery of Mexico City; (3) outer periphery of Mexico City; (4) rest of Central region; and (5) rest of the country (Figure 10.4). The first three groups correspond to the metropolitan scale of Mexico City; the fourth to the regional level, and the fifth group to the addition of regional scopes.

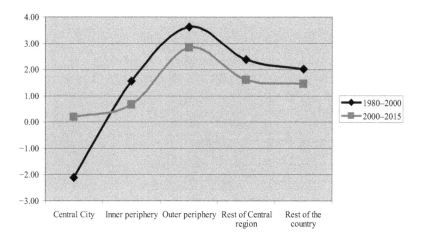

Source: Based on data from the population and housing census.

Figure 10.4   Mexico: Population growth rate, 1980–2015

The rate of population growth was differential within the country, leading to deconcentration and demographic concentration processes. The territorial units with the greatest dynamism in the periods 1980–2000 and 2000–2015 were the municipalities belonging to the outer periphery of Mexico City, which had intra-metropolitan residential mobility and received migrant population. The second most dynamic group was the rest of Central region, which speaks of a pattern of deconcentration from the Mexico City metropolitan area towards its hinterland region, but also a concentration pattern from the rest of the country towards the Central region.

The growth dynamics of the central city of Mexico City was in the period 1980–2000 a phase of deurbanization, due to the absolute loss of population. In 1980, the inhabitants of the central city numbered 2.6 million people, while in 2000 they decreased to 1.7 million. However, during the 2000–2015 period, the stage changed to redevelopment. The population had a marginal growth, from 1.7 to 1.8 million people. This change in the metropolitan stage was due to the implementation of urban policies that promoted housing production in this area, and discouraged the production of new housing on the southern outskirts of the metropolitan area. This policy was implemented by the government of Andrés Manuel López Obrador, when he was the head of government of Mexico City (2000–2006).

The population and housing census for 2010 provides information on changes in the municipality of residence between 2005 and 2010. If the population changed housing within a metropolitan area, then there is talk of intra-metropolitan residential mobility. Conversely, if mobility involved switching from one city to another, then it was internal migration. This information allows us to understand spatial patterns of mobility (Table 10.3).

Table 10.3   Mexico: territorial mobility of population, 2005–2010

Origin	Destination					
	Central City	Inner periphery	Outer periphery	Rest of Central region	Rest of the country	Total origin
Central City	30 233	119 651	9 958	33 928	33 138	226 908
Inner periphery	117 850	804 558	162 217	209 429	217 899	1 511 953
Outer periphery	2 340	71 972	50 639	14 355	17 715	157 021
Rest of Central region	2 741	20 043	2 330	35 658	225 602	286 374
Rest of the country	53 795	259 774	38 708	585 619	3 220 938	4 158 834
Total destination	206 959	1 275 998	263 852	878 989	3 715 292	6 341 090

Source: Author's calculations with data from the census of population and housing 2010.

The population that changed its municipality of residence between 2005 and 2010 totaled 6.3 million people, which meant a mobility rate of 11.3 people per 1000 inhabitants per year. Of the total movements, 2.4 million corresponded to intra-metropolitan residential mobility occurring within the 59 metropolitan areas of the country, while 3.9 million were due to internal migration. Residential mobility in Mexico City totaled 1.4 million people, the most relevant absolute flow being between territorial units of the inner periphery, with a flow of just over 800 000 people, while the most important relative displacement was from the central city to the inner periphery, with an out-migration rate of 13.9 persons per 1000 inhabitants annual.

The population that left the central city and the outer periphery had as its main destination another territorial unit of Mexico City itself, while the population that left the inner periphery had as its predominant destination a territorial unit of the rest of region. On the other hand, the outer city was the area with the most population dynamism in the country since the 1980s. By 2010, this expansion was more contingent on residential mobility than internal migration. For every migrant received from the rest of the country, there were a total of 4.2 people who moved to that area from more central areas of Mexico City.

The rest of the Central region was an important arrival area for internal migration flows with primary origin in the rest of the country. This area had 2.3 in-migrants from the rest of the country for each one from Mexico City. The central region was the territorial area of concentrated deconcentration: deconcentration from Mexico City, and concentration from the rest of the national territory. This central region took advantage of the agglomeration and reach economies generated by Mexico City.

Concentrated deconcentration of the population contrasted with the decentralization of manufacturing employment (Table 10.4). In 1980, total occupational demand in manufacturing was 2.1 million people, of whom 911 000 were in Mexico City, 291 000 in the rest of the Central region, and 945 000 in the rest of the country. Mexico City concentrated 42 percent of national manufacturing employment, against 14 percent of the rest of the Central region, and in the rest of the country the remaining 44 percent.

The years 1980 to 1998 meant the end of the industrialization model of import substitution and the insertion of Mexico into globalization. Manufacturing employment doubled from 2.1 million to 4.2 million workers, but in Mexico City it remained in the order of 900 000 employees, and even the central city had deindustrialization. Mexico City's share of the national total decreased from 42 to 21 percent. The zero occupational growth in Mexico City contrasted with a dynamic in the rest of Central region similar to that of the country as a whole, and a significant expansion in the rest of the country, especially in border towns or near the northern border of the country. In this area, employment increased from 944 000 to 2.8 million workers, and its share of the national total increased from 44 to 65 percent. Manufacturing showed centrifugal forces from Mexico City to the rest of the country.

Table 10.4   Mexico manufacturing employment, 1980–2013

Area	1980	1998	2013	1980	1998	2013
		People			*Horizontal percentage*	
Total	2 146 620	4 232 322	5 073 432	100.0	100.0	100.0
Mexico City's Central City	236 585	170 944	107 230	11.0	4.0	2.1
Mexico City's inner periphery	655 428	672 516	565 907	30.5	15.9	11.2
Mexico City's outer periphery	19 036	48 310	58 070	0.9	1.1	1.1
Rest of Central region	290 769	583 274	771 471	13.5	13.8	15.2
Rest of the country	944 802	2 757 278	3 570 754	44.0	65.1	70.4

Source: Author's calculations with data from the economic censuses.

During the period 1998–2013, manufacturing employment in the country lost dynamism and only increased from 4.2 million to 5.1 million workers. On this occasion, Mexico City again showed deindustrialization, but now not only in the central city: also in the inner periphery. Total employment in the megacity decreased from 892 000 employees in 1998 to 731 000 in 2013. For 2013, its share of the national total stood at 14 percent. The rest of the Central region continued with a growth rate similar to that of the country as a whole, and its number of workers in industry exceeded that of Mexico City, achieving a 15 percent share in total national employment. The rest of the country remained as the area with the highest growth in manufacturing employment, reaching 3.6 million workers in 2013 and with a 70 percent share of total national employment. The location of companies was not only in the North Frontier region, but also in the West. The deindustrialization of Mexico City meant centrifugal forces to the rest of the national territory.

FINAL REMARKS

The geography of the population and economic activities and their change over time are issues of great relevance in urban and regional studies, since they allow illustration of the patterns of concentration or demographic deconcentration, as well as of centralization or economic decentralization. This knowledge serves for the formulation and implementation of public policies that aim to produce a more balanced social and territorial development.

Mexico demonstrated processes of concentrated deconcentration of the population and decentralization of manufacturing employment in the period 1980–2015. Population deconcentration between regions accounted for about 3.4 percent of the total population in 2015, or just over 4 million people; while economic decentralization was 5.1 percent, or $62 billion. Economic decentralization outperformed population deconcentration, especially by the relocation of manufacturing to the North Frontier and West regions, and by the decline in oil activity in the South and Southeast region.

If the scale of analysis is changed, then demographic deconcentration and economic decentralization are more evident. For example, the country's population had a relative growth of 70 percent between 1980 and 2015, but 15 urban agglomerations tripled their population volume, largely due to the dynamism of manufacturing or tourism activity. In the interior of Mexico City, the central city lost an absolute population and then regained to some extent its demographic attraction; while its outer periphery showed significant dynamism, as well as the rest of the regional urban system.

These processes were carried out without the intervention of territorial policies, except perhaps the promotion of housing production in the central city at the beginning of the 21st century. It appears that Mexico's 2018–2024 federal government will seek to resume the role of territorial planning, an activity absent since the establishment of the trade opening strategy. This intervention could help to reduce the conditions of poverty and, above all, the inequality that exists all over the country.

REFERENCES

Aguilar, G. and I. Escamilla (eds), *Problems of Megacities: Social Inequalities, Environmental Risk and Urban Governance*, Mexico City: UNAM/ International Geographical Union, 1999.

Anderson, B., *World Population Dynamics: An Introduction to Demography*, Boston, MA: Pearson, 2015.

Boisier, S., "Postmodernismo territorial y globalización: regiones pivotales y regiones virtuales," *Ciudad y Territorio. Estudios Territoriales*, No. 102, pp. 597–608, 1994.

Champion, A., "A changing demographic regime and evolving polycentric urban regions: consequences for the size, composition and distribution of city populations," *Urban Studies*, Vol. 38, No. 4, pp. 657–677, 2001.

De Mattos, C., "Globalización y metamorfosis metropolitana en América Latina: de la ciudad a lo urbano generalizado," *Revista de Geografía Norte Grande*, No. 47, pp. 81–104, 2010.

Duhau, E., "Evolución reciente de la división social del espacio residencial en la Zona Metropolitana de la Ciudad de México. Los impactos de la renovación habitacional en la ciudad central y de la formación de una nueva periferia," in M.E. Negrete (ed.), *Urbanización y política urbana en Iberoamérica. Experiencias, análisis y reflexiones*, Ciudad de México: El Colegio de México, pp. 311–357, 2016.

Fujita, M. and P. Krugman, "The new economic geography: past, present and the future," *Papers in Regional Science*, Vol. 83, No. 1, pp. 139–164, 2003.

Geyer, H. and T. Kontuly, "A theoretical foundation for the concept of differential urbanisation," *International Regional Science Review*, Vol. 17, No. 2, pp. 157–177, 1993.

Hiernaux, D., "En la búsqueda de un nuevo paradigma regional," in B. Ramírez (ed.), *Nuevas tendencias en el análisis regional*, Ciudad de México: Universidad Autónoma Metropolitana, Xochimilco, pp. 33–48, 1991.

Krugman, P., *International Economics, Trade and Policy*, New York: Harper Collins Publishers, 1991.

Malecki, E., *Technology and Economic Development*, London: Longman, 1997.

McCann, P., *Modern Urban and Regional Economics*, Oxford: Oxford University Press, 2013.

Meltzer, J., *Metropolis to Metroplex*, Baltimore, MD: Johns Hopkins University Press, 1984.

Nallari, R., B. Griffith and S. Yusuf, *Geography of Growth. Spatial Economics and Competitiveness*, Washington, DC: World Bank, 2012.

Ordorica, M., "Four scenarios for the population for Mexico for the late 21st century constructed through an expo[(exponential)] function," in J.L. Lezama and J.B. Morelos (eds), *Population, City and Environment in Contemporary Mexico*, Mexico City: El Colegio de México, pp. 27–43, 2006.

Pacione, M., *Urban Geography: A Global Perspective*, London: Routledge, 2009.

Ramírez, B., "Modernización y reestructuración territorial," *Ciudades*, No. 13, pp. 3–9, 1992.

Rodríguez, J., "Spatial distribution, internal migration and development," *Revista de la CEPAL*, No. 96, pp. 137–157, 2018.

Rodríguez, J., "El efecto de la migración interna sobre la estructura y las disparidades etarias en las grandes ciudades de América Latina," Córdoba, Argentina, Universidad de Córdoba, PhD thesis in Demography, 2019.

Sobrino, J., "Ciclos económicos y competitividad de las ciudades," in G. Garza and M. Schteingart (eds), *Los grandes problemas de México. II. Desarrollo urbano y regional*, Mexico City: El Colegio de México, pp. 127–171, 2010.

Suarez-Villa, L., "Metropolitan evolution, sectoral economic change, and the city size distribution," *Urban Studies*, Vol. 25, No. 1, pp. 1–20, 1988.

11. Mexico: GVCs network development and the emergence of interactive cities

Clemente Ruiz Durán[1]

One unexplored dimension of city growth has been the link with global value chains (GVCs). The purpose of this chapter is to explore their interactions, and to measure how the development of suppliers has led to the growth of cities, and to the emergence of networks where supplier development has become the core of the expansion.

Traditional trade involved producing goods "from start to finish" in one country and exporting them; countries that industrialized in the 19th and 20th centuries had to build full supply chains domestically before becoming internationally competitive. An "unbundling" began in the 1970s as parts of the value chain were offshored. But, from the 1980s, a "great unbundling" has occurred. Production has fragmented; production stages that were originally housed in a single factory have dispersed across borders. As the trade economist Richard Baldwin notes, now factories – not just goods – cross borders, uniting advanced and emerging economies. Globally, competitive firms produce their inputs in the most cost-effective locations, bring everything together through complex logistics systems, and serve global markets. Firms that are not in this game struggle to compete (World Economic Forum, 2016).

This is the world of GVCs. It bundles up traditional trade in goods with foreign direct investment (FDI) and the international flow of services, people and ideas. What used to be concentrated in advanced countries has spread to middle-income and poor countries. Its enablers are technology, driving down transport and communication costs; and policy: the opening up of markets around the world. Today, emerging economies do not have to build whole supply chains to be competitive

[1] This research is supported by PAPIIT IN310519, with the collaboration of Jorge García-Morales, Elías Sosa-Onofre and Rodrigo Chavez de la Vega.

internationally; rather, they can join GVCs by inserting themselves into niches and performing specialized tasks along the value chain. In 30 years, the world has gone from products "made in one country" to those "made in the world," and from "trade in goods" to "trade in tasks" (Gereffi, 2018, p. 401).

Manufacturing is at the heart of GVCs. The first and still the most extensive GVCs are in information and communication technology (ICT) products, linking production hubs in North America, Europe and East Asia to serve global markets. This has powered industrial revolutions in East Asia. GVCs integrate exports with imports; imported inputs account for increasing value-added in exports. FDI drives GVCs; multinational enterprises are their "system integrators." And GVCs are increasingly about services, including services that feed into global manufacturing. Business, communication and infrastructure services (such as financial, telecommunications, transport and professional services) are the fastest-growing parts of international trade; they coordinate international production and are the glue within GVCs.

LOCATION POLICIES AND THE EMERGENCE OF GVCs: GEOGRAPHY MATTERS

One of the most important processes that has accompanied GVCs has been the opening of a new geography, which has modified the existing paths of growth; industry used to concentrate in specific areas, but step-by-step transformation has opened new locations that have given birth to a network economy, one where linkages pushed traditional locations to get connected to markets within the country and with the rest of the world. Forces of production have evolved and modified all patterns of behavior. The challenge for governments has been to adapt to this new reality, giving a new role to regional and local governments that have emerged as the keystones of the GVCs era.

Mexico's geography transformation began at the end of the Revolution. In 1925, Calles created the National Road Commission (CNC) to build the first "petrolized" roads to connect the country (Waters, 2006). In 1936, the United States (US) and Mexico opened the Pan-American Highway, at the crossroads of Laredo, Texas and Nuevo Laredo, Tamaulipas, that give birth to a new era of international trade.[2] Later, in the

---

[2]   The official route of the Pan-American Highway through Mexico (where it is known as the Inter-American Highway) starts at Nuevo Laredo, Tamaulipas (opposite Laredo, Texas) and goes south to Mexico City along Mexican Federal Highway 85.

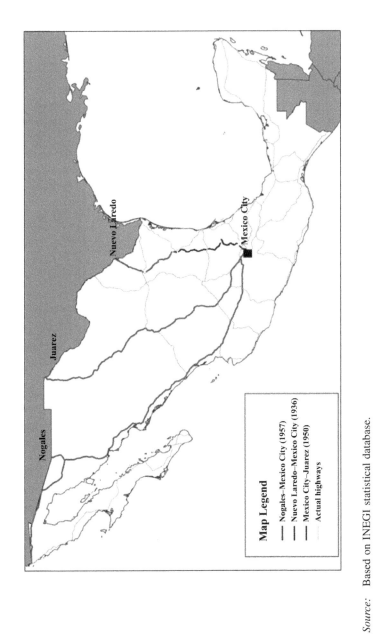

Within the map:

Map Legend

—— Nogales–Mexico City (1957)
—— Nuevo Laredo–Mexico City (1936)
—— Mexico City–Juarez (1950)
···· Actual highways

Nogales

Juarez

Nuevo Laredo

Mexico City

Source: Based on INEGI statistical database.

Figure 11.1 Main locations of industrial development previous to GVC development

1950s, the import substitution industrialization (ISI) that emerged after World War II gave birth to a new trend of country modernization and interconnectedness which relied on attracting transnational corporations to become partners of local businesses to consolidate the domestic market, mainly around large cities and along the main highways connecting Mexico City with the border cities of the US (Figure 11.1).

The 1980s financial crisis brought a change to the industrialization model centered on the domestic market: an era of trade liberalization emerged to transform Mexico into an export platform. For that purpose, a Free Trade Agreement was signed with the US and Canada in 1994, and in 1995 Mexico joined the World Trade Organization. Changes transformed the country into a key location for world trade with a privileged geographical advantage: Mexico City is only 1607 kilometers from Houston, compared to Sao Paulo which is 7833 kilometers and Buenos Aires which is 8136 kilometers. So, the parameter for new investment of GVCs was hubs located near the border or as far south as the Mexico City hinterland. However, the location decision became more complex, as the equation incorporated not only closeness to export locations, but also interconnection to a domestic market of 125 million people and the availability of a well-trained labor force with an average of nine years of education.

Garza describes this process as follows:

> Within the framework of the country's economic models, the urbanization process gradually moved from an organization with a system of highly hierarchical cities in a closed economy to a structure of urban–rural networks more decentralized and diversified with the new trade liberalization era. This evolution has been characterized by convergence cycles and divergence, and in the current neoliberal stage, inequality has predominated with the increase in regional gaps, but also with the development of new metropolitan nodes and the emergence of urban networks, not exempt from serious socio-economic and environmental problems. (Garza, 2010)

In 1995 there were around 244 cities of different sizes within the locus described, so choices of location were related to facilities provided by the city itself (municipal governments) and the state governments (Sánchez, 2016). But the final decision was related to how each industry decided to form a connected network within a region; that is, a form of industrial organization guided by transnational corporations that takes into consideration policies of federal entities regarding land use, industrial parks developed and infrastructure (hard and soft).

TRACKING GVCs' LOCATION AND INTERACTIONS

To analyze the impact of GVCs in the growth of cities, three industries were selected: transport equipment, electronics and medical devices. These three are interconnected through the supply chain, and have been some of the fastest-growing manufacturing industries in Mexico (Table 11.1).

Table 11.1   Dynamic GVCs in the Mexican economy

	Automotive industry		Electronics industry		Medical devices	
FDI 1999–2018 (millions of dollars)	53 297		26 707		1 165	
	1993	2018	1993	2018	1993	2018
Exports	7009	161 698	13 778	87 506	1149	7698
Industries GDP (% of manufacturing GDP)	8.3	18.6	10.3	11.7	0.9	1.6
Average hourly earnings (dollars)	5.3	4.3	4.5	4.1	4.3	4.0

Sources: Secretaria de Economica (2019) and Opportimes (2019).

For the mapping of the selected industries supply analysis was based into a two-stage analysis, in the first input–output methodology was used to track activities at a six-digit level considering only those that represent more than 3 percent of the value of the purchases of each activity, as shown in Figures 11.2–11.6. For electronics there were at least 21 activities at six-digit disaggregation, we selected three activities for electronics: computer peripheral equipment manufacturing (334110), major household appliance manufacturing (335220), and computer systems design and related services (541510); for the auto industry the selection was (336320) Motor vehicle electrical and electronic equipment manufacturing (31 activities); for the medical devices was selected: Other navigational, measuring, electro-medical and control instruments manufacturing (334519).

Once the activities were identified, a location analysis of the firms was realized through the *Directorio Estadístico Nacional de Unidades Económicas* (DENUE) to integrate a directory of firms in the industry. Figure 11.7 shows the cities where GVCs firms were concentrated.

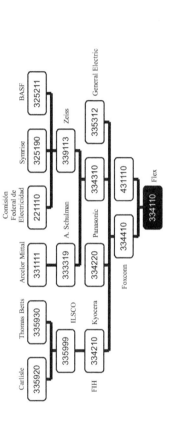

Figure 11.2   334110 Computer peripheral equipment manufacturing (15 activities)

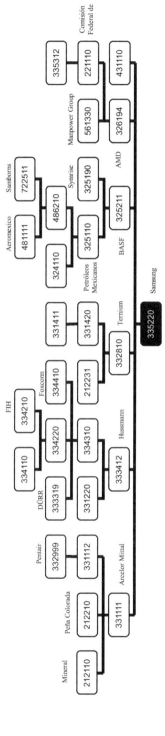

Figure 11.3   335220 Major household appliance manufacturing (29 activities)

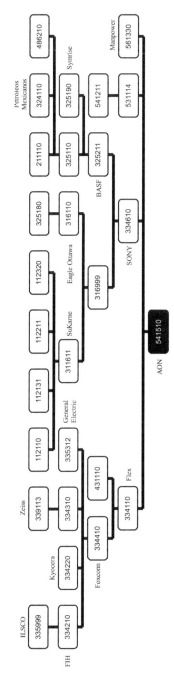

Figure 11.4 541510 Computer systems design and related services (24 activities)

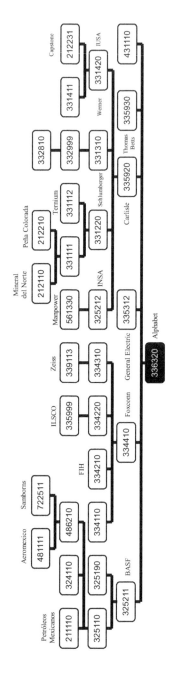

Figure 11.5 336320 Motor vehicle electrical and electronic equipment manufacturing (31 activities)

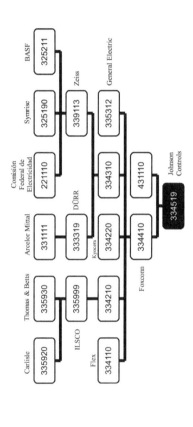

Figure 11.6   334519 Other navigational, measuring, electromedical and control instruments manufacturing

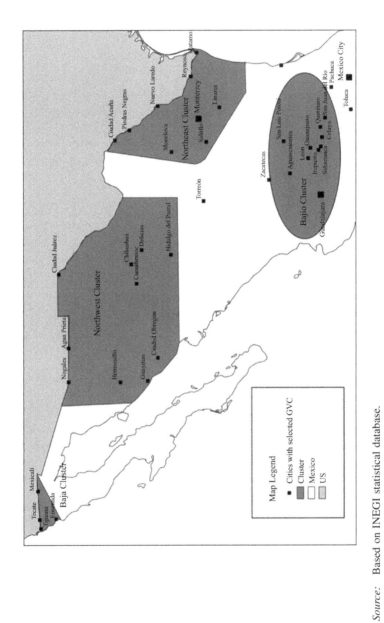

Source: Based on INEGI statistical database.

Figure 11.7 Redefining the geography by GVCs

Regions were formed through a process of cooperation among firms; the location gave rise to interconnections creating interactivity among cities and redefined the geography based on GVCs investment.

GVC IMPACT ON THE GROWTH OF CITIES

Once locations were determined it was possible to analyze how GVCs have affected the growth of cities; the period of analysis was from the enactment of the North American Free Trade Agreement (NAFTA) in 1995 up to 2015, which is the year of latest released data of population by county (*municipio*). The analysis was conducted at two levels. The first was the location of GVC facilities (auto, electronic and medical devices) by metropolitan areas, and how this affected the growth of population in the period of analysis, as can be observed in Figure 11.8.[3]

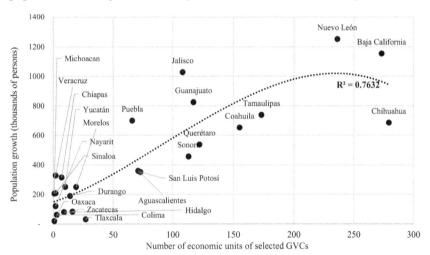

Sources: INEGI (2019) and CONAPO (2018).

Figure 11.8   GVCs and the impact on MA population growth, 1995–2015

GVCs had an additional effect on population growth as suppliers located themselves not only in metropolitan areas but in cities nearby that were

---

[3]   There are 74 metropolitan areas in Mexico as registered by the National Population Council of Mexico (Consejo Nacional de Población) (CONAPO, 2018).

around the terminal plant, which may be called "associated cities," as shown in Figure 11.9.

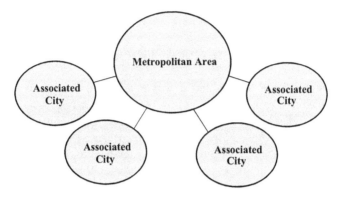

Figure 11.9   Dynamics between cities

The main effect was in the following states: Guanajuato, Coahuila, Sonora, San Luis Potosí and Chihuahua, as shown in Figure 11.10, there was cooperation among firms for the same location and nearby locations, it gave rise to interconnections creating interactivity among cities.

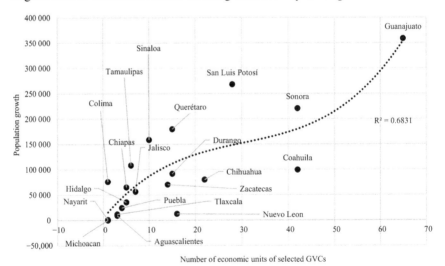

Sources: INEGI (2019) and CONAPO (2018).

Figure 11.10   GVCs and the impact on associated cities' population growth, 1995–2015

GVCs RESHAPING THE CITIES: THE EMERGENCE OF KNOWLEDGE CLUSTERS

The location of GVCs was linked to the promotion policies of local governments through different channels; one of the main tools was the development of industrial parks, that provided investors with land use and utilities to support their operation.[4] Table 11.2 summarizes industrial park expansion between 1986 and 2019: their expansion quadrupled in the period. The difference compared to traditional industrial parks was the emergence of technological parks that brought in technological research as a feature of land development (Mora and Marquetti, 2019; Organizacion de Estados Iberoamericanos, n.d.).

Table 11.2   Industrial parks as a source of MA expansion

	State	Total industrial parks	
		1986	2019
1	Baja California	6	92
2	Nuevo Leon	8	64
3	Jalisco	6	47
4	Chihuahua	11	39
5	Coahuila	7	38
7	Sonora	15	33
8	Guanajuato	4	23
9	Tamaulipas	8	23
10	Puebla	4	19
11	Querétaro	6	13
12	Sinaloa	2	12
13	Hidalgo	5	11
14	San Luis Potosí	1	10

---

[4]   A useful description is mentioned by Mexican Association of Industrial Parks (AMPIP) president Pablo Charvel, of the characteristics of industrial parks: "It is based on privately owned land and has the required permits for the operation of industrial plants and distribution centers, it also has urban infrastructure and water and discharge services, electricity, telecommunications in a mandatory manner, and with options for natural gas, rail transport, water treatment plant and other complementary services; It operates under an internal regulation and has an administration that coordinates security, the proper functioning of infrastructure, the promotion of real estate and the general management of procedures and permits before authorities" (Orozco, 2016).

Table 11.2 (continued)

	State	Total industrial parks	
		1986	2019
15	Aguascalientes	3	9
16	Tlaxcala	1	9
17	Veracruz	3	9
18	Yucatan	4	8
20	Michoacan	2	7
22	Durango	2	5
23	Morelos	2	3
24	Oaxaca	1	3
26	Zacatecas	2	3
27	Chiapas	1	2
31	Colima	2	1
32	Nayarit	2	1
Total		108	484

Sources: Garza (1990) and AMPIP (2019).

One of the main features of the new agglomerations was that they were not traditional assembling plants; rather, they were intermediate schemes with some characteristics of knowledge-oriented clusters, where there was a demand for more skills for the average worker and the need of university trainees that could support development of some technical tasks inside the new GVC factories. Those new requirements led to a rise of average education level and the emergence of research centers for manufacturing; average education increased by three years, reaching ten years in 2018. Also, there was an increase in the number of national researchers registered at state level (Table 11.3): the highest increases were in Aguascalientes, Chihuahua and Querétaro; and the states with the largest numbers of national researchers were Jalisco and Nuevo León, both of them becoming key in the development of new knowledge clusters in the country.

CITIES AS KNOWLEDGE CLUSTERS AND THEIR INTERACTIVITY

The mix of conditions that has emerged among the different regions has evolved into a complex process of cities becoming knowledge clusters

Table 11.3   Average educational attainment and national researchers in GVC regions

	Average educational attainment (years)		National researchers		Research centers
Bajio Cluster	6.7	9.4	2495	6066	4308
Jalisco	7.0	9.5	208	1466	1590
Aguascalientes	7.3	10.0	11	230	245
Guanajuato	5.8	8.5	162	940	1,004
Querétaro	6.8	9.7	49	719	752
San Luis Potosí	6.4	9.0	70	693	717
North East Cluster	7.9	10.1	253	1898	2086
Coahuila	7.8	10.1	69	421	474
Nuevo León	8.4	10.3	154	1,216	1,325
Tamaulipas	7.5	10.0	30	261	287
North West Cluster	7.5	9.9	141	1072	1152
Sonora	7.8	10.2	109	597	625
Chihuahua	7.3	9.5	32	475	527
Baja California Cluster	7.9	9.8	195	841	919

Sources: INEGI and CONACYT database.

where cities interact among themselves, led by the development of electronics, auto and medical devices, each one with specific characteristics that make it different. The following paragraphs describe how they have become knowledge clusters.

Bajio Cluster

Bajio is a geographical, historical, economic and cultural region that comprises part of the cities of Aguascalientes, Guadalajara, Guanajuato, Leon, Celaya, Irapuato, Salamanca, Querétaro and San Luis Potosí. Within this region, the main industries that have shaped the cluster have been a combination of electronics, software, digital creative industries, auto and aeronautics, all of them interacting within the supply chain. Exports of the region reached $81 billion in 2018; the auto industry and electronics exports jointly account for 80 percent of the exports of the region (see Table 11.4):

Guadalajara, Jalisco holds the largest amount of electronics manufacturing services (EMS) manufacturing operations in the country with 12 original equipment manufacturers (OEMs) and more than 380 specialized suppliers that exports about $150 billion annually. Some of the companies in Guadalajara include Plexus, IMI, IKOR, Flex Ltd., V-TEK, InterLatin, Sanmina, QSS, JABIL, Molex, OMP Mechtron, and Talos. Much like the rest of Mexico, Guadalajara is home to a diverse base of EMS manufacturing that gives the state a global competitive advantage. (Tetakawi, 2019b)

Guadalajara, Aguascalientes, Guanajuato and San Luis Potosí house one of the largest auto industry clusters in the country, with facilities in El Salto, Jalisco – Honda; Aguascalientes – Nissan I and II, Mercedes Benz, Infinity; Guanajuato – GM, Volkswagen, Mazda, Honda, Toyota; San Luis Potosí – GM and BMW; and in Querétaro, which has become a manufacturer of critical components such as wire harnesses manufactured in San Juan del Rio.

Querétaro houses one of the largest aero clusters in the country, made up of 85 companies and organizations: 24 companies TR1, TR2 and TR3; 8 special process companies; 4 OEM (original equipment manufacturer); 5 MRO (maintenance, repair and operations); 12 research and design centers; 19 special services companies; 6 companies providing raw materials; and 7 academic institutions (Internacional Metalmecanica, 2018). Bombardier and Safran are the largest companies in the cluster.

Bajio became the house of the electro domestic network, the main plant developed in the state of Querétaro. In 1986, Mabe entered into an important joint venture with General Electric Co. to produce appliances for the US market. As part of an effort to move away from controlling Mexican operations from the US, GE decided to enter into the joint venture with a 48 percent minority stake. While GE hoped to gain access to Mexico's low-cost labor pool, Mabe was given greater access to the world's largest consumer market through GE's US distribution network. By the mid-1990s, more than two-thirds of all gas ranges and refrigerators imported into the United States were designed and manufactured by Mabe in Mexico; while 95 percent of those sold under the General Electric names were designed in Mabe's San Luis Potosí plant, the biggest kitchen plant in the world. As a result, Mabe became the leading brand in Mexico, moving ahead of Vitro's Acros brand with a domestic market share of 50 percent. As the company continued to grow, exports and production remained concentrated in Latin America. By the mid-1990s, Mabe was one of the leading appliance manufacturers in the world, with annual growth between 15 and 20 percent. In Mexico, Mabe dominates the market; while in Latin America, Mabe commanded a 70 percent market share in home appliances. The group also entered into several joint ventures and alliances with other regional manufacturers. NAFTA reinforced the Central Mexico home-appliance network in the states of Guanajuato, San Luis Potosí and Querétaro, bringing in US firms (for example, Whirlpool and Onnera Solutions), and attracting Asian firms such as Daewoo and Samsung. Today, besides home appliances these states house electronic components for the auto and aeronautic industries.

North East Cluster: Monterrey–Saltillo

Monterrey was one of the traditional manufacturing centers of Mexico; the GVC era brought to the region the consolidation of a joint cluster with Saltillo, the capital city of the state of Coahuila, and with Reynosa, Tamaulipas. Exports of the region in 2018 reached $107 billion, half from the auto industry, and one-fifth from electronics (see Table 11.4).

In its 2016 report the World Economic Forum (2016) recognized the effort of the state to build strong capabilities to develop GVCs, attracting more than 2200 companies in the sectors of appliances, automotive, information technologies, aerospace, electrical, electronics and metal manufacturing, among others, making Monterrey an active player in the GVCs of these sectors. Its strength comes from its interaction with a large educational and knowledge network (Tecnológico de Monterrey, Universidad Autónoma de Nuevo León, Universidad de Monterrey among others). The average schooling is 11 years, 2.4 years more than the national mean, and 18 percent of the city's population has finished either bachelor or graduate degree. In 2004 it became an International City of knowledge with the intention of promoting technological development. To support innovation there is an Innovation and Technology Transfer Institute and a Technological Innovative Park. Derived from this broader initiative, 12 strategic economic clusters have been formed in the sectors of nanotechnology, biotechnology, aerospace, medical services, energy, automotive, electronic and electrical appliances, information technologies and software, agrobusiness, logistics and transportation, sustainable housing, and multimedia and creative industries.

Saltillo has high levels of manufacturing activity due to its location, highly educated workforce, affordable labor and advanced infrastructure. According to CoahuilaMex, the state of Coahuila overall has produced more than 578 000 vehicles and 49 000 tractor trailer trucks. Additionally, there are more than 22 industrial parks in the area.

Saltillo's automotive manufacturing sector is one of Mexico's largest, which is why it is often referred to as the "Detroit of Mexico." In fact, 90 percent of the city's economic base is comprised of automotive industry firms and it is a key center for servicing the global automotive industry. Some notable manufacturers in the city include the Chrysler Motors plant (876 workers), Chrysler Motors Ramos Arizpe plant (1552 workers), Chrysler assembly plant (2479 workers), Chrysler van assembly plant (891 workers), Chrysler die plant (250 workers), Daimler-Freightliner assembly plant (3802 workers), and the General Motors Ramos Arizpe complex (3800 workers). In response to the area's strong manufacturing sector, there are currently 18 industrial parks and five industrial complexes as well as one manufacturing community, La Angostura Manufacturing Community, which is owned and operated by the Offshore Group. With so many manufacturers located in Saltillo, businesses have access to a strong network of both suppliers and larger OEM producers (Tetakawi, 2019a).

Tijuana Cluster

Tijuana is the largest city in Baja California, with a successful infrastructure and transportation network that crosses into the rest of Mexico and the US. Among its many advantages, access to the global market through major international seaports, airports and highway infrastructure creates a competitive import–export market in Tijuana. As one of the biggest border crossings in Mexico, Tijuana has a steady growth of employment that also bleeds into the United States. Tijuana's industrial development has amounted to more than US$25.6 billion of foreign direct investment for the period 1999 to 2018 (see Table 11.4).

The region supports over 550 companies from over 20 countries that employ more than 185 000 people. Success in operational practices has pushed Tijuana to maintain a high volume of the export manufacturing base in Mexico. The city has become a manufacturing powerhouse for many industries; these include medical devices, electronics, aerospace, automotive and semiconductors. There have been four main areas developed in the city, as follows.

First, Tijuana's medical device manufacturing industry is 30 years old and maintains an established local supply chain network, making the city the biggest medical device manufacturing hub in the country. As of 2016, there were 67 companies, that had a US$599 million production value, employing about 42 000 people. The medical device companies include BD, Welch Allyn and Thermo Fisher. The city is responsible for 67 percent of the country's exports in the industry, that in 2018 reached US$7698 million (Opportimes, 2019). With more than 44 of these companies calling Tijuana home, the industry has named the northern Mexican city a "medical device cluster," with 91 percent of the medical device industry direct foreign investments (DFI) coming from the United States (Co-Production International, 2016).

Second, electronics manufacturing in Tijuana produces a wide range of goods, spanning appliances, electrical components, media equipment and semiconductors. The electronics manufacturing industry has been established for around 50 years and provides 50 000 jobs over 122 companies. TVs and semiconductors are the most-produced goods in the industry. Over 20 million TVs are manufactured a year, creating a $419 million production value. Semiconductors are the base of the supply chain for the electrical and electronic devices, hosting 71 companies and providing over 20 000 jobs. Electronics manufacturing companies in Tijuana include Plantronics, Kyocera, Philips, Foxconn Sanyo, Samsung and Panasonic.

Third, the range of the aerospace industry in Tijuana has turned into its own ecosystem of supply chain and tier-level companies over the past 40 years. Tijuana's aerospace cluster aerospace cluster is four times larger than the industry operations in other regions of Mexico, with a highly skilled workforce in the 39 existing companies.

Fourth, the automotive industry in Tijuana is also a manufacturing powerhouse that specializes in truck chassis, stamped metal parts, seat belts, sound speakers, carbon fiber body kits and electronic sensors. The industry employs 14 600 employees over 50 companies, and those automotive companies include Hyundai, Toyota and Goodridge.

Northwest Cluster: Sonora–Chihuahua

Hermosillo, Nogales, Chihuahua and Ciudad Juárez have become key cities in the development of GVCs in northwestern Mexico; they interact through various channels. This region has achieved exports by 69 billion dollars in 2018 and accumulated 47 billion dollars in foreign direct investment between 1999 and 2018 (see Table 11.4). One key industry is the auto industry, where the Ford facilities in Hermosillo and Chihuahua interact; the first has a stamping and assembly plant, and the second has a motor plant, although they are independent under the Ford Production System (FPS). Both of them interact with Ford plants in the US. The Hermosillo plant produces the Fusion hybrid model and Chihuahua manufactures gasoline and diesel motors. Production was on the rise between 2010 and 2015, reaching 515 395 units. Since then there has been a continuous decrease, and in 2019 production reached only 249 605 units, a decrease of more than 50 percent, weakening the northwestern cluster.

Nogales has become a key exchange hub between Arizona and Sonora, Mexico. Nogales, Arizona is a service center enabling businesses to easily understand and navigate the myriad laws, regulations and agreements governing cross-border trade. Nogales, AZ is also adept as a logistics, warehousing and service hub for manufacturing operations in Nogales, Sonora known as *maquilas*.

While manufacturing may occur in Mexico, however, these operations have warehousing and distribution operations on the Arizona side of the border, first for receiving components and sub-assemblies to move into Sonora, and later for cross-docking and warehousing operations. By this method, northern-moving goods are transported to parent companies or distribution sites. Many companies use third parties and customs brokers to manage logistics. Others own and operate their warehouses. *Maquilas* account for the primary regional economic impact from manufacturing. Truck crossings attributable to *maquilas* are about 500–600 northbound daily and 200–300 southbound daily. On a typical day in Nogales, AZ and Nogales, Mexico, chassis, motherboards and mining equipment move south while manufactured products including vehicles move north.

The monetary impact of the *maquilas* for greater Nogales, AZ, including direct and secondary activities, is more than 1100 jobs and $206.8 million. About 35 percent of Nogales, Sonora *maquilas* are owned and operated by out-of-Arizona parent companies, while only 20 percent have a parent company in Nogales or Santa Cruz County (Nogales-Santa Cruz EDF, n.d.).

Electronics has revamped the manufacturing specialities; the west part of Mexico specializes in manufacturing aerospace, hi-tech, information technology (IT) and electronic sub-assembly parts (Tetakawi, 2019b). Exports reached $19 788 million in 2018; two-thirds came from Chihuahua, mainly from plants in Ciudad Juárez. In a unique study of the El Paso–Ciudad Juárez region, the Institute for Policy and Economic Development at the University of Texas at El Paso examined customer–supplier linkages between Ciudad Juárez manufacturing operations and El Paso industry. The study provides insight into areas for development among these Mexican industry clusters, oriented towards fostering regional economic expansion, competitiveness, and industry health and stability. According to the Institute's study, the top manufacturing clusters in terms of employment in Ciudad Juárez, Mexico are as follows: the automotive industry is the largest sector with 82 000 jobs; semiconductor/electric parts provides 31 000 jobs; electrical equipment has 17 000 jobs; medical equipment 12 000 jobs; and other related industries add another 40 000 jobs (Russell, n.d.). Clusters of manufacturing in Ciudad Juárez, Mexico in all likelihood will continue with their steady expansion. Rising costs for manufacturers in China, as well as for those in the United States, make the city a preferential venue for low-cost nearshore production.

Table 11.4   México: exports 2018 and foreign direct investment by state 1999–2018 (millions of US dollars)

	Exports	Auto industry	Elect-ronics	Medical devices	FDI (1999–2018)
Bajio Cluster	81 226	47 029	17 722	n.a.	91 038
Jalisco	20 406	2 458	12 365	n.a.	29 906
Aguascalientes	9 618	7 927	1 073	n.a.	9 359
Guanajuato	24 914	19 895	405	n.a.	21 622
Querétaro	11 110	5 176	2 938	n.a.	16 006
San Luis Potosí	15 178	11 573	941	n.a.	14 145
North East Cluster	107 453	52 800	21 005	n.a.	92 171
Coahuila	40 906	26 224	3 341	n.a.	21 119
Nuevo León	39 507	19 304	7 836	n.a.	50 646
Tamaulipas	27 039	7 271	9 828	n.a.	20 406
North West Cluster	69 672	19 788	31 544	n.a.	47 912
Chihuahua	51 944	13 062	28 078	n.a.	32 812
Sonora	17 728	6 725	3 466	n.a.	15 100
Baja California Cluster	38 662	7 389	16 465	4 917	25 623
Exports from the cluster regions	297 013	127 005	86 737	n.a.	256 744
Total exports	387 443	161 698	87 507	7 698	–
Total FDI	–	70 072	33 149	1 252	541 526
Total FDI in the cluster regions	–	53 297	26 707	1 165	81 169
Exports of CGV regions as % of total	76.66	78.54	99.12	n.a.	–

Sources: Secretaria de Economia (2019) and Opportimes (2019).

COROLLARY, JANUARY 24, 2020

GVCs have had a positive impact on the growth of cities in Mexico; they have not only contributed to an expansion of metropolitan life in Mexico, but have also pushed the development of knowledge clusters. Geography has been reshaped by GVC clusters that have contributed to a new dynamic of production mainly in the central and north part of the country, fostered by the creation of NAFTA, which has been renegotiated under the name of USMCA (United States–Mexico–Canada Agreement).

The new treaty could help to give larger effects of GVCs in regional development, as there are key facts that claim for an increase in regional content (country of origin rules now cover 75 percent of regional components), labor provisions to improve wages in Mexico through the improvement of union laws, improvement in intellectual property and digital trade, and it also includes new provisions to deal with the digital economy, such as prohibiting duties on things like music and e-books, and protections for Internet companies so that they are not liable for content produced by their users (Office of the United States Trade Representative, n.d.).

Cities in Mexico could benefit from the expansion of new GVCs and clusters of production, as in all cases there will be a push for interaction among them which could bring in new urban development; the challenge must be to ensure that all new urban development is knowledge conglomerates, rather than traditional urban expansion. The quest for government is to set clear guidelines for future expansion, through technological parks that could help to develop innovations within the new clusters.

REFERENCES

AMPIP (2019). Industrial Parks Directory. Retrieved from Mexican Association of Industial Parks: https://ampip.org.mx/en/industrial-parks-directory/.

CONAPO (2018). Delimitación de las zonas metropolitanas de México 2015. Retrieved from Consejo Nacional de Población: https://www.gob.mx/cms/uploads/attachment/file/344506/1_Preliminares_hasta_V_correcciones_11_de_julio.pdf.

Co-Production International (2016). *Medical Device Manufacturing in Tijuana and Mexico*. May. Retrieved January 2020 from Coastline: https://www.coastlineintl.com/wp-content/uploads/2017/12/White-Paper-Medical-Device-Manufacturing-in-Mexico_2016.pdf.

Garza, G. (1990). Impacto regional de los parques y ciudades industriales en México. *Estudios demográficos y urbanos*, 5(3), 655–675.

Garza, G. (2010). La transformación urbana de México, 1970–2020. In G. Garza and M. Schteingart, *Desarrollo Urbano y Regional.* México, D.F: El Colegio de México, pp. 31–87).

Gereffi, G. (2018). *Global Value Chains and Development: Redefining the Contours of 21st Century Capitalism.* Cambridge: Cambridge University Press.

INEGI (2019). Instituto Nacional de Estadística y Geografía. Retrieved from DENUE-Descarga masiva: https://www.inegi.org.mx/app/descarga/.

Internacional Metalmecanica (2018). Querétaro concentra 85 empresas del sector aeroespacial en su aeroclúster. August. Retrieved January 2020 from Internacional Metalmecanica: http://www.metalmecanica.com/temas/Queretaro-concentra-85-empresas-del-sector-aeroespacial-en-su-aerocluster+126856.

Mora, D., and Marquetti, H. (2019). *Política industria, clústeres y parque tecnológicos: La experiencia reciente de México.* Retrieved January 2019 from Eumed: http://www.eumed.net/libros-gratis/2015/1475/index.htm.

Nogales-Santa Cruz EDF (n.d.). *Ambos Nogales – An Advanced Manufacturing Cluster.* Retrieved January 2020 from Nogales-Santa Cruz County Economic Development Foundation: https://nogales.com/industry/manufacturing/.

Office of the United States Trade Representative (n.d.). *United States–Mexico–Canada Trade Fact Sheet Modernizing NAFTA into a 21st Century Trade Agreement.* Retrieved January 2020 from Office of the United States Trade Representatives: https://ustr.gov/trade-agreements/free-trade-agreements/united-states-mexico-canada-agreement/fact-sheets/modernizing.

Opportimes (2019). *Mexico es el 4t exportador de aparatos de medicina.* May. Retrieved January 2020 from Opportimes: https://www.opportimes.com/mexico-es-4to-exportador-de-aparatos-de-medicina/.

Organizacion de Estados Iberoamericanos (n.d.). *La experiencia de los parques tecnológicos en México.* Retrieved January 2020 from OEI: https://www.oei.es/historico/divulgacioncientifica/reportajes147.htm.

Orozco, P.C. (2016). The giants of the industry. Reforma Newspaper, Interviewer. September. Retrieved from: https://comercial.reforma.com/libre/comercial/campanas/industrial_parks/download/INDUSTRIAL.pdf.

Russell, A. (n.d.). Principal clusters of manufacturing in Ciudad Juarez, Mexico. Retrieved January 2020 from TECMA: https://www.tecma.com/clusters-of-manufacturing-in-ciudad-juarez/.

Sánchez, A. (2016). Sistema de ciudades y redes urbanas en los modelos económicos de México. *Problemas del Desarrollo. Revista Latinoamericana de Economía*, 47(184), 7–34.

Secretaria de Economia (2019). Información estadística de flujos de IED hacia México por entidad federativa desde 1999. December. Mexico.

Tetakawi (2019a). The benefits of manufacturing in Saltillo, Coahuila. Retrieved January 2020 from Tetakawi: https://go.tetakawi.com/hubfs/Tetakawi%20E books%20GO/Tetakawi-Manufacturing%20in%20Saltillo%20Ebook.pdf?hsCta Tracking=29d7fa09-3386-4b15-bdf3-316f707a82aa%7C2a435772-8db7-4153-b7da-5d4ddc80bcc5.

Tetakawi (2019b). The top 5 industries manufacturing in Mexico. April. Retrieved January 2019 from Tetakawi: https://insights.tetakawi.com/top-5-mexican-manufacturing-industries.

Waters, W. (2006). Remapping identities: road construction and nation building in postrevolutionary Mexico. In M.K. Vaughan and S. Lewis (eds), *The Eagle and the Virgin: Nation and Cultural Revolution in Mexico, 1920–1940*. Durham, NC: Duke University Press, pp. 221–241.

World Economic Forum (2016). *Competitive Cities and their Connections to Global Value Chains*. June. Retrieved January 2020 from WEFORUM: http://www3.weforum.org/docs/WEF_2016_WhitePaper_GAC_Competitive_Cities_.pdf.

12. Mexican cities' innovative industry and competitiveness in the age of the modern city: changes between 1993 and 2013

Isela Orihuela

INTRODUCTION

Cities have experienced changes throughout their history which have defined their role in the world economic, social, political and environmental spheres. These changes have been related to the introduction of new ideas, forms and technology to undertake the challenges imposed by development that transform the society, its relations and its representation in space. One of these main transformations was focused before, during and after the industrialization era, identified as pre-modernity, modernity and postmodernity (Harvey, 1989; Giddens, 1990; Kumar, 1995).

The industrialization process changed the way society and economy worked, making transformations in the production process and in the organization of activities and people, creating new institutions and imposing new ways of territorial distribution and use of resources, which meant positive and negative impacts in every sphere of development. Through time, all those changes were in the hands of different actors, with diverse institutions, under their own rules, that made cities, nations or regions the protagonists of those changes and the representatives of their spatial expression.

In the 21st century, the globalization process can be seen as another of these key transformations in the world. The term "modernity" can be applied to the periods before and during this process. Globalization is a step forward in the phases of capitalist development, where the productive forces and the spatial division of labor have been readjusted. The main characteristics of globalization are: (1) presence of more international transactions than intra-national ones; (2) national frontiers as limits for goods and services flows; (3) hierarchical organization of the spatial division of activities; and (4) decentralized production, shown in production flexibility, technological innovation, capital mobility and telecommunications development (Budd, 1998).

Cities are the areas where the characteristics and effects of this process are more visible; their level of competitiveness defines their role in the world economy, and innovation is one of the main factors influencing competitiveness. Globalization, together with information technology progress and structural change, has modified the patterns of city competence. The urban hierarchy is changing radically, and competitive advantages, more than comparative ones, are now the attributes of urban areas which improve market niches, and attract as well as retain investment, people and public resources (Gordon, 1999). Therefore, higher levels of competitiveness mean better conditions for people and productive activities in cities, and innovation is one of the key elements that generates higher productivity and that can take cities to better positions in the world economy.

This chapter has the objective of showing the changes experienced in Mexican cities in relation to innovative industry from 1993 to 2013. It first refers to the role of cities in economic development in the era of globalization, and the importance of innovation and city competitiveness. Next, it explains the changes of innovative industry, in terms of employment and production, in the main cities of Mexico. The chapter then presents the position of Mexican cities in the Index of Competitiveness, in the Index of Innovation and some data representing the place of Mexico City around the world. Some comments are added at the end.

GLOBALIZATION, INNOVATION AND URBAN COMPETITIVENESS

Globalization is not only a matter of internationalization, which implies the crossing of borders, but also implies a functional integration. Therefore, quantitative as well as qualitative change is involved (Dicken, 1998). Three main areas are involved: economic, for the new organization of firms and services in a worldwide scale; cultural, for the adoption of lifestyles and patterns of consumption; and political, related to the changing role of the government to regulate and control these trends (Allen and Massey, 1995).

In globalization, there are surplus accumulation forces, new markets and global production that transform social and economic life; expansion of transnational corporations; use of technological innovations and promotion of capital from governments across the world; and the increasing importance of the financial and services sector (Farazmand, 1999; Goldsmith, 1993).

Cities have become the leaders of economic activity, as they have the personnel, technology, knowledge and financial resources needed for development. Cities are the engines of their national economies, as they concentrate productive activity, employment generation and wealth (OECD, 2006). Some global cities in developing countries have emerged, such as Sao Paulo, Mexico City, Hong Kong and Seoul, and they are changing positions in the hierarchical system of cities, in the context of globalization.

Cities have become leaders at the urban, national and global level (Sassen, 2019). From a world perspective, cities are classified as alpha, beta or gamma, based on world corporate service provision (Beaverstock et al., 1999). In a regional space, cities in Europe, for example, can be metropoles, europoles, eurocities or smaller cities according to different degrees of concentration of international functions (Meijer, 1993). More-over, in a more specific level of analysis, in Mexico, Mexico City is being consolidated in the national urban system, while frontier cities are emerging with an increasing specialization in export industry.

There are four aspects that differentiate cities in the urban system: the hierarchy; specialization or differentiation of activities; the functional division of labor or organization; and the particular networks with other cities. The relationship and development of these aspects define the city's place in the national, continental or global system; the strengths and weaknesses of the systems; the attributes of the place to attract more investment; and the level of economic integration (Gordon, 1999).

The place of cities in the world economy can be defined through their level of competitiveness. This refers to the capacity of cities to generate economic growth and social development while taking care of the environment. It means that cities promote a social, technological, envir-onmental and institutional context for a better performance of economic activities (Cabrero et al., 2005), and that cities compete to attract productive investment to generate employment, increase wages, increase and consolidate cultural amenities, social cohesion, governance and better conditions for their residents (Ni and Kresl, 2007).

Innovation is one of the more important engines to generate competi-tiveness, growth and employment in all countries. According to the Organisation for Economic Co-operation and Development (OECD) (2006), since 1970, more than half of the economic growth of developed countries was the result of innovation, and this increases according to the tendency of economies to become more intensive in knowledge. Know-ledge is considered essential for technological development and the productivity of capital and labor, and cities are the conducive spaces to create, concentrate and expand it, since it is in those places that there are higher levels of human capital, goods, infrastructure and processes of production and exchange that promote innovation and productivity (Lambooy, 2002; Polèse, 2005).

Companies rely heavily on their capacity for innovation, which is achieved by investment in the creation and dissemination of knowledge, and this is related to urban competitiveness as it stimulates the rapid growth of markets, and in all countries, regardless of their level of development. In this way, the basis to generate competitive advantages and economic growth is in direct relation to the ability to innovate and learn continuously (Pinch et al., 2003; Forsman and Solitander, 2003).

One of the elements that shows how knowledge has been used in innovation is high-tech production, where industries use less labor and capital and invest more in generating and applying knowledge in processes, organization and products. Innovation and competitiveness vary from country to country and from city to city depending on the conditions of the national and local economy, infrastructure, public services and, in general, the amenities needed for promoting economic growth and social cohesion.

Latin American countries, in general, have a system of cities each of which is based on a primary city, which in the case of Mexico is Mexico City. This implies a territorial pattern with high concentration of people and economic activities in only a few places of the territory, but it is also possible to find a wide diversity of productive activities thanks to the variety of geographical, economic and social contexts around the country (Orihuela et al., 2015). Therefore, it is important to study those differences to have a better idea of the specific characteristics that give cities different positions of competitiveness and innovation in relation to others in their country. The following section presents the main changes in innovative industries in the cities of Mexico.

EVOLUTION OF PRODUCTION AND EMPLOYMENT IN INNOVATIVE CITIES OF MEXICO, 1993–2013

This section presents the main changes that have occurred in production and employment of manufacturing in general, and innovative industries in particular, in Mexico and in the main cities of Mexico. These cities include the 56 metropolitan areas recognized by the government of Mexico in 2010 (SEDESOL et al., 2010), and another 18 cities that are not metropolitan areas but are among those having the highest levels of population and economic production in the country; in total, 74 cities. The information derives from the Economic Censuses of Mexico (INEGI, 1994, 1999, 2004, 2009, 2014).

The innovative industries are those having higher participation in knowledge and less in capital and labor, compared to the rest of the economic sectors. This chapter uses the classification from the OECD (2003), which divides industries in high and medium-high technology. Hence, the sectors from the Mexican economy are identified in Table 12.1.

Table 12.1   Sectors of high and medium-high technology in Mexico

Level	Type of industry	Sector ID in Mexico
High	Electronics Computing Pharmaceutical Aeronautics Scientific and precision instruments	334 Computing equipment 3254 Pharmaceutical 3364 Aeronautical equipment
Medium-high	Electrical machinery Transport equipment Mechanical machinery and equipment Chemical	325 Chemical industry (without pharmaceutical) 333 Mechanical machinery and equipment 335 Electrical machinery 336 Transport equipment (without aeronautical)

Source: Based on the classification of OECD (2003).

Production of manufacturing industry in Mexico has increased in absolute terms, as Figure 12.1 shows, and it has exhibited a similar pace through the years. Meanwhile, production of innovative industry has increased as well since 1993. In absolute terms, it has passed from 235 billion pesos in 1993 to 2792 billion pesos in 2013. However, as Figure 12.1 shows, the pace has been slower in each period. In 1993, the production multiplied four times, and in the following periods it grew slower and slower until the last period, when it increased only 0.7 percent. In comparison to the manufacturing industry, although both have increased, the innovative industry has shown a major deterioration. In relation to the main cities of the country, the production of total manufacturing and that of the innovative industry has followed the same path, and they are similar in the rhythm of growth, which is less intense in the last period.

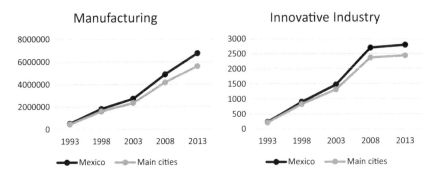

*Figure 12.1   Production of manufacturing and innovative industry in
                México and main cities, 1993–2013*

The proportion of innovative industry in total manufacturing shows a
similar pattern through the years in relation to the absolute values, as
Figure 12.2 shows. There has been growth in the production at the
national level from 1993 to 2008, in Figure 12.2, when the production
passes from 45 percent to 55 percent, respectively. After that, it decreases
in the period of 2008 to 2013, when the participation diminished to 41
percent. Figure 12.2 shows that in the case of the cities, the proportions
are close in all the periods; in 1993 they had a proportion of 47 percent,
it kept growing until 2008, when it reached 57 percent, and then fell to
43 percent in 2013. This means that from the total manufacturing and
innovative industry in the country, approximately half was produced in
the main cities of the country from 1993 to 2013, with a decreasing
tendency from 2008.

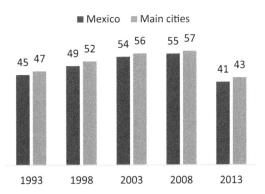

*Figure 12.2   Participation of innovative industry production in total
                manufacturing in Mexico and main cities, 1993–2013 (%)*

In relation to employment in total manufacturing, in absolute numbers, Mexico shows increases throughout the period, although the pace of growth is less each time and presents a negative rate of growth in 2003 of −0.16 percent, which recovers in the following years when it reaches 2.2 percent in 2008, but falls again in 2013 with a growth rate of 1.7 percent (see Figure 12.3). In the cities, there are growing numbers in the whole period except in 2003, when the fall for the main cities reaches −0.6%; however, during the rest of the years there is only growth. In innovative industry, Mexico shows a growth path from 1993 to 2013, with less acceleration through the years and some important falls in growth. In the period 1993–1998, it had its major increase with an annual growth rate of 6.4 percent, which fell in 2003 to 0.5 percent, grew again in 2008 to 2.1 percent, and fell again to 0.3 percent in 2013. On the part of the cities, employment has a similar pattern in all the years; however, it experienced a fall to a 1.35 percent rate of growth from 2008 to 2013.

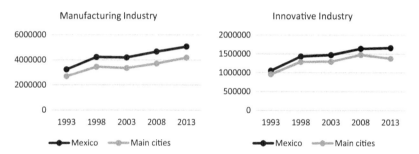

Figure 12.3   Employment in manufacturing and innovative industry in Mexico and main cities, 1993–2013

In relative terms, innovative industry employment in Mexico, as part of manufacturing in the country, had only slight growth during the whole period, when it changed from 32 percent in 1993 to 33 percent in 2013 (Figure 12.4). It showed growth in 1998, when it registered a rise to 34 percent, and again in 2003 to 35 percent, maintains its level in 2008 but falls in 2013. In the cities, there is a growing path from 1993 to 2008, when the proportion of employment increases from 36 percent to 40 percent, nonetheless, there is a fall in 2013 to 33 percent. In comparison to the national numbers, the proportions of employment of innovative industry in total manufacturing are greater in the cities than in the whole country, but both of these fell in 2013.

Regarding the cities, the participation of manufacturing employment in the national manufacturing has passed through different patterns (Figure 12.5). In 1993, the manufacturing industry in cities represented 83

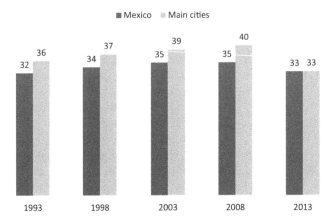

*Figure 12.4   Participation of employment of innovative industry in
            manufacturing, 1993–2013*

percent of the national total, then fell to 82 percent in 1998, and fell
again in 2003 to 80 percent, maintained the same in 2008, and grew to 83
percent in 2013. If we take into account the whole period, the levels of
2013 are the same as in 1993. In the case of the innovative industry, the
tendency is not quite the same. The employment in cities began with a
proportion of 91 percent of the total innovative industry in the country,
then falls to 90 percent in 1998, to 88 percent in 2003, rises to 90 percent
in 2008 and falls to 83 percent in 2013. In the whole period, innovative
industry lost 8 points as part of the national total. In comparision,
manufacturing industry falls on two occasions, 1998 and 2003, while
innovative industry falls three times, in 1998, 2003 and 2013. Industrial
employment is concentrated in the main cities of the country but it had
been more concentrated until 2008 in the case of innovative industry. In
2013, innovative industry has the same levels as manufacturing in the
cities of Mexico but has lost more participation than manufacturing in
general.

   When comparing both production and employment in innovative
industry in cities as part of the national manufacturing totals, production
has had more participation than employment, where the highest point of
production reaches 57 percent while employment takes 40 percent. In the
case of participation of innovative production and employment of cities
in their national counterparts, the levels of both are similar, but production began in 1993 at 91 percent and fell to 87 percent in 2013, while
employment had a mayor loss in the period with 91 percent in 1993 and
83 percent in 2013 (Figure 12.6). In both employment and production in

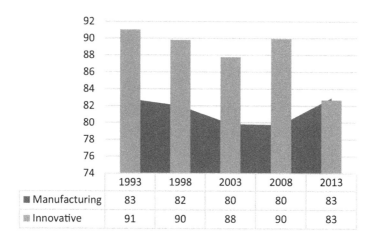

	1993	1998	2003	2008	2013
■ Manufacturing	83	82	80	80	83
▦ Innovative	91	90	88	90	83

Figure 12.5   Participation of employment in the cities of Mexico in the national total per sector, 1993–2003

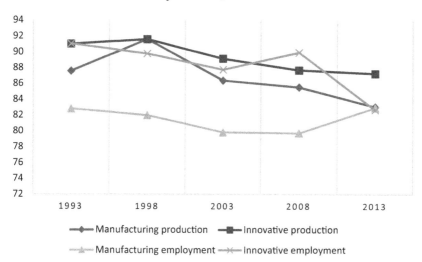

Figure 12.6   Participation of cities in innovative and manufacturing production and employment in national totals, 1993–2013

innovative industry and in manufacturing production, there is a tendency to diminish their participation in the national totals, and there is growth in manufacturing employment only at the end of the period.

According to the data presented in Figure 12.6, more than 80 percent of the employment and production of innovative industry of the country are concentrated in the main cities; approximately half of the total industrial production in Mexico is generated in the main cities of the country, and industrial employment in cities represents a third of the national totals. The following section presents the cases of some of these cities and their conditions of competitiveness.

INNOVATION AND COMPETITIVENESS IN SOME CITIES OF MEXICO AND POSITION OF MEXICO CITY AROUND THE WORLD

This section presents three cases of cities, which have participation in different types of innovative industries in terms of production or employment in 2013 and with different sizes. The purpose is to show the position of these cities in relation to urban competitiveness and then to analyze in more detail some of their main characteristics. This section is based on data from the Index of Competitiveness of Cities in Mexico 2003, 2007 and 2011 (Cabrero et al., 2005; Cabrero and Orihuela, 2009, 2013a), which measures the situation of cities in four groups of variables: economic, institutional, demographic and urban-environmental terms.

Taking the national average in production and employment, as shown in Figure 12.7, there are four types of combinations of innovative industry: high production–low employment, high production–high employment, low production–low employment, and low production–high employment. Most of the cities are in the low production–high employment quadrant and there are no cases of high production–low employment. The three cities selected were: Mexico City (high production–high employment), Queretaro (high employment–low production), and Juárez (low production–high employment).

Mexico City has participation in all the types of innovative industry production that have been analyzed above, but mainly in chemical and pharmaceutical; and in terms of employment it has more participation in chemical, pharmaceutical and transport. Queretaro has its main production in electrical industry and its main employment in mechanical, computing and aeronautical. Juárez has its main production in aeronautical and computing industry and its main employment in electrical industry. Comparing the three cities, Table 12.2 shows their main characteristics and positions in each component of competitiveness.

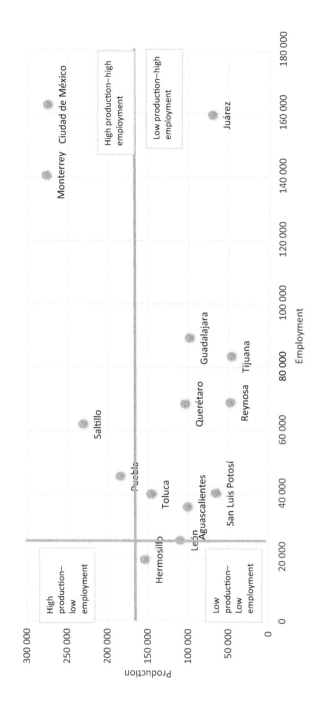

Figure 12.7   Types of combinations of innovative industry

Table 12.2   Characteristics of competitiveness

City	Position of competitiveness (out of 74 cities)				
	Average	Economic	Institutional	Socio-demographic	Urban
Mexico City	1	25	42	22	1
Queretaro	4	11	3	12	11
Juárez	12	13	17	21	30

In terms of urban competitiveness, the Index of Competitiveness of Cities in Mexico shows that Mexico City holds the first position of the 74 cities in 2011; Queretaro is 4th, and Juárez is 12th. Figure 12.8 shows the position of each city in each component of competitiveness through time, and the size of the diamond shows the average competitiveness.

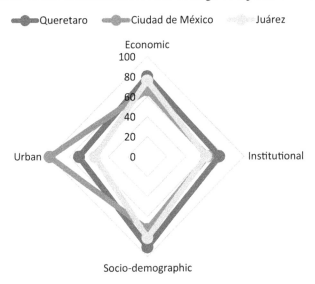

Figure 12.8   Competitiveness diamond for three cities

Figure 12.8 shows that Mexico City has a wider diamond, where it has strengthened the urban component through time, and holds the first position of all cities in these variables; it also has increased in socio-demographic terms, while in the economic part it has diminished a little bit and the institutional has the main decline. The economic component is among the top 20 of the competitiveness of the study. Its development profile is based on a high proportion of modern trade and service, which also shows an economic structure that is specialized in the services sector. On the other hand, its level of production per capita is below the first 15 places. The institutional component was where it shows its lowest position. Financial, investment and per capita income are disadvantaged compared with the rest of the cities. In addition, the mechanisms of transparency and improving regulatory are also at a disadvantage. With respect to the socio-demographic component, it is located among the top 15 positions of the study. Its employment structure is based on the tertiary sector and shows a low level of unemployment. The urban component was where it obtained its best position, to occupy the first position in the cities of the study set. It is one of the cities with more telecommunications infrastructure, as well as scientific research. It also presents a high level of coverage of services in homes. However, the level of public safety and environmental quality do not favor it.

Queretaro shows a more equilibrated diamond, where all four components have a similar proportion. Even though it is visible that the economic component has been steady through the years, the socio-demographic has increased and the urban and institutional have fallen. Economically, it is characterized as one of the cities with greater per capita production. The wage level is among the top ten best cities. It has an economic structure based on the industrial sector. It has an important participation of modern industry in the local economy, as well as of modern commerce. The institutional component is where it has its most disadvantageous position of the four components. Mainly affected is its low position in relation to lack of urban planning mechanisms, systems of regulatory improvement and transparency mechanisms. However, it is among the top ten in terms of financial capacity, income and investment per capita. In the socio-demographic component, Queretaro is one of the cities with a lower level of shortages and poverty. Its employment structure is based mainly in the secondary sector of the economy. Moreover, it is one of the cities with greater human potential. On the other hand, it presents a low level of formal employment and has a disadvantage in terms of the level of criminality. In the urban aspect, it is among the cities with the highest proportion of industrial infrastructure. It also has a good level of infrastructure for scientific research, and personnel to carry out these activities. However, it has a low level of infrastructure for educational, financial and hospital services.

In Juárez, the diamond is the thinnest of the three cities, with more participation in the socio-demographic component than in the economic, and has maintained the urban but fallen in the institutional. In the economic component it is characterized by having an economic structure based on the industrial sector. The participation of industry and modern services helps in maintaining their competitiveness. In addition, it is one of the cities with the highest wage levels, being located within the first five places. The institutional component is where it has its lowest position of the four components. This is due to its high level of public debt and its low proportion of income and investment per capita. This is also influenced by the lack of updating of its planning and transparency mechanisms. However, Juárez shows self-sufficiency in local finance through its high financial capacity and its low level of dependence on other levels of government. In the socio-demographic component, it is located among the top five positions. This is mainly due to its having a low level of marginalization and an employment structure based on a higher proportion in the secondary sector. The city also has one of the lowest levels of poverty of the cities, and its average standard of living is among the top ten. The levels of formal employment and of crime favor the city. In the urban component the city is positioned among the top 15. It is characterized by being among the cities with the best quality of services in housing and infrastructure for telecommunications. However, it displays disadvantageous positions in terms of infrastructure for financial, educational and hospital services.

In a more profound analysis, an Index of Innovation for the 74 cities was developed (Cabrero and Orihuela, 2013a, 2013b). It takes into account aspects related to human capital, centers of research, patents, high-tech and medium-tech production, Internet connection, cellular phones, human development, students at universities, transparency and growth rates, among others. The most representative variables in the model were those related to human capital, centers of research, patents, production and population size.

The results of the index were divided into three groups according to their position in the index: high, medium and low. Table 12.3 shows the positions of the 74 cities. In the "high" section, there are 13 cities, in which Mexico City is in the first place. It has the major concentration of researchers, centers of research, patents, innovative production and population. The rest of the cities are clearly below the levels of Mexico City. Queretaro is in 5th place with important proportion of patents, telecommunications infrastructure and innovative production. Juárez is in the middle section within a group of 28 cities; it has important participation in innovative production, but lesser so in patents, telecommunications and research centers.

Table 12.3   Levels of innovation in Mexican cities

Level of innovation	Position	City	Index value
High	1	Ciudad de México	100.0
	2	Monterrey	65.6
	3	Guadalajara	60.8
	4	Chihuahua	58.0
	5	Querétaro	55.8
	6	Hermosillo	55.8
	7	Tijuana	55.4
	8	Puebla	54.9
	9	Mexicali	54.8
	10	Saltillo	54.6
	11	Los Cabos	54.4
	12	La Paz	53.9
	13	San Luis Potosí	53.5
Medium	14–41	28 cities	52.6–47.4
	23	Juárez	50.3
Low	42–74	33 cities	46.9–32.2

Therefore, the innovation in Mexico depends on an interaction of knowledge generation, infrastructure for telecommunications, population size, and high and medium high production. These results are coincident with the competitiveness index, where from the 25 first cities in with high levels of competitiveness, 19 appear also in the first places of the innovation index.

In a world perspective, the position of Mexico City is interesting. The Global Urban Competitiveness Report 2018–2019 (Ni et al., 2018), mentions that Mexico City is in position 135 out of 1007 cities; it is fourth in population size; 193 in sustainable competitiveness; connectivity is ranked 32, human capital 39, infrastructure 175, financial services 18, industrial systems 33, and human resources 30. In accordance to the Index of MostConnected Cities, Mexico City is in 14th place. The position of Mexico City has fallen, in the competitiveness report, since it was in place 129 in 2017 in that same Index (Ni et al., 2017). The first places in the Indexes of 2017 and 2018 are occupied by New York, Los Angeles, Singapore, London and San Francisco.

FINAL COMMENTS

Cities are increasing in number and population. In the listing of competitive cities, there are no small cities (with less than 100 000 people), medium-sized cities are the majority but falling in number (with less than 1 million people), and big cities are increasing in number (with more than 1 million people).

Economic specialization has changed in cities during the period studied. Cities specialized in industry are increasing, and represent 33 percent of the total. Those in commerce are decreasing; in services there are only three cases; industry and commerce are steady; industry and services have disappeared; and commerce and services are decreasing but still represent 42 percent of the total. There are more medium-sized cities in industry, and more big cities in commerce and services.

Innovative industry is increasing in the country, but it is concentrated in small cities that are close to big or medium-sized cities but depend more on airports. Therefore, those small cities are not counted in this study. This happens at least in the case of Queretaro, where an aeronautics cluster has been built in the small city of Colon.

The aeronautics industry is more interested in building networks among government–university–enterprise complexes. First, a big enterprise located in the city, then other related enterprises came, and then higher education institutions and high schools located there, and the benefits are spreading in the local and regional population. That is not the case for the automotive industry, which has been located in other cities of the country where that kind of relationship is more difficult to find, and the benefits are more visible for the industry itself and not for the local and regional population.

The positions of the cities of Mexico around the world are most visible in the case of Mexico City, which is among the 25 percent of cities with the best position in competitiveness, and among the first 40 in global connections. Although there is much to do in relation to competitiveness, there are innovation processes taking place in the country that are showing similar patterns to those in other countries of the world, including those cities ranking in the first places of the Global Urban Competitiveness Report. As innovation needs a supportive system to attain better results, an interrelation between economic, social, legal and environmental favorable contexts needs to be built to give better conditions for both productive and social development.

REFERENCES

Allen, J. and D. Massey (eds), *Geographical Worlds*, Milton Keynes: Open University Press, 1995.

Beaverstock, J., P. Taylor and R. Smith, "A Roster of World Cities," *Cities*, Vol. 16, No. 6, pp. 445–458, 1999.

Budd, L., "Territorial Competition and Globalisation: Scylla and Charybdis of European Cities," *Urban Studies*, Vol. 35, No. 4, pp. 663–685, 1998.

Cabrero, E. and I. Orihuela, "Índice de competitividad de las ciudades mexicanas," versión 2007, in E. Cabrero (ed.), *Competitividad de las ciudades en México. La nueva agenda urbana*, México: Secretaría de Economía-CIDE, 2009.

Cabrero, E. and I. Orihuela, "Índice de competitividad de las ciudades de México versión 2011," in Enrique Cabrero (ed.), *Retos de la competitividad urbana*, México: CIDE, 2013a.

Cabrero, E. and I. Orihuela, "Innovación en ciudades de México: ¿Hacia ciudades del conocimiento?," in Enrique Cabrero (ed.), *Retos de la competitividad urbana*, México: CIDE, 2013b.

Cabrero, E., I. Orihuela and A. Ziccardi, "Ciudades competitivas, ciudades cooperativas: conceptos clave y construcción de un índice," in C. Arce, E. Cabrero and A. Ziccardi (eds), *Ciudades del Siglo XXI ¿Competitividad o cooperación*, México: Miguel Ángel Porrúa-CIDE, 2005.

Dicken, P., *Global Shift: Transforming the World Economy*, 3rd edition, London: Paul Chapman, 1998.

Farazmand, A., "Globalisation and Public Administration," *Public Administration Review*, Vol. 59, No. 6, 1999.

Forsman, M. and N. Solitander, "Knowledge Transfer in Clusters and Networks," *Journal of International Business Studies*, Vol. 3, pp. 1–23, 2003.

Giddens, A., *The Consequences of Modernity*, Cambridge: Polity Press, 1990.

Goldsmith, M., "The Europeanisation of Local Government," *Urban Studies*, Vol. 30, Nos 4–5, pp. 683–699, 1993.

Gordon, I., "Internationalisation and Urban Competition," *Urban Studies*, Vol. 36, Nos 5–6, pp. 1001–1016, 1999.

Harvey, D., *The Condition of Postmodernity*, Cambridge: Polity Press, 1989.

INEGI, *Censos Económicos*, México: INEGI, 1994.

INEGI, *Censos Económicos*, México: INEGI, 1999.

INEGI, *Censos Económicos*, México: INEGI, 2004.

INEGI, *Censos Económicos*, México: INEGI, 2009.

INEGI, *Censos Económicos*, México: INEGI, 2014.

Kumar, K., *From Post-Industrial to Postmodern Society*, Oxford: Basil Blackwell, 1995.

Lambooy, J., "Knowledge and Urban Economic Development: An Evolutionary Perspective," *Urban Studies*, Vol. 39, Nos 5–6, pp. 1019–1035, 2002.

Meijer, M., "Growth and Decline of European Cities: Changing Position of Cities in Europe," *Urban Studies*, Vol. 30, No. 6, pp. 981–990, 1993.

Ni, P., M. Kamiya, S. Jianfa and G. Weijin, *Global Urban Competitiveness Report, Report Series by Global Urban Competitiveness Project*, Beijing: National Academy of Economic Strategy, UN-HABITAT, 2018.

Ni, P., M. Kamiya and H. Wang, *Global Urban Competitiveness Report*, Report Series by Global Urban Competitiveness Project, Beijing: National Academy of Economic Strategy, UN-HABITAT, 2017.

Ni, P. and P. Kresl, *Global Urban Competitiveness Report*, Report Series by Global Urban Competitiveness Project, Beijing: Social Sciences Academy Press, 2007.

OECD, *OECD Science, Technology and Industry Scoreboard 2003*, Paris: OECD Publishing, 2003.

OECD, *Competitive Cities in the Global Economy*, Territorial Reviews, Paris: OECD Publishing, 2006.

Orihuela, I., C. Becerril, L. Rodríguez, H. Solano and C. Tello, *Estudios metropolitanos. Actualidad y retos*, Mexico City: Instituto Mora, 2015.

Pinch, S., N. Henry, M. Jenkins and S. Tallman, "From 'Industrial Districts' to 'Knowledge Clusters': A Model of Knowledge Dissemination and Competitive Advantage in Industrial Agglomerations," *Journal of Economic Geography*, Vol. 3, No. 4, pp. 373–388, 2003.

Polèse, M., "Cities and National Economic Growth: A Reappraisal," *Urban Studies*, Vol. 42, No. 8, pp. 1429–1451, 2005.

Sassen, S., *Cities in a World Economy*, 5th edition, New York: SAGE Publications, 2019.

SEDESOL, CONAPO and INEGI, *Delimitación de zonas metropolitanas en México 2010*, México: SEDESOL, CONAPO, INEGI, 2010.

Index